Following the Sun

A Practical Guide to Egyptian Religion
Revised Edition

Sharon LaBorde

Following the Sun : A Practical Guide to Egyptian Religion, Revised Edition. Copyright Sharon LaBorde. All rights reserved. This book, or parts thereof, may not be reproduced in any form without written permission except by a reviewer who may quote brief passages in review, or by individual users posting online video blogs.

First edition, 2010.

Revised edition, 2017. All rights reserved.

Cover design by Sharon LaBorde

www.golden-age-productions.com

ISBN: 978-1-365-85833-8

Printed in the USA by Lulu Press

Acknowledgments

This book could never have happened without the assistance, encouragement, and opportunities that were afforded me by some very special people. These "guilty parties" include Nic M. and Trixie Davis, who invited me to that first Pagan Pride Day (I know Ken was watching over all of us); Krys Garnett, who generously provided photos of major Egyptological sites and scans of obscure books (a 'voice offering' to Ra and all your patrons); the various online communities of which I have been part, including Children of Kemet, Het Shemsu, and the Following the Sun forum; and particularly to Tony Kail and my dear friend Matt Kirkby, who pointed me in the right direction when it came time to publish.

And most especially to Daryn– my husband, my beta-reader, my editor, my cheerleader– my everything!

To the Osiris, King NebkheperuRa, son
of Ra Tutankhamun, that he may celebrate millions
of jubilees into eternity

Table of Contents

Preface to the New Edition   7

I. Introduction   11

Part One – Building a Foundation:
Background of Ancient Egypt

II. Exodus, Ethnicity and Other Controversies   27

III. You've Got to Know Where You've Been
   (To Know Where You're Going)   58

IV. The World According to Them:
   Ancient Egyptians' Religious Worldview   77

V. Who's Who of the Egyptian Gods   99

Part Two – Practice Today:
Ancient Wisdom, Modern Lives

VI. Building And Using Your Own Sacred Space   147

VII. Prayers, Spells and Rites   164

VIII. Do-It-Yourself Egyptian   179

IX.	The Egyptian Liturgical Year	205
X.	Some Sacred Texts	253
XI.	Conclusion	259
	Online Resources	263
	Bibliography	264
	Index	269

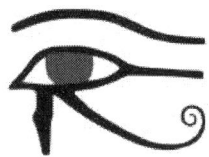

Preface to the New Edition

Following the Sun was first published in June 2010, just six months after Richard Reidy's work on Kemetic Reconstructionism, Eternal Egypt, was published. I would like to think that these two books represent for Kemetic Pagans what Margot Adler's Drawing Down the Moon and Starhawk's The Spiral Dance have for a previous generation of Pagans; both of those books were first published on Samhain (Halloween) 1979, and together they exposed many readers to Paganism, Wicca and Goddess spirituality for the first time. Indeed, in the years since I first released Following the Sun, I have spoken to or corresponded with many Kemetics and Egyptian Pagans who keep both Following the Sun and Eternal Egypt on their bookshelves. But it is still too soon, as yet, to know fully whether this comparison will ring true - even though seven years, as measured on the Internet, is a rather long time.

During that time, both society at large and "the Kemetic scene" have further evolved. Technologies that were already present in 2010 - blogging, YouTube and social media in particular - have supported an upswell of Pagans practicing some form of Kemetic, or Egyptian, Paganism. (The subtle differences of meaning between these two terms will also be revisited in this edition.) While technically these people could be termed 'Independent Kemetics', because they do not claim membership in an established community such as Church of the Eternal Source; Kemetic Orthodoxy; the Kemetic [Reconstructionist] Temple co-founded by Richard Reidy; or the Ausar-Auset

Society (among others), these unaffiliated practitioners still communicate with fellow Pagans online, and their beliefs and practices are influenced by this collective experience. This new edition of Following the Sun owes much to the concerns they have expressed.

One social issue that has grown painfully urgent in recent years and holds a direct bearing upon Kemeticism is racial disparity, particularly in the United States. The Black Lives Matter movement first formed to address continued race discrimination in law enforcement and the justice system, but its message has been applied to many other aspects of life, including Kemeticism. This renewed awareness has not come without controversy. A deep divide still separates Afrocentric Kemetic beliefs and practices from other forms of Kemeticism; one need only peruse 'Kemetic' video listings on YouTube to see these stark contrasts firsthand. While addressing that divide in greater detail reaches beyond the scope of this book, the discussion of ethnicity in ancient Egypt found in Chapter Two has been greatly expanded. Recent research on Nubia, some of it published after the first edition of Following the Sun appeared, has been incorporated in order to give a more inclusive answer to the question of racial identity in ancient Egypt.

Kemetic Paganism's relation to Wicca, and comparative practices between the two, has also been reconsidered. While Wicca represents only one form of modern Paganism, within Wicca itself one finds a kaleidoscope of beliefs and practices. No two covens or circles are alike, even if one coven formed as an offshoot of another. General observations about Wicca in the first edition reflected my exposure to a limited number of Wiccan practices; in this new edition, I can relate a broader spectrum.

The section on holiday observances in Part Two has been expanded in response to feedback from readers. While my second book, Circle of the Sun, includes detailed rituals meant for use by either Kemetic or Wiccan readers, I am including more background information here in Following the Sun especially for Egyptian-themed (or Tameran) Wiccans to use in adapting the Wheel of the Year. Kemetic practitioners could also find it useful material for working with members of open circles or eclectic

Pagan groups. One theme expressed in both books that, to some extent, still holds true today is the distance between other forms of Paganism and Kemeticism/Egyptian Paganism. Despite our growing numbers, we still find relatively little mention in "mainstream" discussions of Paganism. My continued hope is that together we can change that oversight, and claim our place among the "mainstream" of modern Pagan faiths.

One critique of <u>Following</u>'s first edition, however, will *not* make its way into this revision. All of my historical material is researched to the fullest extent of my ability; but with only one exception, I deliberately forego the use of footnotes in my text. My sources can be found either from direct citation or in my bibliography. In my experience, footnotes not only make reading more cumbersome, but also frequently tell me nothing that the bibliography doesn't already. As Egyptologist Ann Macy Roth wrote in her article *Ancient Egypt in America: Claiming the Riches*, "myriad footnotes do not in themselves constitute scholarship." My aim has always been to make legitimate, up-to-date research on ancient Egypt easy for non-academics to read, understand, and enjoy. Dressing up my writing in footnotes and lengthy citations does a disservice to that goal and to my audience. <u>Following the Sun</u>, <u>Circle of the Sun</u>, and however many books will eventually follow them, are all first and foremost intended to be a benefit to their readers.

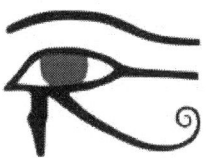

Introduction

I tend to be the oddball wherever I go. Whatever the situation, I always seem to be either too young, too educated, too eclectic, or else too *something* unique compared to the rest of my group. I've even managed to throw members of a local Pagan community – surely a bastion of counter-culturalism if ever society has one – for a complete loop. Our crowning moment of con-fusion came during a celebration of Mabon, the autumnal equinox. While the service was hosted by an area Wiccan coven, free spirits of all stripes were in attendance: Christians, Druids, "non-denominational" Pagans, Germanic Heathens, and myself, the token devotee of Egyptian deities. Before the ceremony got underway, one of our regulars made informal introductions for a newcomer. She gestured toward each person where it applied:

"We have people who follow the Druidic path, the Germanic path–" Next she motioned toward me. "The path of Isis–"

I had to correct her. "Egyptian, actually."

"Oh yeah, Egyptian," she smiled apologetically. "Isis was just the first word I could think of."

Our Germanic friend certainly didn't mean any harm, but her flub illustrates the unique sort of limbo in which we Egyptian Pagans often find ourselves within the larger Pagan movement. Wicca is the largest and best-known form of modern Paganism, and its devotion to the Goddess in all Her forms enthusiastically includes the Egyptian goddess Isis. Egyptian-themed, or

11

Tameran, Wicca has yielded books such as <u>The Circle of Isis</u>, <u>Mysteries of Isis</u>, and <u>Offering to Isis</u>. One can even join and seek ordination in the Fellowship of Isis, an international organization begun in Ireland in 1976. As a result, when most people think of Egyptian Paganism, generally the worship of Isis is what first comes to mind. I've even been asked, on account of my *ankh* and *udjat*, or Eye of Horus, pendants, if I was 'Isian'. But while there are many Wiccans and other Pagans who revere Isis as their primary goddess, an increasing number of us simply are not 'Isian'. We worship *many* gods and goddesses of the ancient Nile, some deities more closely than others. Some of us are Wiccan; many of us are not. Our faith can be considered 'Pagan', inasmuch as its prototype predates Christianity; but not all Egyptian adherents specifically identify themselves as 'Pagan' or 'Neopagan'. So what are we? Even among ourselves, that question sometimes poses difficulties as we strive to carve our own identity as a faith. Lack of accurate information, popular stereotypes about Egyptian culture and a lack of scruples on the part of some religious groups all tug at the movement and pull it toward varying extremes.

Modern Forms of an Ancient Religion

Even what name to give our religious movement presents challenges and uncertainties. Online groups commonly refer to it as Kemeticism, or Kemetic religion, referring to the ancient Egyptians' word for their own country, *Kemet*. However, Tameran Wicca borrows a synonymous Egyptian word, *Ta-mery*, or "beloved land", so which name is more valid? Furthermore, how many people outside of 'Kemetic' circles are even familiar with the term? Out of an entire crowd attending a Pagan Pride Day event at which I spoke a few years ago, which included a kaleidoscope of Pagan adherents, authors, coven and community leaders, the sole person who had even heard of the word "Kemetic" was a forensic investigator who specialized in unusual religious paraphernalia. No one else had encountered the term before, even folks who knew about the Fellowship of Isis. Say the word "Egyptian", however, and the recognition is instant. So for the purposes of this book, the more inclusive term *Egyptian*

Paganism will be used to refer to this modern revival of the ancient faith.

Yet here again, that very description brings up another point of debate. Egyptian Paganism is not alone in seeking to renew ancient forms of worship. Other groups draw from Greek, Roman, and Celtic traditions, and like Egyptian adherents they use archaeology and scholarship as a starting point for rebuilding these belief systems. Collectively, these new faiths are known as *Pagan Reconstructionism*. But just how far should we go in our attempts to 'reconstruct' ancient societies' religions and even social structures, as some groups have tried to do? Implementation varies, but most Egyptian Pagans and Kemetics agree – at least in principle, if not always in practice – that the exact manner in which Egyptian religion and society were originally structured cannot be duplicated in modern society without serious ethical implications. Ancient Egypt, for example, made no separation between church and state. Its people lived in essentially a feudal system, led by a hereditary king whose divine authority could not be challenged, and its courts offered no appeals process. The freedom to elect leaders, legally challenge their decisions and believe differently than them form the basis of our modern government and even many religious organizations. To 'reconstruct' ancient religions strictly around their original prototypes is to disregard how our world has advanced to the present age.

Not surprisingly, most of the forms or 'sects' of Egyptian religion have evolved around one of several approaches to these issues. While this is by no means an exhaustive survey, the three primary branches of Egyptian Paganism are as follows:

Tameran Wicca – Despite being a growing tradition within Wicca, Tameran Wicca is actually not among the traditions listed in many well-known books on Wicca in general. As its name suggests, Tameran Wicca uses the same basic structure: the Wheel of the Year, sabbat and esbat ritual formats, and use of certain ritual tools. But instead of invoking European pantheons or an eclectic mix, Tameran Wicca focuses on Egyptian gods and goddesses. Tameran Wicca can be further subdivided into *Isian* and *Kemetic*, based on theological emphasis:

Isian Tradition – Isian Tradition grew out of a British Traditional lineage with the founding of the Star of the Gold Cross coven in 1974. As its name suggests, Isian Wiccan Tradition concentrates its veneration on Isis as the premiere goddess. Duality is explored through Osiris and Isis as the God and Goddess respectively.

Kemetic Wicca – A more recent development, Kemetic Wicca shifts its focus away from the duality of Isis and Osiris and toward the divine Mother-Father-Child concept of a Triad. The Goddess in Kemetic Wicca can become Hathor, or Sakhmet, or one of several others, and They are not viewed as purely manifestations of Isis.

Kemetic Reconstructionism – The largest sect in terms of its internal diversity, Kemetic Reconstructionism is also known as *Kemetic Revivalism*. What it seeks to reconstruct or revive specifically are religious beliefs and practices of Egypt before the Greco-Roman Period, during the classical Pharaonic era. Some Kemetic Reconstructionist groups are Afrocentric; most are not racially oriented. Some adherents regard themselves as part of a unique movement within Reconstructionism, known as *Kemetic Traditionalism*.

While it classifies as Egyptian Paganism, some Kemetic Reconstructionists eschew the use of the word 'Egyptian' as "non-native" (even though 'Kemetic' is itself a modern usage). Kemetic Reconstructionism generally uses native names of deities, as deciphered from hieroglyphic texts, although modern spellings vary widely and some are unique to particular groups. Kemetic Reconstructionism also observes calendars based on the ancient Egyptian year and draws from translated ancient texts for rituals. Some groups pattern their organization after ancient Egypt's social hierarchy, even to the point of being led by a pharaoh-like figure. Other Kemetic Reconstructionists shy away from what they consider the potential abuse of power by such a pharaoh-like figure.

Eclectic Neo-Egyptian – Outside of Tameran or Kemetic faiths, other groups and traditions have formed that follow Egyptian motifs, but blend more liberally and often take the Egyptian path in totally new directions. In the last two decades, groups have sprung up that teach 'Egyptian Yoga', 'Kemetic Diets', and offer 'Kemetic' spa retreats. Many, but not all, of these groups are Afrocentric in theme.

Beyond these primary forms of Egyptian Paganism, other belief systems have borrowed from Egypt since the days of the Greeks and Romans. Indeed, some followers of modern Greek (or *Hellenistic*) Paganism have adopted Egyptian beliefs and deities much as the ancient Greeks did under the Ptolemies. They use the more commonly-known Greek names and attributes for Egyptian deities (much to the consternation of Kemetic purists) sometimes combining them with Greek counterparts. In a similar vein, *Hermeticism* utilizes Egyptian characters and motifs but blends them with Greek elements, Eastern religions and Kabbalah mysticism. The system is reputedly based on Late Antiquity writings attributed to Hermes Trismegistus, who is in turn linked to the Egyptian god Thoth (Djehuty). Hermeticism is best known through the Hermetic Order of the Golden Dawn, which was most active in the late 19th and early 20th centuries. Related to Hermeticism are Rosicrucianism and Thelema.

Regardless of whether you follow one of these three sects of Egyptian Paganism, a new variation that has not been described, a religion that borrows Egyptian elements or a different faith entirely, this book has been written with you in mind. Its aim is twofold: first, to present the most recent scholarship on ancient Egyptian religion in a manner that is both easy for average readers to understand and relevant to modern religious perspectives. Too often, important discoveries in the field of Egyptology only get exposed in specialist publications;

meanwhile, those who are interested in active Egyptian worship face scattered references written in intimidating specialist jargon by scholars whose own credibility would be at stake were they to breathe or type a word about modern Paganism. Confronted by such a dearth of pertinent information, too many Egyptian seekers must rely on what little they can find – be it out-of-date, inaccurate, or even outright misleading. No more.

This book's second aim is to offer examples of prayers, services and holidays that are built upon the same research and can be easily implemented or adapted to suit readers' needs. Excerpts from translated ancient texts, where given, also list their original sources so that anyone can find these academic references to study for themselves. Just as it is difficult to find accurate scholarship on the ancient religion, it is also just as daunting to locate reliable references for modern worship. Often the only way that a beginner to Egyptian faith can learn how best to arrange a shrine, conduct a simple service or even approach their chosen deities is to join a group that teaches its own interpretation. At best, this route limits a newcomer's options to study and compare different approaches. At worst, the beginner is misled into dependency by "experts" who demand compensation – monetary and otherwise – in exchange for their "knowledge". For Egyptian Paganism, as for all aspects of life, freedom of information allows freedom of choice.

So Why Egyptian Paganism?

Faced with this lack of accessible and reliable information, and the lack of an established niche within the landscape of emerging religions, why are more and more people turning to Egyptian Paganism? Especially in our post-Millennial world shadowed by the twin specters of fundamentalism and xenophobia, making the deliberate choice to stand apart from the majority – even a "majority within the minority" such as Wicca – still carries a stigma of deviance about it. Yet despite these challenges, the number of people who practice a form of Egyptian Paganism grows with each passing year. Why? What draws this increasing number of faithful to revere and worship gods and goddesses thought by most to be relics, mere shadows of an age gone by?

Quite simply, it is because these Gods and Goddesses have stepped out of the shadows and begun to speak again. They speak, and increasingly, people hear.

Unlike many other Pagans, Egyptian adherents frequently do not convert directly from Christianity to Egyptian Paganism. Some begin in another tradition of Wicca, where often a beautiful, unmistakably Egyptian figure – male or female – approaches them during a ritual, a trance, or in a dream. Thus begins a new relationship with a Goddess such as Bast or Sakhmet, or a god such as Anubis or Set. Surprisingly, more and more people have begun to embrace Egyptian Paganism after having considered themselves atheist. They report having given up on spirituality entirely, wondering if any such higher beings exist – only to discover a Presence in their lives that they could not ignore. Through investigation and personal revelations, these presences reveal Themselves as an Egyptian god or goddess. Still others do convert from a Christian background, feeling dissatisfied with an atmosphere of stifling dogma and a lack of personal connection to either their church community or any sense of the Divine. For these individuals, Egyptian gods and goddesses are more approachable, accessible – and especially, caring.

These deities who manifest Themselves in people's lives come to have a profound and positive impact upon them. People who adopt Egyptian Paganism have shared stories of being guided through difficult situations; overcoming or healing from abuse; finding much-needed inner strength and confidence; even deciding not to commit suicide. For survivors such as these, it is no exaggeration to say that an Egyptian God or Goddess saved their lives. Their subsequent decisions to dedicate themselves to a chosen God or Goddess have inspired many devotees to go back to school, sometimes but not always in Egyptology; to learn new skills ranging from belly-dancing to web design; to pursue their artistic talents, from painting to the jeweler's arts; as well as to take up the pen and write (this book being a case in point!). In coming years, we can look forward to seeing many new and valuable contributions to our global society by these people who have been inspired by their guides and saviors, the Gods and Goddesses of Egypt.

What Is – And Isn't – Egyptian Paganism

Truly, embracing Egyptian Paganism is heeding the Gods' call. But unlike the popular image of ancient religion, where worshipers slavishly prostrate them-selves before domineering graven images, true Egyptian religion is a celebration of life, gratitude, and mutual bond between the Gods and humankind. It is a faith that cherishes morality and balance, not hedonism or blind servitude. While some adherents practice derivatives of ancient magic (called *heka* in the Egyptian language), Egyptian Paganism is not a religion of witchcraft and it certainly does not condone 'hexes' or 'black magic'. But unfortunately, because Egyptian Paganism expresses devotion through practices long abandoned by post-Industrial America and Europe, misunderstanding and misconceptions about the faith abound. Before exploring any further into the specifics of Egyptian Pagan beliefs, it is high time we separated what is fact from what is fiction.

What Egyptian Paganism Is *Not* About

Delineating what Egyptian Paganism does *not* focus on requires more immediate attention than what it *does* focus on, owing to the many misconceptions about Egyptian civilization created by our popular culture. Ever since the Greek era, observers have taken their own impressions of Egypt away with them, often incorrectly. Hollywood monster movies and modern Egyptomania 'conspiracy theories' have only added more layers of confusion. Let's examine some of the more commonly-held myths:

Egyptian Paganism is not obsessed with death. So many concepts associated with Egypt have a funerary association: mummies, tombs, and the so-called Book of the Dead (which, to the ancient Egyptians, was called "The Book of Going Forth by Day"). But researchers in the field of Egyptology refer to this as a "mortuary bias" in our collection of remaining artifacts. This material imbalance does not reflect what the Egyptian faith directed most of its energies toward, which was living and not dying. Like their ancient counterparts, modern Egyptian Pagans are primarily concerned with how to live. Their first preparation for a good afterlife is to live a just, happy life.

Egyptian Paganism does not worship dogs and cats. Two of the most famous deities to come from Egypt, Anubis and Bast, are embodied by the dog (or jackal) and cat respectively. Consequently, many casual observers – and a few more interested parties – assume that worshiping Anubis or Bast in Their animal forms is the crux of Egyptian religion. There is in fact more to being an Egyptian Pagan than being a "cat person", or having a preoccupation with anthropomorphic canines. Scores of Egyptian deities have animal avatars, ranging from falcons to cows to crocodiles, while some are known only by human forms. The sun god Ra was known to assume the incarnation of a tomcat, ram, and even a scarab beetle. (Incidentally, those "flesh-eating scarab beetles" of the early 2000's *Mummy* franchise are pure fiction. Scarab beetles are actually harmless, subsisting on dung.) Part of the complexity, and indeed profundity, of Egyptian Paganism is that it seeks to understand the nature of divinity through a multitude of forms.

Egyptian Paganism is not strictly a Goddess religion. Isis is certainly the most famous of Egyptian goddesses, having transplanted into other faiths as early as the Greco-Roman era. But in Egypt, She did not stand alone. Whereas most traditions of Wicca choose to focus either primarily on the Goddess aspect of divinity or on the duality of God-Goddess, Egyptian Paganism looks to the ancient prototype of a divine family. Isis, for example, forms a triad with Her husband Osiris and son Horus. Another popular goddess, Sakhmet, is wife to Ptah and mother to Nefertem. Scores of such family triads were worshiped across ancient Egypt, and continue to be worshiped by modern Egyptian Pagans today.

Egyptian Paganism is not a "shamanic" religion. Some books and popular misconceptions have tried to compare the apple of Egyptian religion to the oranges of Native American spirituality and shamanism. Not only is authentic Siberian shamanism different from Native American religions, (many American Indians don't even like to use the word 'shaman',) but both are also totally unrelated to ancient Egyptian society and beliefs. The ancient Egyptians did not practice *animism*, or the personification of natural elements, which is a common feature of shamanism. Egyptian services were officiated by priests and priestesses, not shamans; and the extended family, not a tribe, was the most important unit in Egyptian society. Whatever concept of "tribe" their Neolithic ancestors may have held would have been extinct by the time the first pharaoh ruled a united Egypt.

Egyptian Paganism does not "belong" to any one race, ethnicity or continent. Google the word "Kemetic" and inevitably pages will turn up for Egyptian-themed black pride rallies and clubs, as well as articles attacking modern archaeology as 'Euro-centrically biased' attempts to cover up the 'true' source of all civilization, being ancient Egypt. Even setting aside the academic flaws of such arguments – which are many – the viewpoint unfairly tries to co-opt ancient Egypt as the intellectual "property" of one group of people. At the height of Egypt's civilization there were a variety of races and ethnicities living and working under the pharaohs. While their physical relics belong to modern Egypt, their written and spiritual legacy belongs to the world; it belongs to *all* of us, to protect and to cherish.

A king, "nisut" or pharaoh figure is not necessary to practice organized Egyptian Paganism. The Egyptian king was known by the native titles *per a'ah,* or 'Great House' (root of our word "pharaoh"), and *nisut* ('king'). Because the king was also considered the living embodiment of the god Horus, some groups insist that the office of *nisut* remains essential to having an Egyptian congregation. They also cite the ancient pharaohs' role as high priest of every god. Aside from the considerably dangerous potential for abuse of power from such a position – a charge that has already been leveled against the Kemetic Orthodox in particular – this claim ignores Egypt's own history. Following the Persian invasion, for example, the country had no *nisut*. Petosiris, the high priest in his hometown of Hermopolis, reorganized local temples himself and performed traditional kingly duties in groundbreaking ceremonies. But he never took on any kingly titles to do so. Petosiris recognized, as do growing numbers of Egyptian Pagans today, that faith in the gods does not require a king by any name.

A caveat: ***Egyptian Paganism as an "African Traditional" religion.*** Both Afrocentrists and the Kemetic Orthodox tradition argue that, because Egypt lies on the African continent, ancient Egyptian religion must be counted as an "African Traditional Religion". Geographically speaking, this argument would be correct. However, the label also suggests Egyptian religion bears direct kinship with Voudon, Santaria, Candomble' and other African Diaspora religions that are derived from the Yoruba traditions of western Africa. Despite many attempts to meld living Yoruban religious practices with what we know of Egyptian practices, the connections are far from seamless. Most notably, we have no records of ritual possession as practiced in Voudon ever being practiced in pharaonic Egypt. Adherents of Diaspora religions have pointed out parallels between Egyptian deities and *orishas* from Diaspora traditions; but followers of Hinduism, Celtic Paganism and Hellenism have likewise found parallel roles and symbolism within the Egyptian pantheon, so the case for direct evolution based on similar elements grows thin. While the heading of "African Traditional Religion" might *technically* apply to pharaonic Egyptian religion, using that category also suggests a number of connotations that either do not fit, or might even be misleading. For that reason, I continue to recommend that Egyptian religion - and especially its modern derivative forms of Egyptian Paganism - be kept in its own category for clarity's sake.

What Egyptian Paganism *Is* About

To relate everything that the Egyptian religion celebrates could fill ever so many volumes of books. But now that we have cast off many of the false impressions of this faith, and begun to move past the "strange" exterior that so many have given it, we can start to discover the far richer reality of its ancient roots and modern realization. It's time to uncover what Egyptian Paganism actually is: what it values, how it seeks the divine, what it offers to those who embrace it.

Egyptian Paganism is a religion of life. Rather than focusing heavily on the hope of salvation in the next life, Egyptian Paganism focuses on finding comfort and understanding in this life. The material world in which we live is embraced, not shunned; the Gods and Goddesses have given it to us so that we can improve upon it and build a lasting legacy within it. When They judge us at the end of life, it will be based upon what good deeds we have done, not what earthly pleasures we have avoided. Their message for us is one of positive action and hope. Further, the Egyptian liturgical calendar is filled with festivals honoring fertility, love, renewal, good triumphing over evil, the anniversary of creation and births of deities. While there are also festivals honoring the blessed dead, at the same time they also celebrate what it means to be alive.

Egyptian Paganism looks to a variety of approachable Gods and Goddesses. The ancients left us scores of prayers directed to a multitude of deities; from the most exalted creator gods Amun, Ra and Ptah, down to the local goddess of the Theban peak, Meretseger. These prayers, which speak to us even today, describe the Gods as "hearer[s] of prayers" who "come at the voice of the poor". While They do sometimes punish, They are also swift to forgive. The only 'placation' They truly require of us is ethical conduct, respect and acknowledgment. What They ask of humanity is not servitude or blind adoration, but simply to be involved in our lives. We are the partners of the Gods and Goddesses in managing the created world. They benefit when we call on Their names, and we in turn benefit from Their intercession.

Egyptian Paganism is open to all ages, races, disabilities, genders and orientations. Ancient Egyptian society is noted for the surprisingly modern status of its women; at a time when most other societies treated women as property, an Egyptian woman could own an estate, make her own will and testify in court. As their society grew more cosmopolitan, other races came to be viewed as sharing in the gods' protection. These progressive beliefs continue to be expanded today. Modern Egyptian Pagans include men, women, and transgenders; African-Americans, Caucasians and Native Americans; and all sexual orientations. All genders, disabilities and races are equal in the eyes of the gods. While ancient writers expressed disapproval of homosexuality, modern Egyptian Pagans have found acceptance and equality among fellow worshipers and before their chosen gods, Who do not condemn their sexual orientation as 'sinful' or abhorrent. Nor is there ageism in Egyptian Paganism, which both celebrates a child who became a king and warns that "painful in the sight of Ra is a youth who reviles an old man".

Egyptian Paganism promotes the ethical treatment of our fellow beings. In the famous "Monologue of the Creator", Ra states that "I made every man like his fellow; and I did not command that they do wrong". He and the other gods and goddesses hold each person accountable to the same standard of truth and equanimity. Called *ma'at*, it is an ethical standard that promotes fair dealing with others and condemns acts of malice. The Wisdom Texts that provide another basis for Egyptian Pagan morals advise against treating others with harsh words or stingy attitudes. Instead, they promote generosity, gentleness and the value of people over material things. Indeed, a person is considered just who "feeds the hungry and clothes the naked," and "has not caused any to weep". Humankind was said to spring from the tears of Ra; it is up to us whether we become His tears of sadness, or tears of joy.

Indeed, true Egyptian Paganism does not fixate on morbidity, zoolatry or ruler worship. It *does* celebrate love, life, and equality, and its values are universally human. We have cast aside the pulp fiction and taken a first look at the real religion; now we can begin to acquaint ourselves more intimately with its origins as left to us by the ancient Egyptians them-selves. We will start to build a more solid frame of reference for Egyptian Paganism today by re-examining four of the biggest controversies surrounding the subject, then taking a brief overview of the religious history of classical Egypt. From there, we will try to step inside the Egyptians' world and perceive it through their eyes. Finally, we'll get to meet each of their major gods and goddesses in turn, to see what each of Them has to tell us.

Part One - Building a Foundation: Background of Ancient Egypt

As a form of *Pagan Reconstructionist* faith, Egyptian Paganism looks to the past as a source of wisdom that our modern, post-Industrial society often seems to lack. But to reach its buried layers of pharaonic civilization, we must first sift through centuries of misconceptions and foreign influences. It's time to reach back, through the mists of faded memory, into an age when our forebears still stood in awe of the world around them and the Gods who created it.

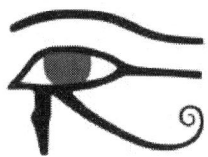

Exodus, Ethnicity and Other Controversies

Many people in both Europe and America first encounter ancient Egypt not through history class, but through church. Every kid who goes to Sunday school or participates in a Pesach (Passover) Seder learns the Biblical tale of Moses, who confronted an unnamed Pharaoh and led his Hebrew people out of slavery. Even beyond houses of worship, Hollywood has permanently fixed an image of Rameses II as actor Yul Brenner from *The Ten Commandments* in the public mind. (The animated film *Prince of Egypt* and live-action *Exodus: God and Kings* both attempted, and ultimately failed, to upstage Yul Brenner's memorable performance.) While the story serves as a powerful theodicy for both the Judeo-Christian and Muslim faiths, it could hardly be treated as a careful historical account. Yet the Exodus story is still viewed as precisely that – a fantastic, but somehow factual, account – or else, in the extreme opposite view, as a malicious fabrication meant to smear a prestigious ancient culture. Amidst these polarized beliefs, a balanced view of the Egyptians and *their* side of the story gets buried somewhere in the sand dunes. Break out your shovels, it's time to start digging.

The main problem with the Exodus tale, in all its translations and Hollywood remakes, is that in order to portray the Hebrews as devout and heroic, it paints the Egyptians as amoral and devoid of religious devotion. The Muslim Qur'an goes a step further and states the Egyptians worshiped Satan. Nothing could be further from the truth. Greek tourists and writers, most notably Herodotus, observed that Egyptians were the most devout worshipers they ever met. The Egyptians believed in the triumph of order and righteousness, or *ma'at*, over evil and chaos; they held themselves to moral standards which they believed they would be tested upon after death in the Hall of Two Truths; and they expressed personal piety on tablets and personal monuments which survive to the present day. It must be remembered, the Exodus story was told from the very beginning with an overall goal in mind: to convince its audience of the supremacy of the Judaic, later the Christian and Muslim, religious belief systems over polytheism. At the time of the tale's inception, the gods of the Egyptian empire represented some of the biggest kids on the block.

But we know that the tale of Exodus is not a complete fabrication, because we have ample archaeological evidence that some of the ancient Hebrews' ancestors once lived in Egypt. Tribes from Canaan (modern-day Israel and Palestine) migrated and settled in the Egyptian Delta region during the late Middle Kingdom and the Second Intermediate Period. An Egyptian tomb painting from Beni Hasan pictures them driving their flocks of sheep and goats, with women dressed in distinctively patterned dresses and men playing the same kind of lyre referred to in the Old Testament as the "harp of David". They made their capital at a city in the eastern Nile delta now called Tell ed Da'ba, better known by its Greek name, Avaris. Their burials and grave goods are all distinctively Canaanite (Dever, 2001). Native Egyptians referred to these intruders as *Heqau Khasut*, the "Rulers of Foreign Lands" (or perhaps simply 'Foreign Rulers'), because they set up a rival dynasty of kings now counted as the Fifteenth, or *Hyksos,* Dynasty. The names of these Hyksos kings were recorded in later Egyptian kings lists, including one 'Yaqub'[1] - which matches the Hebrew name we now render as 'Jacob'. Whether Jacob the Hyksos King is the same as Jacob, father of Joseph who owned the 'Technicolor dream coat', can never be known for certain.

Eventually the Egyptians ousted the Hyksos, marking a time of heightened nationalism and a series of conquests that made Egypt the first major empire in history. Their path into Canaan became known as the "Ways of Horus", Horus being embodied by the pharaoh leading military campaigns. The vassal states they maintained in Canaan wrote frequent letters, impressed in cuneiform script on clay tablets, to the reigning pharaoh; an entire cache was discovered at Akhenaton's capital and are now known as the Amarna Letters. These letters have been studied by Biblical archaeologists as well as Egyptologists, and in particular William G. Dever has cited them to vividly describe Canaan at the dawn of what would become ancient Israel in his work, <u>Who Were The Early Israelites And Where Did They Come From?</u>. Religious fundamentalists often claim that the Egyptians never recorded their devastating losses due to the Ten Plagues, thus dismissing the lack of physical evidence for them; and yet we find proof that an ancient Israel did indeed come to exist from none other than royal Egyptian records.

We even know by what time this early Israel would have been known because of a famous stela commissioned by Pharaoh Merenptah, son of Rameses II. Its hieroglyphic text records the king's victories in Libya and Canaan, claiming, "Israel is laid waste, its seed is not," and uses a determinative sign indicating a group of people (Dever, 2001). Merenptah's claim might have been a bit exaggerated, but his inscription is in fact the oldest historical reference to Israel anywhere in the ancient world.

So we know that a group of Canaanites now considered to be the Hebrews' ancestors had in fact settled in Egypt at one time, but eventually left to return to the desert hills of Canaan. They probably did make some sort of 'Exodus' out of the Nile delta, but it was hardly in the dramatic Cecil B. DeMille fashion. Both the Judeo-Christian fundamentalists who insist on a literal reading of the Book of Exodus, and Pagans and post-modern scholars who categorically deny that *any* sort of mass Hebrew migration out of Egypt occurred, all share the common flaw of assuming that accounts from the Torah/Old Testament and Qur'an are the only way to tell the story. But once the religious texts are cross-checked with actual artifacts and knowledge of Egyptology, the setting and characters of a much more realistic - not to mention *fair* - Exodus story present themselves.

To give a name to our Pharaoh and a location to his capital, let's start by examining a minor detail from the Bible.

Exodus 5:7-19 describes Hebrew slaves making mud bricks with straw as a binding agent. This practice was common throughout Egyptian history, even up to recent times. However, mud brick was only used for housing and secular building projects – temples and monuments were made of stone, as they were meant to last for eternity. Their construction required skilled architects and draftsmen familiar with sacred texts, who would certainly not have come from the ranks of slaves; this is another reason why the Hebrews did not build the pyramids. So, the Israelites were put to work on an expanding city, named in some Bible translations as *Pi-Rameses*. This "City of Rameses" has been identified with Avaris. Not only was it the Hyksos' capital city, but also Rameses II's home-town; after he took the throne, or perhaps during a co-regency with his father Seti I, he moved the Egyptian capital from Thebes to Avaris. Moving an entire national bureaucracy would have required massive local manpower to be mobilized, and the Hebrews whose ancestors had settled in the region certainly fit the bill.

Interestingly, the Qur'an provides a better source for details of events between Rameses II, his court and his confronter Moses. In Surah 26:18-19, Rameses actually says to Moses, "Did we not cherish you as a child among us, and did you not stay in our midst many years of your life? And you did a deed of yours which (you know) you did, and you are an ungrateful (wretch)!" Clearly, then, Moses had been raised in the Egyptian court, probably as a "Child of the *Kap*". The *Kap* was an elite school for princes and nobility; not only were future pharaohs and high administrators educated there, but also the children of Nubian chieftains who would later return home to act as local governors. This policy of Egyptian "re-education" was effectively used throughout the New Kingdom period, and quite likely Moses was sent there in the hopes that he might one day act as a regent for his Hebrew brethren. The "ungrateful deed" Rameses referred to is related in Exodus 2:12, when Moses killed an Egyptian overseer and then fled into the desert. While Moses may have been a *Kap* alumnus, he was not the potential king's heir Hollywood painted him to be, able to get off scot-free.

Rameses II, generally accepted to be the Pharaoh of the Exodus. Photo by Krys Garnett

Having never stood trial for his offense, Moses returned to Egypt a wanted man.

The timing of Moses' return was significant. He came before Pharaoh during a festival, and issued his challenge of a contest between religions during the day of feast while the sun was still up (Surah 20:59). At that time the barque shrine of the local god, possibly Seth or even the national god Amun-Ra, would have been parading through the city where people could make offerings or petitions. This would have heightened the effect of Moses' demonstration, directing his challenge not only at the king but also at the god himself. And, had this festival been the Egyptian New Year, it would have held the added bonus of including Moses in the traditional holiday amnesty granted to convicts by the king.

What happened next is important, and the Qur'an restates it several times. The Pharaoh confers with his officials, who warn him: "This is indeed a sorcerer well-versed. His plan is to get you out of your land: then what is it you counsel?" (Surah 7:109-110). What were they so afraid of? Very likely, a memory from their own recent history. Moses' claim of a single, supreme god who had no effigy and no home temple probably sounded eerily reminiscent of the god Aton, whose only representation was the sun and whose sole high priest was Akhenaton. So hated was Akhenaton's memory that his monuments were erased or destroyed, and by Rameses II's time he would have simply been called "the criminal of Amarna". His Aton revolution completely upset the priestly bureaucracy, and it was a young Tutankhamun who finally placated them by restoring traditional religion. Almost a century later, Rameses II was not about to let a perceived ghost from his country's past threaten his right to rule.

So the viziers suggested to him that they stall Moses and his brother Aaron long enough to round up magicians to challenge them. These 'magicians' would most likely have been *Sesh Per Ankh* priests, or "Scribes of the House of Life", from the local temple. The *Per Ankh* was a temple library of spell and amulet manuals, religious texts and hymns. Most large temples had a *Per Ankh*. One of the *Sesh Per Ankh* (a corruption of which became the Coptic word for 'magician') would have been trained in the sleight-of-hand tricks so commonly used in ancient times, such as making rods appear to turn into snakes. As the Qur'an relates, these *Sesh Per Ankh* priests knew a potential promotion when they saw one: "they said, 'Of course, we shall have a (suitable) reward if we win!' He [Pharaoh] said: 'Yes, (and more) – for you shall in that case be (raised to posts) nearest (my person)'" (Surah 7:113-114). If they won the contest, they would be named as viziers; or perhaps one of them might become High Priest of Amun, a powerful position that later rivaled the throne itself. No longer the priestly equivalent of middle-class, they could then expect lavish accommodations for their entire family and funerary monuments commissioned from the king's workshop. One well-performed trick could secure their future for eternity.

Before getting underway, Rameses had a further warning for Moses: "If you do put forward any god other than me, I will certainly put you in prison!" (Surah 26:29) Of course, both the Bible and the Qur'an relate that Moses won. The *Sesh Per Ankh* priests were actually so astonished and afraid that they "fell down prostrate in adoration" (Surah 7:120). Naturally, Rameses didn't find this very amusing. He demanded, "Do you believe in him before I give you permission?" (Surah 7:123). Clearly, Rameses was a man who expected and got the solemn reverence of his subjects. For a runaway criminal of non-Egyptian blood to return and challenge his divine authority was tantamount to treason.

But rather than have Moses executed by impalement, put in prison or his nose cut off, (all standard punishments of the day,) Rameses let him return to his Hebrew people and granted him further audiences. He may not have cared for Moses' manners or his message, but he probably considered Moses a servant of a foreign deity. In fact, by Rameses II's day, Canaanite deities had worshipers in Egypt, and Egyptian deities had made their way into Canaan. Amulets of the Egyptian dwarf god Bes have been found in ancient sites in Israel; and an Egyptian stela pictures a Canaanite-style goddess, frontally nude and standing on a lion, who is named three ways as 'Anat, Astarte and "Qudshu", the "Holy One", a title also used by the Hebrew goddess Asherah. (More on her in a moment.) So Rameses already knew about a variety of gods and goddesses from his subject states in Canaan, and as high priest of all the gods honored in Egypt, he probably invoked some of them himself. This makes his famous line in Chapter 5 of *Exodus*, "I do not know your God," all the more telling. How could Rameses not have known about Yahweh, unless this was the first time anyone had ever invoked 'Yahweh' in front of him in the first place?

As Dever explores in his 2005 book, <u>Did God Have a Wife? Archaeology and Folk Religion in Ancient Israel</u>, that might have been precisely the case. Perhaps one of the most disconcerting (for modern monotheists) revelations that archaeologists have made, which Dever details in much depth, is that most of the ancient Hebrews *were actually polytheists*. They venerated Ba'al, who was also known in Egypt; Asherah, the mother goddess; and her consort El, who is recorded in *Genesis* as the God of the Patriarchs. But then the name 'El' is supplanted by 'Yahweh' (translated as "I Am"); recall how in Exodus 3:14 Moses encounters his God through the burning bush, and Yahweh explains that 'I Am' is the name he would be known by from that time on. But ironically, even Moses' fellow Hebrews didn't readily take to Yahweh; in Exodus 32:4 they melted down their gold jewelry to make a statue of a calf to worship. This would probably have represented El, who was also known as "Bull El". At a site in Israel dated to the 12th century B.C. - right around the time of Rameses II and company - archaeologists unearthed a cast bronze bull statue that resembles the description from Exodus (Dever, 2005). Eventually Yahweh replaced El in Israelite religion, but inscriptions in ancient Hebrew invoke "Yahweh and His Asherah" (p.162) alongside Ba'al and El. In light of this new perspective on the religious practices of the ancient Hebrews, we can hardly consider the Exodus a clash between Judaic monotheism and polytheism. At most, Moses would have been leader of a 'Yahweh tradition' that only later gained supremacy in the state religion of ancient Israel.

So then came the plagues – or did they? The Qur'an briefly mentions that nine took place, as well as drought. The Bible makes no mention of drought, focusing instead on the other plagues. Useful as they may be for dramatic effect, though, their place in history is problematic. Recent research has found that Rameses II ruled during a time of plenty, when the fullness of Nile floods produced bumper crops and Egypt enjoyed one last flowering of prosperity. None of the widespread disasters chronicled in the Plague accounts could have taken place during his reign. We do have evidence of some calamities, but none of them occurred even chronologically close together. For example, an earthquake did destroy one of the temples at Deir el-Bahari, but not until after Rameses II's time. Drought was also known to occur in Egypt, but that too happened long before and long after Rameses II. Plagues of disease did sometimes strike Egypt, including bubonic plague which some believe was carried into Akhenaton's capital city of Amarna by foreign visitors. Scholars also suspect some sort of epidemic took place during Amunhotep III's reign, because he erected scores of statues of Sakhmet, "Lady of Pestilence" and "Mistress of Fear". These votive statues do offer tremendous insight into the Egyptians' response to natural disasters. Such calamities were seen as a manifestation of the goddess Sakhmet's anger, and the Egyptians would have sought to appease her and correct whatever transgressions upset her. The Qur'an even supports this: "But when good times came, they said: 'This is due to us'; when gripped by calamity, they ascribed it to evil omens connected with Moses and those with him" (Surah 7:131). Clearly, a series of pestilences fell far short of converting the Egyptian population to Judaism.

Sakhmet, "Lady of Pestilence"; from the Mut Precinct at Karnak. Photo by Krys Garnett

So, did the plagues actually take place? Probably not quite as the Bible and Qur'an describe them, and not even in the time frame described. The final plague, being the death of every firstborn in Egypt, certainly could not have happened without leaving telltale archaeological clues. Such wholesale death would have overwhelmed the entire nation, but we have no mention in any personal monuments of such a catastrophe. By contrast, we have a plethora of records from the end of the Old Kingdom describing starving villagers, economic turmoil and widespread despair. Folk tales of disastrous phenomena over the course of several centuries probably passed through generations of Hebrews, to be compressed later into what became the *Book of Exodus*. Indeed, no "plagues" struck Rameses II's Egypt except one. Judeo-Christianity and Islam paint him as an inveterate swaggerer and deal-breaker, but it could be that the death of his beloved firstborn son Amun-her-khopeshef, combined with the weight of royal responsibilities, was enough to make a grieving Rameses let the Hebrews go.

1. The Hyksos King Yaqub may have also been the inspiration for a claim made by some Afrocentric Kemetic groups that an evil scientist named Yaqub created the European races from genetic experiments performed upon Africans; but while this idea sheds some light on a few modern conspiracy theories, it could hardly be treated as sound science.

This prince of Rameses II, holding an emblem of office, served in his bureaucracy and may have predeceased him; from Abu Simbel. Photo by Krys Garnett

Atonism: The World's First Monotheism?

Just as many people today still hear about Egypt in a Bible school context first, scholars of the 18th and 19th centuries who first traveled to Egypt understood its ancient culture from a similar frame of reference. Some of the very people renowned today as pioneers of Egyptology, such as Jean Francois Champollion, the Frenchman who translated the Rosetta Stone, and his successor Emmanuel de Rouge', were also devout Christians hoping to find support for their religion's tenets within Egyptian ruins. The 19th-century British Egyptologist E. A. Wallis Budge, whose translation of the *Book of the Dead* and other books on Egyptian religion are easily accessible today, was also a staunch Christian who actually hoped to disprove Darwin's theories through archaeological records. So pervasive was this dogmatic bias among the first generations of Egyptologists that many of them insisted on interpreting the entire Egyptian religion as sort of 'monotheism in disguise'. So as details slowly came to light of a unique pharaoh, Akhenaton, and his worship of the sun disk Aton in place of all other gods, these early scholars were intrigued. Here was an ancient historical figure who believed much as they did – or so they thought. Modern scholars are re-examining how we understand Atonism and its founder, but those colored "first impressions" are still difficult to shake. Ultimately, the uniqueness of the Amarna period and the superficial resemblance between Atonism and modern monotheistic religions has helped make it one of the most controversial periods of ancient Egyptian history.

Flip through virtually any book that discusses Atonism and you will find the parallel cited between the "Hymn to the Aton" and Psalm 104 of the Bible. For example, the verse of Psalm 104:24 says,

"Oh lord, how manifold are thy works!
In wisdom hast thou made them all;
the earth is full of thy creatures."

The Great Hymn to Aton is a bit more long-winded, saying:

"How many are your deeds,
though hidden from sight,
O sole god beside whom there is none!
You made the earth as you wished, you alone,
All people, herds and flocks;
All upon earth that walk on legs,
All on high that fly on wings..."

Based on their similarity of content, some have claimed that the Aton Hymn actually inspired the Psalm. This alluring conclusion even prompted the famous father of psychoanalysis, Sigmund Freud, to suggest a link between Akhenaton and Moses. But despite the overwhelming lack of evidence to support this line of thought, armchair Egyptologists for the last century have continued to add to it – one recent book even claims that Akhenaton's maternal grandfather Yuya was the Biblical Joseph, and that Akhenaton himself was a "Hebrew pharaoh". Most of these theories go on to claim that either Atonism was the original inspiration for Judaism and Christianity, that Judaism inspired Atonism, or that the traditional Egyptian religion was itself a monotheism (which will be discussed below). As with the story of the Exodus, all of these suppositions fail to examine Atonism and Egyptian spirituality from within, on their own merit. Understanding Atonism's place in the evolution of Egyptian religion proves how both really relate to modern monotheism.

For starters, books written for beginning audiences give the false impression that Aton was a deity created overnight. In actuality, Aton was referred to as an aspect of the sun god Ra centuries before Akhenaton in the Pyramid Texts. Aton manifested as the physical disc or globe of the sun, "glittering" in the sky. This shining attribute would later figure heavily into the sun worship of Akhenaton's father, Amunhotep III.

The office of pharaoh had always held ties to the sun god – either Horus, Ra, or their combined form Ra-Horakhety – since the dawn of recorded history. This divine connection was most celebrated during the Old Kingdom or Pyramid Age, when "Son of Ra" was officially adopted into the king's names and titles. By Amunhotep III's day, people looked back upon the Old Kingdom as a golden age of stability and achievement. Pharaohs were especially nostalgic, because their Old Kingdom predecessors had ruled absolute as living gods. Amunhotep III's own father Thutmose IV left inscriptions which suggest that he felt a close personal connection to the sun god in his sphinx aspect, Hor-em-Akhet. New scholarship also concludes that Thutmose IV, father of Amunhotep III and grandfather of Akhenaton, was the first of his line to portray himself as equal to the gods while he was still alive.

His son took this idea and figuratively ran with it. Amunhotep III adopted the title "Dazzling Disk of Aton" to describe himself. He also borrowed a motif from his great-great aunt, Hatshepsut, and built a chapel portraying his divine conception by Amun in the guise of his father. While Hatshepsut is thought to have done this to proclaim her legitimacy as a female pharaoh, Amunhotep III may have done it to continue the idea that his father was divine – acting as an avatar of Amun – and thus that Amunhotep himself was divine.

Who were these pharaohs trying to aggrandize themselves to? The common people of Egypt already looked to their kings as the earthly representations of gods. But another faction was steadily building power within the court, and in a sense it was the monster that the pharaohs themselves created: the priesthood of Amun. In the early days of the Eighteenth Dynasty (Amunhotep III's family line), kings brought back spoils of war and donated them reverently to Amun's temples. Hatshepsut herself acted in tremendous piety, erecting obelisks and chapels throughout Thebes and constructing her famous temple at Deir el-Bahari. All of this expansion, donating land, cattle and material wealth to Amun, made the high priests in the god's service some of the wealthiest men in the nation. The resources and manpower at their command gave them much the same sway as corporate lobbyists hold today in American politics. In fact, Amunhotep III broke with tradition and made a non-royal woman his queen by marrying Tiya, daughter of Yuya, a high priest of Min (a god connected with Amun), and Tjuya, a priestess of Amun. Queen Tiya was a powerful woman in her own right, and Amunhotep seemed to love her like no other; but the marriage held deep political implications. Suddenly the Amun priests had unprecedented access to the throne and whomever occupied it.

Interestingly, Amunhotep III had two sons; the oldest was named for his grandfather Thutmose, but died while still in his teens. His younger son was named after him as Amunhotep IV, but would later become known to the world as Akhenaton. Probably before ascending the throne, Akhenaton married another powerful and beautiful woman, Nefertiti. At one time it was thought that Nefertiti was a foreign princess married to the pharaoh to cement a treaty, but new research contends that she was actually from the same family of Amun priests as her mother-in-law Tiya. If indeed true, it further underscores the pressure being exerted upon the throne by the Amun priests.

At first, Amunhotep IV/Akhenaton stuck to orthodox themes, commissioning some work in the temple of Amun at Karnak and to Osiris in Abydos. But he heavily emphasized solar gods, especially Ra-Horakhety – remember that link to Old Kingdom pharaohs? Some Egyptologists have portrayed Akhenaton as an idealist and a dreamer, seeking a better way to worship; but given the background of pressures he faced as king, he was more likely a brooding young man determined to continue his father's legacy, recapture an era of glory and re-consolidate a bureaucracy that was growing beyond his control. He was probably looking for a place to make his fresh start when he had an intense personal revelation that would later be recorded on boundary stelae for his new city, Akhet-Aton: riding into the desert in his chariot, he saw the sun come up through a break in the cliffs that mimicked the shape of the hieroglyph for "horizon". We will never know what emotions moved Akhenaton that fateful morning, but the moment was so significant he performed services on its anniversary for rest of his life.

Within three years of that event he had a new city built and moved some twenty-thousand people into it. By doing this, he effectively transplanted all of the bureaucracy that owed its allegiance to him away from the Amun faction back at Thebes. But he still managed to "pull strings" with the Theban clergy, at one point even sending the high priest of Amun on an expedition into the desert! During this early period of transition the old temples were allowed to continue operating, and even the verbose title given to Aton included the names of other gods: "The living one, Ra-Horakhety who rejoices in the two horizons in his name of Shu, which is from Aton". Clearly Atonism was not a true monotheism at this initial stage. In fact, it wasn't even that great of a departure from the current religious climate. Remember the Great Hymn to Aton's words? It addressed Aton as:

"...sole god beside whom there is none!

You made the earth as you wished, you alone,

All people, herds and flocks;

All upon earth that walk on legs,

All on high that fly on wings..."

Compare the Aton Hymn's words with those of a hymn to *Amun*:

"You are the Sole [or Unique] One, who made all that exists...

He who made pasture for the cattle and fruit-trees

for men. He who made the food for the fish in the

river and the birds which live in the sky..."

The similarity is remarkable. In fact, modern scholars now acknowledge that Atonism as a religious movement actually has its precedents in the worship of Amun as primary creator god. This phase of Egyptian faith is defined as *henotheism*; which is still essentially polytheistic, but focuses on one deity at a time depending on the situation. At the start of his reforms, Akhenaton essentially changed the "window dressing" of developing henotheism from worship of Amun-Ra to worship of Aton. He also eliminated the need for a priestly bureaucracy, as the only pictorial representation of Aton was the sun globe, and Akhenaton acted as his sole high priest. Numerous stela were carved of the royal family basking beneath Aton for private shrines, though. The people worshiped Akhenaton, and he in turn offered their devotion to Aton.

Year Nine of his reign marked a big change in policy. The severity and scale suggest that it was perhaps a counter-reaction to the Amun priesthood balking at their loss of prestige. By Akhenaton's decree, no longer would the old gods coexist with Aton. Agents of the king were sent out across the country to hack out the names of Amun, his consort Mut, and even the plural of "god" wherever they found it. Not even his father Amunhotep III's monuments were safe. Temples were shut down, and suddenly the Amun priests found themselves completely out of a job. Meanwhile, life continued at Akhet-Aton, where the king made regular public appearances and encouraged celebrations in the name of Aton, the "sole god beside whom there is none". But the common folk living in his city still clung to their household gods, as figurines of Bes and Tawret found in the site attest.

This is the period many consider to be the world's first monotheism, but it still differs too greatly in its ideology to have been the forerunner of Judeo-Christianity. Akhenaton worshiped a universal god, but his people were meant to direct their reverence to him. In another interpretation, Akhenaton sought to replace the older divine triads by offering himself and his queen Nefertiti as objects of devotion, prototypes of a new divine couple with Aton above. This interpretation would mean Atonism was still by definition a poly-theism. By contrast, Judaism eliminated the concept of a divine family or any earthly manifestation of a deity altogether. But Akhenaton's bold experiment failed after his death, as his city was abandoned and his temples were dismantled. It took another three millennia for audiences to appreciate, whether for good or ill, his personal passion and political shrewdness.

But what about the rest of Egypt's religion, both before and after Akhenaton? Was it an almost-monotheism? And what of the terms sometimes applied to it, such as *monolatry* and the aforementioned henotheism? Much has been misconstrued about these ideas. Egyptian religion was not a monotheism at any point outside of the latter half of the Aton revolution. While early scholars bent of finding support for Judeo-Christian beliefs tried to re-frame Egyptian faith as a monotheism, their arguments were based on shaky evidence that has since been disproven, such as interpretation of the Wisdom Texts and the meaning of the word *netjer*, or "god". But language such as the Hymn to Amun does suggest an exclusive focus on a particular deity, without going so far as to deny the existence of the other gods. This is the definition of henotheism, and also of monolatry; the two terms can be used interchangeably. 'Henotheism' in particular has also been used to describe Hinduism, to which Egyptian religion has been more recently compared. However, outside of the scholarly realm, the term 'monolatry' has wrongly been used to self-describe Kemetic religious movements that interpret the various gods and goddesses as simply different aspects of an original deity. Not only does this idea re-package the same position once used by the early Egyptologists, but it also does not fit the definition of monolatry – it is more accurately called *pluriform monotheism*. Meanwhile, many Wiccans have adopted the Greco-Roman view that all deities are essentially the same, regardless of which name is used to address them. "Isis of Ten Thousand Names" is presented this way in *The Golden Ass* by Apuleius. This belief system is sometimes wrongly called 'henotheism', but is more appropriately termed *inclusive monotheism*, because it reveres oneness despite a multitude of possible presentations.

Such a plethora of labels and '-isms' can grow confusing. Even Egyptologist Erik Hornung, author of the definitive text <u>Conceptions of God in Ancient Egypt: The One and the Many</u>, noted how bewilderingly easy it is to reduce Egyptian religion to an '-ism' or mere slogan. Perhaps the best way to understand ancient Egypt's faith is through a visual metaphor. Atonism is like a web camera; it stays trained on just one view, being Aton, which never shifts. Traditional Egyptian religion, meanwhile, is like a movie camera; it can zoom in for a close-up on just one deity, or pull back to a 'medium shot' on a family triad. Occasionally a 'long shot' encompassing many deities is also used. But a complete, dynamic picture of the whole religion, as in film, requires all three angles in order to work.

Were the Ancient Egyptians Black?

In the original opening to this section, I wrote that "Here in the United States, race is always a thorny issue." Looking back, that sentence feels like something of an understatement. Despite electing our first African-American president to two consecutive terms, in our public discourse we have come to realize that racial equality has not yet been fully realized. What does this have to do with Egyptian Paganism and Kemetic spirituality? To some practitioners, it has *everything* to do with Kemeticism, so we have to try to understand the controversy of ethnicity in ancient Egypt more fully if we hope to build a greater sense of accord among Kemetic and Egyptian Pagans of varying stripes. To gain a more solid background on the question, we need to re-examine two related topics: first, the history of archaeology as a scholarly discipline, and how it views itself; and second, the rise of the Afrocentric movement.

While this observation drastically condenses several developments within the early field, it can be said that archaeology as we know it today developed during the 1800's when wealthy European and American men realized that they could learn more about ancient cultures by studying objects in their find sites than they could by simply absconding antiquities like so much buried treasure. (Rosalie David's <u>Discovering Ancient Egypt</u> and Lise Manniche's <u>City of the Dead</u> describe this history in sometimes painful detail.) But as these early archaeologists began piecing together remnants of ancient Egyptian civilization, they interpreted those clues through their own values and experiences - which we now qualify as 'Victorian', 'imperialist', Judeo-Christian, and, yes, racist and sexist. Their value judgments influenced many initial ideas about Egyptian religion, culture, and ethnicity.

One early theory held that Egypt's original, pre-Dynastic inhabitants were a primitive assemblage of tribes who were united by an invading 'Dynastic race' that came from ancient Mesopotamia (in what is now Iraq), who brought with them the tools of writing and civilization. The 'Dynastic race' theory is rife with racial and even religious bias; if one holds as truth the Biblical view that all humanity sprang from the ancestors of the Patriarchs, then surely humans must have all come out of ancient Mesopotamia, including the 'proper', Dynastic ancient Egyptians. But by the late twentieth century this idea fell out of favor, especially as further digs in the Abydos region of Egypt revealed a native 'Dynasty 0' that developed writing and social stratification on its own. By the 1980's, archaeology as a discipline began to realize just how subjective much of its early work had been. By adopting strategies from anthropology and sociology, modern archaeologists attempt to draw more nuanced conclusions about ancient peoples and redress the biases of earlier generations of scholars.

Unfortunately, much of their published work remains highly inaccessible to the public at large, because it stays locked away in academic journals that only graduate students can access; new books from 'post-processual' archaeologists published on the open market remain fairly expensive; and because their writing style and jargon are all but incomprehensible to readers not familiar with both sociology and philosophy. What does remain cheap to buy or even free to download, however, is the outdated, racist, sexist, Christian imperialist - and *prolific* - work of pioneer Egyptologist E. A. Wallis Budge. Sadly, anyone coming to the subject of ancient Egypt from a spiritual perspective who has no prior knowledge of Egyptology's 'growing pains' will probably assume that Budge's Egyptian Magic, The Egyptian Book of the Dead, The Egyptian Heaven and Hell, Dwellers on the Nile, and literally at least a dozen other titles, all represent our current state of knowledge. (Even some books that still contain useful information, notably Winifred S. Blackman's 1927 work The Fellahin of Upper Egypt, also express markedly racist or prudish value judgments; but at least this fact is pointed out in the foreword to a 2000 reprint by native Egyptologist Salima Ikram.) Those of us seeking an alternative to the Judeo-Christian worldview might find the inherent biases in this corpus of older work confusing or downright annoying. But imagine the reaction of African-American readers when they pick up books by a thoroughly colonialist, Victorian English Egyptologist who makes denigrating comparisons to 'primitive African tribes'. Enter the Afrocentric movement.

'Afrocentrism' is thought to have been first coined as a term by African-American scholar and civil rights activist W. E. B. DuBois. It began to gain popularity as a philosophy and a way of interpreting history in the 1970's, which not coincidentally is also the same time-frame in which the Ausar-Auset Society began. (The term *Kemetic* is thought to have been coined by the Ausar-Auset Society.) Afrocentrism, in its most basic essence, seeks to re-examine history from an African and not a European point of view, and promote the contributions of Africans to world history and culture. Controversy arises, however, over the proposed extent of African ethnic and cultural contributions: such as, that the Olmec civilization of Central America rose to prominence because of African contact; that the Phoenicians and ancient Greeks were either influenced by or 'stole from' African cultures; that certain South Asian phenotypes are the result of African genetic influence; and most pertinently for our discussion, that the ancient Egyptians either migrated out of Nubia, or else were overtly 'black' (as in 'sub-Saharan African'), and that the lighter complexion of modern Egyptians is the result of successive invasions beginning with the Hyksos and continuing up through the Ottoman Turks. Furthermore, the most strident proponents of the 'black Egyptians' view charge that even modern archaeologists and the government of Egypt itself have all engaged in systematic attempts to 'cover up' the 'true identity' of the ancient Egyptians.

While these ideas can appear highly attractive to African-Americans who grow up bombarded by negative stereotypes and systemic racism, the scholarship behind some of these claims is highly flawed, or at the very least paints too broad and sweeping of a picture. Understandably, the modern inhabitants of Egypt take great offense at the suggestion that their ancestors were essentially guilty of invasion, theft and ethnic cleansing; to them, the claims of Afrocentrists are just as imperialist as the old European views of Orientalism. (Similarly, native Mesoamerican scholars reject the idea that African settlers were behind the achievements of the Olmec peoples.) Modern scholars have repeatedly tried to point out that 'race' as we imagine it today is a thoroughly modern invention - 'modern' in this sense meaning within the last few centuries of human history. We can also point out that skin tone, facial features and hair textures in any given population can vary widely, and that from this perspective 'blackness' is often simply in the eye of the beholder. But the Afrocentric meaning of 'black' carries a much more charged meaning and sense of identity. To address it we have to set aside northern Egypt's long historical ties to the Levant (modern Syria and Israel-Palestine), Libya and the Mediterranean, instead delving into the Nile Cataracts and Nubia, much closer to the heart of Africa.

The name "Nubia", which may have come from *nub*, the Egyptian word for 'gold', refers to the territory stretching from the First to the Sixth Cataracts of the Nile; or, from the modern town of Aswan in southern Egypt to Khartoum in modern Sudan. Oddly, "Nubia" as a place name does not appear in texts until Greco-Roman times (O'Connor, 1993). During pharaonic times the northern section of Nubia (called "Lower Nubia" because it lies downstream) was called Wawat. Wawat occupies what is now southernmost Egypt. Further to the south, in Upper Nubia (modern Sudan), lay Kush - often referred to in official texts as 'wretched Kush', for reasons we shall soon explore.

The Predynastic (also called Naqada) Period in Egypt corresponds with an A-Group in Lower Nubia, and Pre-Kerma culture in Upper Nubia. Some Afrocentrists cite the work of archaeologist Bruce Williams, who theorized that an A-Group royal cemetery in Qustul, Sudan held the first 'Egyptian-style', pharaonic kings; thus, they claim, Egyptian culture originated in Nubia. But since then, royal burials in Abydos, Egypt have been unearthed that are even older that the Qustul ones. (This debate is explained in clear, even-handed terms in David O'Connor's Ancient Nubia: Egypt's Rival in Africa.) Probably the fairest conclusion one can make is that Nubian and Egyptian civilizations began to take shape at roughly the same time, sharing some similarities but also distinct differences. But mysteriously, when Egypt unified and its Early Dynastic (or Archaic) Period began, Lower Nubia's A-Group peoples seem to have disappeared. Wawat became a veritable no-man's land for several centuries. It would ultimately provide the perfect place, however, for Egyptian pharaohs to build a series of impressive fortresses.

Before we continue, a quick geography lesson may help put Egypt and Nubia's relationship into perspective. Typically, books on ancient Egypt describe the Nile Cataracts - a series of rocky granite rapids that make heavy boat traffic treacherous if not impossible - as a natural border against invasion. But the Twelfth-Dynasty pharaoh Senwosret III might beg to differ. He led military campaigns into Nubia, setting up victory inscriptions exhorting his successors to defend his borders, then built a sequence of fortresses around the Second Cataract with their headquarters at Semna, a bastion so complex it would not be equaled until Roman times. His official policy was that the *Nehesyu*, or Nubians living in the Nile Valley, could travel as far as the forts to trade goods; there, they would be treated hospitably and allowed to stay the night, but the next day they would have to return south. No *Nehesyu* would be allowed to pass northward, by river or land.

Such a strict policy might easily lead one to conclude that no Nubians ever went into Egypt - but that would not be the case. Even as early as the Old Kingdom (see the next chapter for a fuller explanation of Egyptian history), pharaohs employed Nubians from a desert tribe called the *Medjayu* as archers, mercenaries and security; later, the word *Medjay* would become synonymous with 'police'. Nubian princes were brought into the royal court to learn alongside Egyptians. And later in the Eleventh Dynasty, as some scholars now believe, King Montuhotep II and some of his wives may have themselves been of Nubian descent (Fisher, in Fisher, Lacovera et al, 2012). But in spite of this possible blood connection, he too led armies into Wawat, establishing fortresses and even ordering ritual execration rites against Nubian enemies.

Whenever Egypt's political and military power waned, Nubia's civilization waxed and grew stronger. In Upper Nubia, the kingdom of Kush first began to gain strength during the Middle Kingdom - hence Senwosret III's need for strict border security. The Kushite capital was most likely the city of Kerma, which grew to be the largest city in Africa outside of Egypt itself. Kerma culture reached its zenith during the Second Intermediate Period; while the Egyptians were preoccupied with fighting the Hyksos in the Nile Delta, the Kushites were able to take control of Wawat and conduct raids into Egypt itself. But after finally expelling the Hyksos, the nascent Eighteenth Dynasty kings then turned their attention to Nubia, retaking Wawat and pushing into Kush itself. Kerma was eventually sacked, and Kush became an Egyptian colony.

Scholars debate whether Nubia suffered or benefited from Egyptian control. We do know that Nubian culture began to adopt more distinctly Egyptian elements. Because of temples to Amun built by Egyptian pharaohs in Nubian towns, Amun and his consort Mut took on great prominence in Nubian religion, alongside native gods like the lion-headed Apademak. Egyptian language was spoken in administrative and commercial activities, and Nubian princes continued to travel to the Egyptian capital to be educated as "Children of the *Kap*". But the Nubians gave things their own flair; for example, rituals in Nubian temples offered millet porridge and beer instead of wheat or barley bread, because the more arid conditions of Wawat and Kush make wheat and barley more difficult to grow. The god Anubis was adopted into Nubian religion, but because mummification generally was not practiced in Nubia, they emphasized Anubis' role as a kindly shepherd, something that resonated with their experience as cattle herders.

When Egyptian civilization finally collapsed at the end of the New Kingdom around 1,000 B.C., they lost control over Nubia. But another three centuries passed - called the "Nubian Dark Ages" by some scholars - before the Kushites would return

Conquered Kushites are brought before the Pharaoh; from Medinet Habu. Photo by Krys Garnett

with a vengeance, conquering all of Egypt and establishing the Twenty-Fifth Dynasty.

Because these kings ruled from Napata in Kush, their period of history is called the Napatan Period. Two things are worthy of note during this time: for one, scholars now argue that the Napatan court was so highly literate in Egyptian classical language that their texts comprise a renaissance of Egyptian literature (Doll in Fisher, Lacovera et al, 2012); and secondly, Napatan royal women took on roles of unprecedented power that often had no parallel in Egyptian custom. King Piankhi's wife actually made a speech at his coronation in Memphis, and King Taharqo's mother travelled from Napata to Memphis to see her son crowned, the crowds kneeling in obeisance to her as well as her son.

Around 625 B.C. the Assyrians invaded Egypt, forcing the Kushites back to their homeland. Egypt suffered terribly under the Assyrians, but Nubian civilization had one more incredible flowering to go, known today as the Meroitic Period.

Named for the new capital city of Meroe, this period saw strong rule by Nubian queens, who bore the title of *Kandake*, as well as kings. (This name would eventually enter Latin as 'Candace', perhaps the origin of the personal name.) It was under the reign of Queen Shanakdakheto that a new Meroitic alphabet, based on Egyptian hieroglyphic signs but developed to sound the native Meroitic language, first appeared. Today we can decipher the sounds, and some words, but little else - for the moment. Scholars are even now working to 'crack the code', using possible similarities from modern Sudanese languages, hoping to revolutionize our understanding of Nubian history.

Remains of cities in the Upper Nubian portions of Meroe show a surprisingly cosmopolitan society, complete with Hellenistic art and Roman baths. Indeed, Rome's empire stopped at Egypt's borders; the Nubians, who developed iron working and horsemanship with greater skill than the Egyptians had, held off the Roman armies long enough to force them to a treaty.

The last known Meroitic pharaoh, Yesbokheamani, died around 300 A.D. What happened after that? Scholars are not sure. Another popular Afrocentric theory, that Egyptian/Nubian culture travelled from the Nile River valley westward to the Niger River valley, has no historical evidence but may have been inspired (via oral traditions) by the aftermath of a war between an early Christian kingdom in what is now the Arabian peninsula and the Kingdom of Axum, in modern Ethiopia, to the distant southeast of Meroe. Refugees from Axum are said to have made their way across the continent to eventually mingle with the Yoruba peoples. Whether Nubians ever joined in this legendary migration, no one knows with absolute certainty (and material record to back their claims). We do know that Islam spread from Egypt southward, and across sub-Saharan Africa, some four centuries after the last Nubian pharaoh ruled Meroe.

So, were the ancient Egyptians 'black', as we would recognize it today? Some of them, in fact, were. But if you were to look at the population of pharaonic Egypt as a whole, they would probably have resembled some of our most cosmopolitan and diverse urban centers today, such as the Latino-African sections of Harlem, New York; Creole neighborhoods in New Orleans; Toronto, Canada, and many more places. Most importantly, the ancient Egyptians completely lacked our baggage associated with racial and ethnic/genetic identity. If we should be modeling anything from their society, it should be their absence of any notions of racial superiority, on whatever 'race' one chooses to focus. Clearly they believed that 'Egyptian-ness' could be imparted and shared, not simply encoded into one's DNA (which they would not have understood anyway).

Furthermore, focusing so exclusively on the achievements of a supposedly wholly 'black' ancient Egypt actually takes away much-deserved attention from their southern neighbors in Nubia. Nubian culture had its own share of artistic achievement, urban development and military tenacity. They shared some cultural elements with the Egyptians, but they also developed their own unique religious practices, language, writing system and forms of self-government. They can also count as their own a substantial number of strong women rulers, more so than Egypt did. Surely the legacy of these *Kandake*'s and their people deserves acknowledgment in its own right.

(For an excellent insight into Nubian civilization, I highly recommend Ancient Nubia: African Kingdoms on the Nile, already cited multiple times in this section. The book is new and costs roughly forty US dollars, but it is worth every penny.)

The Great Sphinx, with the pyramid of Khafra (Chepren) in the background. Photo by Krys Garnett

Aliens, Atlantis and the Great Sphinx of Giza

Fascinated as we are by the ancient civilization of the Nile, we modern folk have certainly come up with some wacky and far-fetched ideas about Egyptians. What we've covered up to this point could best be characterized as 'misconceptions'; ideas that are definitely off-target, but still understandable. This last section is devoted to 'myths', in the non-religious, fabricated sense of the word.

Since medieval Europeans first came to Egypt during the Crusades and dubbed them "Joseph's Barns", after the Biblical tale, the Great Pyramids of Giza and their guardian Great Sphinx have mystified us. (This erroneous belief that the Pyramids were grain silos was even espoused by 2016 U.S. Presidential candidate Ben Carson.) Who built them, and why? Today we understand that the pyramids were tombs of kings, focal points in grand memorial temples. But how did such a simple people build such massive stone monuments without even use of the wheel? Some of the explanations put forth to explain the Pyramids' construction show all the colorful imagination of older mythology without the redeeming moral value. Among the most notorious are that the Egyptians used mental telepathy to move stone blocks, or that visiting aliens actually built them with their own advanced technology. A more admirable – but still completely unsupportable – idea even garnered its own *Discovery Channel* documentary, claiming the Egyptians used wind power. The investigating team proved that wind power could indeed be harnessed to move blocks and even a small cement obelisk into place, but failed to offer any evidence that the Egyptians themselves knew how to utilize wind power for anything beyond sailing vessels.

Modern archaeological research, by contrast, has offered tremendous enlightenment. A cemetery and workers' village recently discovered near the Great Pyramids themselves reveals that workers during the flood season quarried blocks from Giza and nearby Tura, hauling the blocks into place with sheer manpower. They lived on-site, and many also died on-site from accidental injuries. Others suffered long-term debilitation such as spinal compression, joint wear and mangled limbs. Ancient medical papyri demonstrate an extensive knowledge of traumatic wound treatment, experience that was dearly bought by the pyramid laborers. To suggest that someone or something else was responsible for the Giza monuments seems a slap in the face to the literal blood, sweat and tears of these early Egyptians.

Not that tall tales about the Pyramids are anything new. The Greek writer Herodotus recorded stories of Pharaoh Khufu (called "Cheops" in Greek) and his lavish, totalitarian rule; that his Great Pyramid took forty years to complete; or even that he pressed his own daughter into prostitution to finance its construction! Research again proves the victor over hearsay. The pyramid of Khufu probably took between ten and twenty years to complete, less than some modern interstate highway projects. Its construction was probably overseen by the vizier Hemiunu, who was perhaps a royal prince, and it did not bankrupt Egypt's economy. The eventual collapse of the Old Kingdom was actually precipitated by factors such as drought and an overexpansion of tax-exempt lands for temple estates, of which the finished pyramids of Giza were only one part.

If the Giza Pyramids are fodder for tales of the bizarre, then the Great Sphinx is a centerpiece for them. Arabs long called it the "Father of Terror", fearing its weathered visage that gazed across the desert sands. Over the centuries, it has been covered up to its chest in sand and then uncovered several times. The Ottoman Turks and Napoleon's troops are all said to have used it for target practice. Now the most popular, and pernicious, tales to circulate about this monumental sculpture are that it was built either by aliens long before the rise of human civilization, or else by the people of the lost continent Atlantis. The biggest piece of supposed evidence for the Sphinx pre-dating Egyptian civilization is traces of water erosion in the rock around its base, which proponents say came about during an earlier geological epoch before the Sahara desert came into being. Well and good – but even archaeologists have observed that the Sphinx was built out of an outcropping in one of the Egyptians' stone quarries. The original stone shape could have been exposed to the elements long before it became what we know today. Furthermore, rainfall still occurs in rare but torrential bursts in Egypt even today, so further water erosion could have come about at any point while the rock was exposed after the Sphinx was built. In addition, the human-headed lion form is a common heraldric image for the pharaoh that was used throughout their history, along with falcon- and ram-headed variants. The Egyptians were quite capable of developing the icon themselves without external guidance. Another tenuous sliver of evidence used by alien proponents are the still-unidentified shapes of some hieroglyphs that resemble helicopters and spaceships. Surely this must prove alien involvement in the Giza monuments? In truth, we can't even decide for certain what the *ankh* symbol represents; guesses range from a stylized sandal strap to a combined male-female element. Just because one symbol looks like a spaceship to us does not mean it couldn't have represented something else entirely to an ancient Egyptian. Objects they would have recognized as everyday tools would seem exotic to our post-Industrial eyes. To assume that their pictograms must represent something we moderners can identify is presumptuous to say the least.

The theories about Atlantis actually have a probable source, one that goes back to those pesky Greek tourists. The Greek reformer, writer and politician Solon, whose travels in Egypt were later chronicled by Herodotus and Plutarch, visited a temple in the Delta city of Sais and asked priests to explain the already-ancient inscriptions on the walls. Included in their stories was Rameses III's war against the Sea Peoples of the Mediterranean. By the Hellenistic era, those events were almost a thousand years old – by our modern count. The Egyptians reckoned dates by the reigns of kings, starting at Year One with each new pharaoh, so needless to say many errors had crept into their system of dating. According to Solon, Egyptian priests counted some eleven thousand years of their own recorded history! (By contrast, modern archaeology estimates written history to date back only 3,200 years B.C.E.) So they presented their Greek guest with an ages-old tale of invaders who came from the sea, as well as a possible account of an island sinking into the ocean as in their *Tale of the Shipwrecked Sailor*. Roll these elements around, throw in some Greek folk tales about cataclysmic floods, and *voila*! We have a 'lost continent' the Greeks call Atlantis. About two thousand years later, some folks come along who don't really know how these pyramid things or the Great Sphinx were built, but they're well-versed in Greek lore; so pressed for an explanation, they assume Atlantians built the ancient monuments. A convenient explanation, but hardly scientific.

One last oddball claim about the Sphinx is that it faces east, not simply because east is home to the all-important sunrise, but because in ages past it would have faced the rising constellation Leo. Supposedly, according to this theory, it was actually built during the "Age of Leo" (as opposed to the "Age of Aquarius"). Aside from the previously discussed issues about the Sphinx's age and original builders, this idea has one other major problem: the Zodiac in which Leo and Aquarius are part is of Greek origin, not Egyptian. The Egyptians didn't even interpret the same constellation imagery as the Greeks. In Hathor's temple at Dendera, a zodiacal ceiling relief combines Greek and native Egyptian constellation groups because it was designed in the

Ptolemaic era. So the Great Sphinx being built to celebrate the "Age of Leo" is an anachronism, because during the "Age of Leo" no one in Egypt would have been aware of the occasion. Instead, they faced the Sphinx east because it embodied Hor-em-Akhet, "Horus in the Horizon", a prestigious ancient avatar of the rising sun.

Before we leave thinking that the Greeks were total morons when it came to Egypt, though, let us recall the Riddle of the Sphinx. Remember how it goes: *What has four legs at morning, two at high noon, and three in the evening?* The answer, of course, is man, who crawls on all fours at its morning of infancy, walks upright at the noon of adulthood and uses a cane in the evening of old age. But do you know where in Egyptian lore that metaphor may have originated?

To find out, you'll just have to keep reading!

You've Got to Know Where You've Been
(To Know Where You're Going)

To examine the history of Egyptian values and religion, and especially to compare it to modern views, is to appreciate the growth of human thought and society. While some of the fundamental elements of what it means to be human have not changed over five thousand years of recorded history, nuances in how people view themselves and the world around them can offer a vivid picture of how far our species has come – and why, in certain definite respects, we can never go back.

Prehistoric Egypt

The roots of ancient Egypt's soaring religious expression, which at its zenith was carved in the stone pylons of Karnak and Luxor, originally lay in prehistoric chiefdoms scattered along the Nile valley and Delta regions. What we know of these small communities comes from their artifacts, as they had no writing. But the basics of religious devotion can be seen in their primitively-carved figurines of goddesses with arms upraised, perching falcons and other animals, and burials that included food, belongings and ritual implements. These prehistoric peoples clearly believed in life after death, divine beings that could take on both human and animal forms, and a direct link between the prosperity of their chiefdoms and the patronage of a deity.

Rulers of these early kingdoms held not only authority over the day-to-day affairs of their villages, but also over religious affairs; one man served as both king and high priest. This contrasts with the American Indians, to whom the ancient Egyptians are sometimes erroneously compared. Most tribes in Native America appointed a chief to lead wars whose role was completely separate from that of the medicine chief or holy man. In the ancient Nile valley, church and state were one and the same under the personage of provincial rulers. These priest-rulers were the prototypes for future pharaohs.

It was from these early proto-pharaohs that many traditions known to classical Egyptian history evolved. For example, the Sed jubilee, celebrated during a pharaoh's thirtieth year of rule as a rite of rejuvenation, harkened back to prehistoric chieftains' required demonstrations of strength upon reaching a certain age. A man unfit to fight and defend his chiefdom's territory was put to death in favor of a successor who could. But it is important to note that a king's success was linked to the success of the entire chiefdom, even the land itself; this reflected his connection to the divine. If the gods favored him, his people would prosper. If they didn't, the people stood in danger of famine or invasion from neighboring kingdoms.

Such invasions no doubt occurred, as well as mergers and alliances, over the centuries until two main kingdoms emerged: Upper Egypt, or the Nile Valley proper, and Lower Egypt, being the Delta. (On a map Lower Egypt is actually above Upper Egypt because the Nile is the world's only major river that flows north, seemingly "upside down".) For a long time it was thought that Upper and Lower Egypt were united as a result of conquest, but modern scholarship suggests that trade and alliance played as much of a role as warfare in the process of unification. But the duality of two kingdoms figured heavily into the Egyptian concept of state. The pharaoh was referred to as "king of the Two Lands", and wore a composite crown made of the two respective crowns worn by Upper and Lower Egyptian rulers.

New archaeological findings also reveal that written language did not come to Egypt from Mesopotamia, as was long believed. It was actually developed locally by order of the first kings of a united nation, the so-called 'Dynasty 0' kings, as a means of recording assets and royal decrees. This discovery seems to complement the ancients' belief that writing was revealed to humankind by revelation from the god of wisdom, Thoth (also called Djehuty). The Egyptians saw no difference in an order from a divine king and revelation from the gods themselves.

Religious and political iconography also traced its beginnings to this time. The famous Narmer palette shows King Narmer in poses that would be echoed throughout pharaonic history: smiting enemies of the state, and wielding agricultural implements in ritual acts to ensure fertility of the land. Even his crown and kilt with a bull's tail in back would be repeated in representations of kings millennia later.

These humble origins formed the bedrock of the great civilization that was to come, one guided by a divinely ordained priest-king and guarded by gods and goddesses who could directly affect the material well-being of the kingdom. Their newfound stability and prosperity would propel the Egyptians' faith to heights they would record in stone.

The Old Kingdom

The first three dynasties who ruled a united Egypt lived during a time called the Archaic Period, where the culture of the nation was still in a formative stage. A bureaucracy formalized under the Third Dynasty king Djoser, whose famous vizier (prime minister) Imhotep designed the Step Pyramid complex at Saqqara. Imhotep also organized the mobilization of massive workforces to complete its construction. The Step Pyramid complex was the first monument to be built in stone, designed to last for eternity. Surrounding the Step Pyramid itself was an entire series of dummy palace buildings and temple facades, recreating shrines of Upper and Lower Egypt and courts for observance of the Sed jubilee. This national outpouring of labor and artisanship for the immortality of its king would be repeated for each new monarch and become one of the major themes of the era.

*Left: **King Djoser wearing a** Sed-festival cloak. *Right: **Dual Shrines of the** Sed-*festival court at the Step Pyramid, Saqqara. Photos by Krys Garnett*

Much of what we consider 'typical' of Egyptian art, society and government took shape under the Fourth Dynasty, which marked the start of the Old Kingdom. Also known as the Pyramid Age, it was truly a golden age of the state. But modern observers looking back upon the Old Kingdom have often struggled to grasp the motivation behind the pyramids and the glory of pharaohs laid to rest within them. Was an entire populace enslaved to gratify one man's ego? In America particularly, where kings are generally equated with despots, this is certainly the first impression. Even the Greek chronicler Herodotus wrote that Egyptians of his day despised the memories of Khufu (Cheops) and Khafra (Chepren), who built two of the three Great Pyramids. But how much of these impressions are true? We simply cannot say for sure. Herodotus wrote that Khufu shut down all of the state temples in favor of his own monuments; this may or may not have been true, but the temples connected to the pyramids may have been used for state religious ceremonies during kings' lifetimes. Meanwhile, other modern scholars have suggested that the rank-and-file citizens of Egypt who built the pyramids saw their work as contributing to their own immortality. By ensuring that their king could live forever, *they* could live forever as his subjects. One archaeologist even compared Egyptians building the pyramids with villagers in medieval Europe building cathedrals. These pyramids were indeed massive shrines that housed the relics of monarchs who lived and died as gods. Regardless of how the workers at Giza may have regarded their kings, the evidence of broken bones and compressed spines found in their own burials bears witness to their effort and dedication.

The supreme level of organization and deployment of manpower needed to build the pyramids has also been credited with making Egypt a more cohesive state. Its economy flourished, and people saw this as a sign of the gods' favor. Inscriptions on personal monuments from the time exhort the values of hard work, service to the king and material rewards.

While in principle, the king was chief priest of every deity, as his earthly responsibilities became too great it was necessary to appoint high priests to act in his name. The height of the Old Kingdom also saw the rise of Ra as sun god *par excellence* and patron of kings, who began using the title "son of Ra". Pharaohs of the Fifth Dynasty built smaller pyramids, devoting more energy instead toward impressive sun temples in Heliopolis, north of modern Cairo, and at Abu Ghurob. Pyramids themselves were considered solar symbols, and as each pharaoh died the pyramid temple erected during his lifetime took on the duties of his memorial observances. All of these temples had their own staff, as well as lands to supply food for daily offerings and the staff's needs. Thus a priestly bureaucracy was born, an entity that would shape and be shaped by politics throughout the rest of pharaonic history.

Prosperity and unity were not to last forever, though. Toward the end of the Old Kingdom, famine struck the nation. After the extraordinarily long-lived King Pepy II ruled for almost a century, the pharaohs' temporal power began to weaken. High priests and regional governors, whose offices had become hereditary, began to act on their own accord and ceased answering to the crown. Egypt slowly slipped into a sort of depression known as the First Intermediate Period, which was characterized by reversals of fortune and weak leadership. One dynasty of kings lasted only about seventy days. Scribes living toward the end of the First Intermediate period described well-to-do families forced to beg for food, villagers resorting to cannibalism, and a national feeling of despair. The faith of many were deeply shaken.

Proverbial seeds of change, however, had already been planted. Our records of it come from the Pyramid Texts, which were first recorded on the chamber walls of King Unis' pyramid. These texts, which are the oldest surviving religious literature in the world, refer to the god Osiris, who was murdered by his brother Seth, then revived as Ruler of the Underworld. In these early references the deceased pharaohs were identified with Osiris in spells meant to allow them divine rule for eternity, but their subjects would soon pick up on other themes presented in the Osiris myth cycle.

The Middle Kingdom

The First Intermediate Period ended when strong pharaohs emerged from the region of Thebes and restored order to the kingdom. While stability returned, however, the national psyche was forever changed. Egyptians began to ask questions that are common to all humanity: is material wealth an indicator of moral character? Is a blessed afterlife among the gods the privilege of a select few? What happens to someone's soul if their body (and grave goods) are destroyed? Does he who dies with the most toys – to borrow a modern expression – still win?

Breakdown of a centralized monarchy during the Intermediate Period actually brought about greater freedoms for non-royalty. Somewhere in the midst of anarchy, as petty nobles declared themselves king in rapid succession, they also discovered what "perks" they had missed out on: not just wealth and status, but also access to religious literature and rites that would allow them to join the gods. As the Middle Kingdom took shape, spells that had once been exclusively royal domain in the Pyramid Texts began to appear painted on wooden coffins and other grave goods of nobility, and anyone else who could afford to have them commissioned. Make no mistake, this was not a sentiment of "equality for all" – it was equality for those who could afford it, which generally meant scribes, priests and other government officials. But the Old Kingdom's royal monopoly on secrets to an afterlife in the gods' company had been forever broken.

We know relatively little about the lower classes from the Middle Kingdom, or practically any other period in Egyptian history, because they were illiterate and often could not afford burials with artifacts that could tell us much about them. Much of what comes to us in literature about the lot of peasants is what scribes and upper classes wrote about them. Discourses of wisdom attributed to this era, such as the "Instructions to King Merikare", advise charity and fair dealing with the less fortunate. Another sentiment, one that can be heard echoed even today, is to be content with one's fortunes as the gods have seen fit to give.

Another excellent work from this era is the "Tale of the Eloquent Peasant", in which a poor man seeks audience with a magistrate to address a grievance. The pharaoh hears reports of what this extraordinarily well-spoken peasant says to his local official, and tells the magistrate to stall him so he will keep talking. (Naturally, he also instructs scribes to write down what the peasant says.) What follows is a series of proverbs, truisms and poetic observations about life, which become increasingly biting as the peasant gets more fed up with being stalled. Finally unable to take any more waiting, he threatens a final act of desperation: he declares that he will "appeal to Anubis" and take his own life. This suddenly put the pharaoh in a moral predicament, so he quickly accepts the peasant's case, restoring the goods that had been stolen from him and amply rewarding him for his wisdom.

The ending of this story underscores a significant theme that developed during the Middle Kingdom: a sense of divine justice that transcended social class. No doubt the inspiration for this change lay with the spreading worship of Osiris – note that Anubis, to whom the Eloquent Peasant threatened a final appeal, was a key player in the Osirian myth cycle. While an embalming that emulated the legendary first mummification of Osiris was still a prerogative of the wealthy, judgment before Him in the Hall of Two Truths was based upon moral standing and not status. Lower classes may not have been able to read spells reputed to offer passage into Osiris' underworld kingdom, but they probably knew an oral tradition of His death and vindication, and held faith that their own good conduct would be judged favorably by Osiris when their day came.

While the sun temples of Ra in Heliopolis continued to receive royal patronage during the Middle Kingdom, a new player emerged in divine politics: Amun. The "Hidden One", Amun was patron deity of the Twelfth Dynasty rulers who hailed from Thebes. Kings bearing the name Senwosret (Sesostris) and Amunemhat had new temples built in Karnak and Luxor, two major suburbs of Thebes. These temples would later explode into the largest religious complex anywhere in Egypt.

The Middle Kingdom ended much as the Old Kingdom had, with weak kings and fragmenting government. But this time outsiders found an opportunity to penetrate the now-permeable borders of Egypt – Asiatic tribes from what is now Israel and Palestine, called the Hyksos. It was long believed that the Hyksos led an armed invasion, but the latest evidence suggests they simply migrated in, bringing flocks and extended families with them, until gradually they had taken over Lower Egypt. They did have a technological advantage over the Egyptians in the form of horse-drawn chariots and composite bows, however. Eventually they established a fortified capital in the Lower Egyptian town of Avaris. Interestingly, one of the Hyksos kings was named (or at least called by the Egyptians) Apophis, after the evil serpent of chaos who tried to swallow up Ra's sun boat in the underworld every night. The Hyksos also venerated Seth, who had a center of worship in Avaris. Seth's alternate names of Sutekh and Setesh came from the Semitic language of the Hyksos, and were later adopted into Egyptian.

Once again, princes from Thebes set about re-uniting their country, this time by leading resistance against their intruders. The eventual expulsion of the Hyksos paved the way for Egypt's grandest – and in some ways, most colorful – epoch.

The New Kingdom

King Ahmose finally succeeded in restoring Egypt's sovereignty. It was a costly undertaking; his father and brother both seemed to have died in battle. While the men fought the

Hyksos, administrative power was actually wielded by the royal women. Queen Ahhotep II was later deified because of her role in the resistance campaign, and in some ways she set a precedent for future royal women of the Eighteenth Dynasty.

Ahmose's successors continued to wage war against not only the Asiatics, but also the Nubians to Egypt's immediate south, and for the first time pharaohs began claiming territory outside of their traditional borders. Not only did this make Egypt the first ancient empire, but it also had an effect upon the nation's religious landscape. As spoils of war and foreign tribute poured into their treasuries, pharaohs in turn donated much of it to the glory of Amun-Ra, who had blessed them with victory after victory. This combined identity of Amun, the ancestral Theban god and Ra, the traditional patron of kings, became the invincible god of the state. His temples in Karnak and Luxor went from being regional religious centers to the equivalent of a national cathedral. Suddenly the priesthood of Amun commanded wealth and prestige that even the clergy of Heliopolis would envy; this would have dire political consequences later.

The avenue of ram-headed sphinxes, representing Amun, connecting Luxor and Karnak temples. Photo by Krys Garnett

When Thutmose II died young with only a toddler-aged heir, his widow took over as regent and a short time later was officially crowned a female pharaoh – Hatshepsut. A descendant of Queen Ahhotep II, she certainly continued her ancestress' legacy of strong leadership. Hatshepsut commissioned massive building projects, including the temple of Deir el-Bahari, to accommodate expanding Theban festivals. New research even suggests she led a short military campaign into Nubia. The arts flowered under her reign, and Egypt's markets became more cosmopolitan. For a long time, though, scholars actually thought she was simply a conniving usurper whose name was later excised from monuments by her bitter stepson Thutmose III. A re-analysis of the historical record now concludes that Hatshepsut and Thutmose III got along normally, and he erased her record only some twenty years after her death in order to aid the legitimacy of his own heir, Amunhotep II. This is purely speculation, but could it be that Hatshepsut left such a strong impact as a female ruler that one of her female relatives could have contended for the throne? Only new findings could tell us for sure.

Political tensions may have subsided following Hatshepsut's proscription, but religious tensions began to mount. Because of the lack of separation between church and state, groups of clergy who received extensive favor from the state could eventually gain enough strength to act independently of the throne, or else exert pressure upon it in turn. This scenario had taken place to a somewhat lesser extent at the end of the Old Kingdom, contributing to its collapse. In the New Kingdom, with the Amun temple complex comprising a veritable state with the state, the same situation was happening again.

Kings of the late Eighteenth Dynasty evidently felt a personal connection to the sun god's older forms of Hor-em-Akhet and Ra-Horakhety; Thutmose IV recorded a prophetic dream he had of Hor-em-Akhet on a stela he placed between the paws of the Great Sphinx. These pharaohs used their devotion politically as a way to subtly push back against the priesthood of Amun.

Finally, Amunhotep IV-Akhenaton dropped the subtlety and declared all-out war on the estate of Amun, the details of which are covered in *Atonism: The World's First Monotheism?*. The irony is that even Akhenaton the universalist underestimated the wishes of the common people. Atonism failed to provide them a satisfactory alternative to the traditional morality tales of the Osiris myth cycle, so they abandoned it after Akhenaton's death.

Now as then, the final burden of the late-Eighteenth Dynasty drama rests upon the last of its line: Tutankhamun. Opinions vary as to how direct a role he played in the restoration of traditional faith, especially considering that he was only nine years old at his coronation. A reversal of his father's policies was inevitable; the Amun priesthood were too powerful to be unseated in a fell swoop and the populace could not be 'converted' to a new religion in less than a generation's time. However, the fact that the teenaged king took to his grave belongings bearing the name of Aton, and that his father's temple in Karnak stayed intact until after Tutankhamun's death, suggests that he was perhaps more religiously tolerant than many of his contemporaries who sought to obliterate any trace of Atonism.

The New Kingdom did not end with him, though. It had one last era of glory under the Nineteenth Dynasty kings Seti I and Rameses II, now known as Rameses the Great.

Amun colossus bearing the features of Tutankhamun; from Luxor.
Photo by Krys Garnett

The Ramesside line came from the Delta town of Avaris and originally served in the military; in fact, Rameses I would have actually have been a young soldier during Tutankhamun's reign. Because they did not grow up entrenched in the marriage, religion and politics of Thebes, they were considerably less beholden to the influence of Amun's clergy. While Rameses the Great addressed Amun-Ra as 'my father' in his monuments, such as the ones recounting his famous battle at Qadesh, his family traditionally worshiped the Archaic form of Set. In a masterful stroke of political maneuvering, he re-appointed the high priest of Osiris at Abydos as the new high priest of Amun in Thebes. He (or possibly his father Seti I) also moved the administrative capital to his hometown, rechristening it Per-Rameses, thus removing himself completely from the internal tensions that doubtless ensued at Thebes. And because he had appointed a priest of Osiris – the brother Seth murdered in the Myth of Kingship – he also managed to allay concerns about his own family's personal devotion. Today he is best known for his military exploits, his scores of children, his rule during the last period of economic wealth and possible role as the Pharaoh of the Exodus; but overlooked is Rameses the Great's skillful manipulation of his country's various politico-religious factions.

No survey of religion in the New Kingdom would be complete without including the major funerary texts to develop during the era – the *Book of the Dead*, a collection of writings that evolved directly from the Pyramid and Coffin Texts; the *Book of Imy-Duat* and the *Litanies of Ra*, which were exclusively royal literature. From the *Imy-Duat* later grew the *Book of Gates* and the *Book of Caverns*. One of the main themes of the *Book of the Dead* was judgement before Osiris in the Hall of Two Truths, in which the ideas of moral judgment that first began in the Middle Kingdom reached perhaps their highest expression. The highlight of its judgment sequences is the "Forty-Two Declarations of Innocence", in which the deceased swear before a divine tribunal that they have not committed crimes against society, the king or the gods. Meanwhile, the main theme of the *Imy-Duat* was an hourly account of Ra's travels through the underworld. The books of *Gates* and *Caverns* added scenes of judgment before Osiris, but emphasis was placed more upon a tribunal against Ra's enemies than upon personal examination of the king! In another view, only the pharaoh was believed fit to witness Ra's punishment of the damned.

Egypt began to decline once more following Rameses II's rule, which lasted some sixty years. A series of wars to defend the nation against invaders and several years of famine drained the economy; political corruption further weakened the state. Organized labor strikes, tomb robberies in the Valley of the Kings and the infamous 'Harem Conspiracy' against Rameses III also took their toll. During the Twentieth Dynasty ruled a whole series of kings named Rameses (one of whom is thought to have died of smallpox), but none could recapture the glory of their "Great" namesake. Mean-while, the Amun priesthood regained its strength, and a high priest named Herihor declared himself king. Thus Egypt's final golden age ended even more feverishly than previous two did, amidst widespread upheaval and confusion.

Libyans and Asiatics conquered by Rameses III. While successful, these wars against the "Sea Peoples" drained the already-weakening Egyptian economy. From Medinet Habu. Photo by Krys Garnett

The Third Intermediate, Late and Greco-Roman Periods

Power in Egypt fragmented and shifted multiple times during the Third Intermediate Period. The son of Rameses XI moved his capital in the Delta from Avaris to another town several miles away called Tanis. Meanwhile, rival kings ruled from Thebes, who tried to bolster their credibility by presenting all of their official proclamations as divine decrees from Amun. The two factions finally joined forces through marriage, but they were eventually supplanted by Libyans who established their own capital in the Delta city of Bubastis. A further three-way split of power in the Delta left Egypt vulnerable for invasion by the Nubians, which marked the beginning of the Late Period.

Anarchy, public corruption and poverty were so rampant in the country during the Third Intermediate Period that the once inviolate burial grounds of the Valley of the Kings were ransacked in broad daylight, with the assistance of the mayor of Thebes! Papyrus records tell us of the inquest and indictments that resulted from the scandal. The ruling priests of Thebes finally gathered the mummies of Egypt's most famous kings – save Tutankhamun, whose tomb lay buried and thankfully forgotten – and placed them in a cache with their few remaining grave goods that had not been looted. From that point on, kings began burying their dead within temple precincts for security reasons. Under earlier eras of greater stability and civil control, the need for such a measure would have been unthinkable.

Kings' power waned, and as a result the public perception of kingship changed. Art from the Third Intermediate and Late Periods ceased to depict the pharaoh alone in monumental scale as master of the cosmos. Increasingly statuary focused on the gods themselves, with the pharaoh as a smaller figure tucked between the falcon legs of Horus, for example. Horus as the image of king grew in such appeal, whereas the pharaoh's personal importance dwindled so greatly, that the kings of Tanis were buried in mummiform coffins with falcon faces instead of human portrait faces. In addition, statues of the gods themselves frequently took on their purely animal forms as opposed to anthropomorphic; the famous statues of Bast as a bejeweled cat date from this time. These changes in artistic emphasis suggest a shift in religious feeling away from state religion toward more introverted, personal belief. Human order was weak and ineffectual, so people placed their faith exclusively in gods who were above human limitations. Animal cults centering around Horus, Bast, Thoth (Djehuty) the ibis and other gods sprang up during the Late Period. Goddess cults took on greater prominence as well. Bast and another Delta goddess, Neith, burgeoned in popularity, as did Isis. It is significant to note that no temples were devoted solely to Isis before the Thirtieth Dynasty, which was the last native dynasty to rule Egypt some four hundred years B.C.E. Meanwhile, Set took a decided plunge in esteem; once the prestigious ancestral god of Seti I and Rameses the Great, in the Late Period his role as a god of evil became more pronounced. Many statues of his were re-carved into Thoth, who had a similarly-shaped head.

The Nubian kings continued worship of Amun, Mut and Khonsu, and delegated authority to female relatives who took on the traditional role of Gods' Wives of Amun. King Shabako also commissioned a stone monument recording important literature from the temple of Ptah in Memphis. But even the tenacious Nubians were eventually driven back into their home area of Kush by invading Assyrians. In 663 B.C.E., the Assyrians sacked once-mighty Thebes, and much of the country suffered similar devastation. The Egyptians had not rid themselves of the Assyrians for long when the even more formidable Persians invaded. Accounts vary on how well the Egyptians fared under Persian rule. Some suggest that temples continued to have state support. But in another account, Persian king Cambyses had the sacred Apis bull in Memphis slaughtered and eaten simply to humiliate its worshipers.

Not surprisingly, people began to look back with nostalgic longing upon bygone days of glory and kings whose names still inspired awe. But even as they did so, their classical heritage began to erode. Due perhaps to a combination of scarce resources and a desire to emulate the past, funeral monuments, coffins and tombs from earlier periods were widely reused by officials and even nobility. Stories composed to celebrate famous kings of the past, such as Thutmose III and Rameses the Great, often confused their titles. Another insight comes to us from the tomb of the high priest in Hermopolis, Petosiris; he described 'outrage' at the vandalism of relics within the temple, as well as efforts to restore them. Petosiris himself had to reorganize temple personnel and daily temple duties, which illustrates the level of chaos that followed foreign invasions. A man of tremendous faith despite hard times, Petosiris recorded advice to future generations about the virtues of living a life devoted to the gods' service. His stalwart example was later admired by not only his countrymen, but also by increasing newcomers to the region – the Greeks.

Alexander the Great was welcomed as a liberator in Egypt. He also pleased the populace tremendously by being crowned as pharaoh in Memphis, then visiting a temple at Siwa Oasis to receive an oracle that he was the son of Amun-Ra. After his death, Alexander's general Ptolemy became king of Egypt, and their dynasty ruled for three more centuries. They materially supported local religion, rebuilding temples to Horus at Edfu and Hathor at Dendera that are the best-preserved in Egypt today; but the Ptolemies themselves did not embrace local customs or beliefs. The highest positions in government were occupied by Greeks and Greek language was spoken in court. Cleopatra VII, last of the Ptolemies and famous for her love affair with Marcus Antonius, was the only one of her line who could speak Egyptian. By contrast, Greek deities and culture mingled freely with that of the Egyptians. During this period of "Hellenization", many Greek traditions such as Zodiac-based astrology and esoterism were blended with native practices, and Egyptian deities were given either new attributes or associations with foreign gods. Greek philosophers and writers became the world's first Egyptophiles, and biographers frequently fabricated a trip to Egypt in order to increase the mystique of figures such as Plato or Pythagoras. Much of the confusion modern scholars and enthusiasts face today in sifting out what is Egyptian from what is not, is a result of the cultural exchange that took place during the Hellenistic era.

Upon Cleopatra VII's death in 30 B.C.E., Egypt became a Roman province. The Romans valued Egypt for its wheat production, which quickly made it the breadbasket of the empire, but they kept a tighter reign over local officials and clergy than did the Greeks. No longer semi-autonomous, they had to answer directly to Roman magistrates. The institution that once made – and ruined – kings for centuries now paid homage to the Roman

Despite its modern fame, Isis' Temple at Philae was actually built late in Egyptian history, during the Thirtieth Dynasty. Photo by Krys Garnett

emperor, just as every other citizen did. Gone forever were the Egyptian priesthood's days of political power and prestige.

Ties to an empire proved a boon, however, to the divine triad of Osiris, Isis and Horus-the-Child. The trio of gods who first democratized ideas of the afterlife almost two millenia before followed trade routes into Rome itself, where temples were built to Isis in particular. While their spread throughout the empire's reaches has been sensationalized in recent years – Isis probably did not reach T'ang China or have a temple at the future site of Notre Dame Cathedral in Paris, for example – it certainly would not be unreasonable to conclude that Romans traveling to distant provinces could have carried with them devotion to the holy family of Abydos.

Into the Modern Era

In the year 384 C.E., Emperor Theodosius ordered that all pagan temples be shut down and converted to Christianity. The last functioning Egyptian temple at that time was Isis' temple at Philae, which afterward became a monastery. It is worth noting that, in addition to some of the last vestiges of ancient paganism, Egypt also nurtured Gnosticism, a form of Christianity that was declared 'heretical' by the Council of Nicea in 325 C.E. Copies of Gnostic gospels, such as the Gospel of Mary Magdalene, have been found in Egypt within the last century.

A uniquely Egyptian form of Christianity was also in existence at that time, one that still has active adherents today: the Coptic Orthodox Church. The Coptic language, spoken in their masses much as Latin is spoken in certain Catholic services, preserves the last form of spoken Egyptian. Their services also make use of sistrums, ancient instruments once considered sacred to the goddess Hathor. Many Coptic Egyptians have recently fled persecution from Wahabi Islamists, seeking a new home in the United States, and they very proudly proclaim their heritage as 'descendants of the Pharaohs'.

Much has already been written about the persecution of pagans at the hands of newly-sanctioned Christians during the first millennium C.E.; the irony, of course, is that Christianity itself started out as an 'underground' movement considered subversive by the Roman upper classes. But the new religion had to have held appeal somewhere in order to take root. Among common Egyptians, one possible source of appeal may have been the relative freedom offered in church communities. In a traditional temple, only a select few priests were deemed fit to behold the enshrined gods. By contrast, in a small, grass-roots Christian congregation everyone attended equally, in theory if not always in practice. Today, the concept of a temple (or church) service being open to all adherents is taken for granted, and its influence is felt even in modern Pagan services. At the outset of the modern era, the idea was revolutionary.

Another probable source of appeal was Christianity's rejection of worldly concerns. By that time, Egypt had been under occupation for the better part of six centuries. Rulers of each new empire tried to establish their legitimacy to the populace by presenting themselves as pharaohs, co-opting the religious aspect of the office for their own gain while they continued to drain resources from the native Egyptians. Christianity, by contrast, offered hope for an eternal kingdom away from the Romans. It must surely have been a tantalizing proposition.

One final development to come out of Europe more recently further separates the ancient Egyptians' era from ours: the Enlightenment Period. Thinkers of the Enlightenment era were the first to conclude that all humanity was inherently equal in rights and dignity, and that each person could choose his or her own destiny. Their radical ideas spurred both the American and French revolutions. Again, today we take these principles as basic elements of society; but imagine trying to stop agents of Akhenaton from defacing Amun's name on a family monument using the arguments of human equality and moral freedom. On the flip side, imagine being one of the last Atonists serving in the Aton temple of Karnak on the day a newly-crowned Horemhab ordered it shut down, then trying to argue that the king had no right to impose his own religious terms. The concept was unheard of in ancient times, yet we cannot – and should not – live without it today. Therein lies the potential danger of Reconstructionist groups, be they Kemetic, Hellenistic, Old Testament-Biblical or otherwise.

As we have seen, religious thought in ancient Egypt was not static or unchanging by any stretch. The Egyptians' views and faith were shaped by their environment, their society, and circumstances that came about within that setting, just as we are so shaped today. We will always share with our ancient Egyptian predecessors a common humanity; we mourn our loved ones who pass on, we fear the unknown, we cry out to the gods for salvation, just as they did. But as writer Thomas Wolfe observed, "You can't go home again". For the sake of our own growth and progress, maybe it's better that we can't.

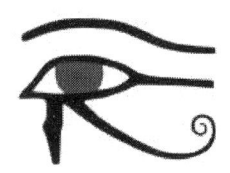

The World According to Them: Ancient Egyptians' Religious Worldview

In order to comprehend just how the ancient Egyptians believed and worshiped, it is crucial that we understand how they saw the world around them. Unlike our modern sense of religion as something apart from the "mundane" physical world, their religion was a practical way of making sense of natural phenomena and the everyday occurrence. They saw no separation between their faith and their day-to-day lives. The Egyptians believed that nature, far from being somehow inferior to the divine, in fact *reflected* the divine and vice versa. In a sense, their gods created not just humankind in their image, but the entire world.

The physical world that the ancient Egyptians inhabited was quite the different environment from what most of us live in today. Many of us live in some form of temperate climate that has four distinct seasons. Those of us who live in desert regions often draw a water supply from a distant river that we may never even see. By contrast, most ancient Egyptians lived their whole lives within sight of the river Nile. They built their settlements on high ground and on the desert's edge, saving the precious floodplain and its arable land for farming. If they needed to travel beyond their village, the river offered them the fastest route; so much that, for a people who lived in the desert, a surprising amount of their language and imagery refers to boating and river vessels.

Now as then, the Nile is considered the life-blood of Egypt. Photo by Krys Garnett

Their dry native climate also did not have four seasons as we know them. Rather, their seasons were based upon the cycles of the river. The period we know as 'winter' was – and still is today – the time in which Egyptians plant their crops. (Indeed, Egyptologists' primary digging season is also during the winter, when temperatures are tolerable enough to work in.) So influential to Egypt is the Nile that even today, modern Egyptians call it *Umm al-Dunyah*, the "Mother of the World".

Seasons of the River

The world's longest river, the Nile actually has two sources. One is Lake Victoria in Uganda, and its other lies in the mountainous highlands of Ethiopia. The Nile is also the only major river in the world that flows north, cutting its way through the arid volcanic mountain ranges of eastern Africa. Beginning around mid-June every year, equatorial monsoons engorged the Ethiopian Blue Nile, sending floodwaters swelling downstream into Sudan. By the end of June, this annual inundation reached the southernmost part of Egypt. Over the next two months, it continued northward to the Nile Delta, which opens into the Mediterranean Sea. The floods crested in late September, and would finally subside by the end of October. This cycle of inundation, which deposited fertile black silt so instrumental to Egypt's prosperous agriculture, continued well into the 20th century, finally ending when the Aswan High Dam was built in the 1960's to control irrigation.

Whereas many ancient agrarian societies marked the start of a new year with the coming of spring, Egyptians began each new year with the flood of the Nile. They observed the start of Inundation with great festivity; even today, Egyptians celebrate a national holiday and throw flowers into the Nile during the time of year when the floods once came. In antiquity, those four months of Inundation were their first season, called *Akhet*. Since no plowing could be done during *Akhet,* this was probably their primary building season for state monuments such as the Pyramids and massive temple complexes. This flood season was also another reason why they built settlements on high ground, out of the swollen river's reach.

Once the Inundation subsided, the Egyptians wasted no time in beginning crucial agricultural work. Their second season, which began around late October or early November and lasted another four months, was called *Peret*, or Emergence – referring either to the land emerging from the receding floodwaters, or to the plants that would soon emerge from the soil. Interestingly, while their season of planting began when most other agrarian societies were concluding their harvest, the major theme of Egyptian holidays during that season was much the same. As they sowed their seeds, essentially 'burying' them in the earth, they commemorated the death and burial of Osiris, who was lord of agriculture and the dead. His powers of rejuvenation manifested in the sprouting of fresh grain, promising new life.

Peret ended around mid-March, when the emmer wheat was ready for harvest. While it was custom to ritually mourn the first sheaves of grain cut, the major holiday of Egyptian harvest was one of fertility. They honored the ithyphallic god Min, celebrating abundance in the crops, animals, and human procreation. With their harvests in, the next season of *Shomu*, or the "Hot" season, began. *Shomu* was the Egyptian summertime. The Nile would sink to its lowest levels, and between March and May the southerly winds brought sand-storms. In Thebes, mid-*Shomu* brought a major festival of the dead known as the

Beautiful Feast of the Valley. Finally, in late June through July, the Inundation returned and the cycle began again.

The Egyptians had no way of knowing that annual monsoon systems blowing westward from the Indian ocean brought the precious floodwaters that fed their land. (In fact, even modern explorers did not successfully trace both Nile sources until the 1800's.) The ancients believed that the Nile originated from a cavern, called the Cavern of Hapy, that opened from the Underworld and was controlled by the ram-headed creator god Khnum. Because of the Nile's importance, one might think it would have been embodied by a preeminent deity. Indeed, many modern readers have struggled to understand whether Egyptian gods were simply personified forces of nature or transcendent personalities, but the Nile's example offers important clues. The fleshy-bodied god Hapy represented the Inundation and abundance, but not the river itself. Several other deities besides Hapy, namely Osiris, Khnum, and the cow-goddess *Mehet-Uret*, or "Great Flood", also played roles in the annual Inundation. But Osiris additionally presided over agriculture and the funerary realm (among other things), so he was not limited to just one aspect of nature. Khnum was also responsible for fashioning mankind on a potter's wheel, and Mehet-Uret was associated with goddesses such as Neith, Nut and Hathor. Clearly, certain deities were *represented* in natural phenomena, but they were not *limited* to those phenomena.

Seasons of the Sun

In addition to the Nile, one other force of nature played a defining role in Egyptian life and provided them with a cycle that aided in their understanding of the cosmos: the sun. Just as the break of dawn heralded a new day's beginning, so too did they imagine that Creation began with the first sunrise. They called this pivotal moment *Zep Tepi*, the "First Occasion", and most Egyptian creation stories centered around the birth of the sun god as either Atum, Ra, Horus, Sobek or Nefertem. Prior to *Zep Tepi*, the cosmos consisted of a dark, still, infinite ocean called *Nun*. This primordial sea of chaos and pre-Creation was punctuated by the light of the first sunrise, which marked the establishment of order and Creation just as a new dawn signals a return to wakefulness and human activity. Indeed, Egyptians regarded each new morning as a reenactment of *Zep Tepi*.

Sunset symbolized death, as one day ended and the sun god descended into the underworld to regenerate. Egyptians believed that, during the hours of the chill desert night, the sun god Ra merged with Osiris in order to rejuvenate and be reborn the following morning. But the process was dangerous, much like the nocturnal desert countryside, full of threatening beings that had to be overcome. Each new dawn meant not only rebirth for the sun god, but also a victorious continuation of order over chaos. Because the sun symbolized an ever-continuing cycle of death, regeneration and rebirth, the Egyptians' beliefs surrounding the afterlife became inextricably linked to the sun god. So long as the sun continued to dawn each morning, the Egyptians felt assured that life would continue after death. For this reason, they buried their dead with symbols of the sun, and sometimes placed their bodies facing east, in order to aid them in their journey toward a new dawn.

Indeed, east was the direction of birth, life, and the *Akhet* (in this context meaning the dawn horizon). Many Egyptian settlements were built on the eastern side of the river, whereas tombs and cemeteries were always built on the western side. Some Egyptians also lived on the west bank, but frequently they were royal tomb workers and their families. The direction of the setting sun became so synonymous with death and the Underworld, or *Duat*, that a common expression for someone dying was to say that they "flew to the West". One of Osiris' titles was *Khenti-Amentiu*, or "Foremost of the Westerners", the 'Westerners' being the dead. Egyptians believed that the entrance to the *Duat* lay somewhere beyond the mountains of the Western Desert, from which no mortal could ever return. Considering that the barren and unforgiving Sahara desert lay beyond Egypt's western mountains, their conclusion made sense.

East and west represented the path of the sun and the two halves of life's perpetual cycle. North and south played a smaller role in Egyptian thought. Unlike the Greeks, the Egyptians did not correspond four elements with the cardinal directions. The northern and southern portions of the country, however, did figure heavily into their concept of duality. Upper and Lower Egypt were two separate territories that united to form a whole, and to acknowledge this union many rituals invoked double elements, such as "Valley [Upper Egyptian] natron" and "Delta [Lower Egyptian] natron". Even Osiris' hall of judgment was called the Hall of *Ma'ati*, or "Two Truths", perhaps reflecting the dual state ruled by living pharaohs. Egyptians saw dualities all around them – river delta and valley; cultivated land and desert wilderness; day and night; life and death. But rather than viewing these elements as opposites in tension, Egyptians generally regarded them as necessary parts of a complete whole. Even death was accepted as simply a part of life. The quintessential duality in Egyptian thought, however, was the dichotomy between good and evil, order versus chaos.

Ma'at versus Isfet

Integral to Egyptian ethical beliefs is the concept of *ma'at* (pronounced 'MAH-aht'). An idiomatic word, *ma'at* translates as "truth", "justice", "order", or "how things ought to be". Symbolized as a goddess bearing an ostrich feather on her head, Ma'at is the daughter of Ra. She illustrates the Egyptian understanding of *ma'at*: at the First Occasion, Ra (or one of the other creator deities) separated order from chaos, creating *ma'at* as his metaphorical daughter. As he is the originator of morality and justice, *ma'at* issues from the Creator. The orderly rhythm of the natural world he created--night and day, the Nile's flood cycle, and cycles of fertility in crops, animals and people – all reflect *ma'at*.

The gods were said to "live on *ma'at*", meaning idiomatically that it was part of their essence and they benefitted from its perpetuation. Temple reliefs pictured the pharaohs offering *ma'at*, represented as little figures of the goddess, to other gods. Symbolically this meant that he ruled the nation in justice and equanimity, maintaining the civilized order created by the gods. In civil court, Ma'at was often invoked so that judgments would be rendered fairly. When a person died, they were judged by Osiris in the Hall of Two Truths by having their heart – considered the seat of intelligence and wisdom by the Egyptians – weighed against Ma'at's ostrich feather. A just heart would equal her feather in lightness, allowing the deceased to gain entry into Osiris' kingdom of the Blessed Dead. Wrongdoing would weigh down the heart, rendering a guilty verdict. The convicted person's life force would then be swallowed up by Ammut, "The Devourer".

The Egyptians' view of *ma'at* tells us something about how they regarded themselves. They did not see humanity as a 'fallen' race in need of redemption; rather, moral conduct ("doing *ma'at*") was the natural course of action that lay within all people's capability. Not only were humans able to do *ma'at*, but they were also held accountable by the gods on their performance. Nor were humans 'conceived in sin', as sexual reproduction was created by none other than Ra himself – one of his many epithets was, "Maker of the Bull for the Cow to Bring Sexual Pleasure into Being". Mortals may not have been as perfect or omniscient as the gods, but they certainly strove to meet a comparable standard. The Egyptian view of universal order and their own role within it was generally a positive, optimistic one.

Opposite to *ma'at* is *isfet*, meaning "sin", "wrongdoing", or "chaos". Just as the Egyptians believed doing good deeds furthered the natural order and equilibrium created by Ra, doing wicked deeds upset order and invited chaos. Today, some belief systems embrace chaos as inevitable; but to the ancient Egyptians, disorder was literally a threat to civilization as they knew it.

So long as the chaotic aspect of the universe remained distinct from ordered creation, the two could coexist in stasis. The Egyptian desert wilderness and teeming marshes along the Nile were two such untamed places beyond the reach of civilization. In fact, famous marsh hunting scenes from the tombs of noblemen are actually metaphorical images of the Egyptians' constant efforts to keep chaos in check.

The original source of pre-Creation was of course Nun, the dark primeval ocean from which Ra first arose. Sometimes personified as a god – even referred to as the "father of Ra" – in certain situations Nun also represented potentiality and the unknown, which can be either good or bad. In the Underworld texts, Ra's sun boat was said to rest on the waters of Nun as he regenerated during the midnight hour. Nun was also the source of the Nile and Mediterranean waters. Indeed, the whole of Creation still floated within the vast ocean of Nun, maintaining a tenuous balance that had to be maintained through constant vigilance. Within the Underworld, however, dwelt one malevolent force determined to upset the balance and throw all of Creation back into chaos: Apophis.

Apophis, or *A'apep* in Egyptian, was an immense green serpent who attacked Ra and his entourage every night in an attempt to swallow up the sun. It required the combined efforts of the gods, even the sometimes-evil god Seth, to defeat Apophis. So threatening was this force of evil and chaos incarnate that he was often referred to in texts as "The Fiend", or "The Evil One" to avoid addressing him by name. Dwelling within Nun, Apophis represented the negative aspect of potential and the unknown; instead of regeneration and progress, Apophis stood for destruction and regression, as he sought to drag the ordered world back into the primordial abyss.

Related to Apophis were the *Mosu Badesh*, the "Children of Rebellion", also called simply "The Rebels". These were enemies of Ra and Osiris, who were judged during Ra's nocturnal journey through the Underworld and then consigned to the "Places of Annihilation" as punishment for opposing *ma'at*. Late in Egyptian history, Seth came to be associated with the *Mosu Badesh* because he had murdered Osiris. The Legend of Horus of Behdet describes the *Mosu Badesh* as essentially henchmen of Seth.

What identified all of these various entities as agents of evil was their course of action: they defied the truth and justice of *ma'at*. The Egyptians did not define 'sin' in purely dogmatic terms. Rather, counterproductive acts that could harm other people, disrupt the rule of law, create disharmony within the human community or threaten civilization all met their definition of sin. Such acts of deviance and negligence, or *isfet*, on the part of mankind would chip away at the sacred order of Creation just as surely as would the workings of Apophis.

Some modern Kemetics have attempted to translate *isfet* as "uncreation" and not "wrongdoing", but this definition is unwieldy and misleading. While chaos opposed creation in the Egyptian worldview, in their language they used *isfet* as a word for both disorder and 'wrongdoing'. In one of the Declarations of Innocence that deceased swore before Osiris, they would state *nen ir-en i isfet*, or "I have not done *isfet*". Further, in Ra's famous monologue from the Coffin Texts, he states, "I did not command that they [humankind] do wrong" – using the word *isfet*. To say, "I did not command them to do wrong," or to say, "I have not worked chaos," makes much more sense than to say, "I have not done 'uncreation'".

Egyptian Concepts of the Soul

The Egyptians had a true talent for representing abstract ideas in pictures and icons, and nowhere is this better illustrated than in their components of the soul. Books written for younger audiences especially tend to "dumb down" explanations of the *ba* and *ka* because their icons are so beguilingly simple. But this approach sells short the Egyptian capacity for tackling the intangible and making it concrete.

The *Ka*

Every living being and all of the gods possess a life force, which was called the *ka*. In the most simple explanation, the *ka* is what separates a living being from a dead body. When someone died, it was their *ka* that 'flew West', and the rest of their soul would ultimately need to reunite with it in order to live on in Duat. Part of the funerary Opening of the Mouth ritual, which dates all the way back to the Pyramid Texts, states that "Someone has gone to be with his *ka*."

The *ka* is often described as a person's "spirit double" because it is represented as a sort of *doppelganger* to the deceased in tomb paintings. The famous illustration on the north wall of Tutankhamun's tomb, for example, shows him embracing Osiris with his *ka* standing behind him with a hand on his shoulder. Similarly, reliefs depicting the conception of Amunhotep III show Khnum fashioning the king-to-be and his *ka* on a potter's wheel, before placing them within the womb of Queen Mutemwiya. Chances are, the Egyptians did not take such an metaphor literally any more than we moderners believe in "the birds and the bees"; they understood that physical bodies came about from the physical union of other bodies. But just as Khnum or other creator gods guided a child's growth in the womb, so too did a person's life force come from the gods, represented as *ka*.

The *ka* was also the part of the soul that required sustenance after physical death. Special officials who made offerings to the deceased in their tomb chapels were called *ka-*servants. A common invocation for the dead called the Voice Offering recited, "A thousand of bread, beer, beef and fowl, and all good and pure things on which a god lives, for the *ka* of" the deceased. The essence of food offered to the spirits of the dead was what fed their eternal life force, or *ka*.

The *Ba*

Everyone possessed life force, but what made an individual unique was their personality. This personality or soul was called *ba*. At death, a person's *ba* and *ka* separated from their body and each other; the purpose of funerary rites was to re-unite them and re-establish their connection with the body. The *ba*, however, could go on to travel outside of the tomb. This might come closest to our concept of a ghost or spirit that sometimes makes contact with the living. Egyptians represented the *ba* as a human-headed bird to evoke this sense of freedom of movement.

The gods also had *ba*'s, which sometimes manifested as their animal avatars. An unexpected or freak event would also be referred to as the *bau* (plural of *ba*), or manifestation of the god. Records from the village of Deir el-Medina tell us that a *ta rekhet*, or wise woman, was often consulted to interpret *bau* and determine how to appease the gods involved. Language in the

Pyramid Texts also suggests that a person's *ba* had a bearing on how strong or forceful of a personality they were. Recitations announcing the successful emergence of the pharaoh into the gods' company would assert that he was "more *ba* and more in control" than even some of the gods themselves!

Another clever example of illustrating a non-tangible concept came from New Kingdom Underworld texts. As Ra descended into the Duat, he was depicted with a ram's head. The word for "ram" was also pronounced *ba*, and by picturing Ra as ram-headed they were not only indulging in a visual pun, but also conveying the idea that the *ba* of Ra had gone into the Underworld to be revitalized and finally reborn.

One more reference to the *ba* comes from reliefs and inscriptions describing state ritual observances. The "*Ba*'s of Nekhen" and the "*Ba*'s of Pe", also translated as the "Souls of Nekhen and Pe", were two groups of mythical celebrants with jackal and falcon heads respectively. These 'souls' represented the respective towns; Nekhen (Hierakonpolis) was the ancient capital of Upper Egypt and Pe was part of Buto, the ancient capital of Lower Egypt. The Souls were associated with the "royal ancestors", being the spirits (*ba'*s) of the reigning king's predecessors. They were also thought to be part of the "Followers of Horus" (*Horu Shemsu*) and had officiants representing them for rites in honor of Horus, such as the Coronation of the Sacred Falcon and the Feast of Victory. The *Ba*'s of Nekhen and Pe also made an appearance at the king's *Sed* festivals.

The *Akh*

When a person died, their *ba* and *ka* separated from their body. If funeral rites were properly done, their spiritual components were re-united to become an *akh*, often translated as a "transfigured" or an "effective spirit". (Older translations by Budge rendered them as "shining ones".) An *akh* spirit could both share the company of the gods and intercede in the realm of the living, hence the meaning "effective spirit". A person's spirit could still manifest as *ba*, but as an *akh* they also had the energy of their *ka*, or life force, plus the benefit of all of the offerings they might be given. Egyptians prayed to and made offerings to their loved ones so that those departed, as *akhu* (plural of *akh*), might act on behalf of the living. Many memorial stelae dedicated to deceased loved ones referred to them as an *akh iker en Ra*, or "effective spirit of Ra". This title meant that the dead person had been transfigured or made an "effective spirit" and now served Ra, perhaps a similar idea to our modern belief in angels.

The fact that Akhenaton spelled his name with the same word, *akh*, at the beginning sheds some light on how he saw his own role. As pharaoh and son of a deified pharaoh, he saw himself as the acting manifestation – the "effective spirit" – of Aton on earth.

The Body

Naturally, a person's body was considered a critical part of their overall being. But the general impression given by literature for the average reader is that the Egyptians really expected a dead person's body to "come alive" again after being mummified and given burial rites. This is a bit misleading. One of the ways Egyptians referred to a mummified body was as a *tut*, or "perfected image"; the same word was also used for statues meant to receive offerings. In essence, they regarded a properly-made mummy as the ultimate vessel for a person's spirit, better than any statue because it had housed that person's spirit during their mortal lifetime. But the Egyptians had also learned from experience over the centuries that bodies wouldn't always stay perfectly recognizable or even intact. Thus they began placing portrait masks over mummies' heads, or commissioning statues to take the place of the body should something ever happen to it. The Egyptians recognized the importance of a person's body as the lynchpin of their temporal existence, and they tried as best they could to preserve that link between the mortal world and the hereafter. For the same reason, what personal belongings had not been passed down as heirlooms were buried with a person to provide them with a further link to the physical realm. Objects a person had touched, used and cherished in life held a powerful connection that their *ba* would recognize. Even we supposedly "rational" moderners still recognize that spiritual connection every time we stare in awe at artifacts displayed in museums that had once been owned, touched, and used by Egyptians who lived millennia ago.

The Name and Shadow

A person's name was also considered an important part of their identity because it expressed something about their true nature. Author Christiane Desroches-Noblecourt wrote that an Egyptian child was named according to the first thing their mother said after giving birth. Certainly names like *Niunenef* ("He takes his time") or *Tay-Tay* ("She's mine") would suggest such a mother's comment. Many Egyptian names expressed a wish for the child's future: *Nakht* ("strength" or "victorious"), *Nofret* ("beauty") or *Senebi* ("health"). Other names were theophoric, meaning they expressed something about a deity: *Amunhotep* ("Amun is satisfied"), *Tutankhamun* ("Living Image of Amun") or *Ramoses* ("Born of Ra", known more commonly as *Rameses*). In the course of their lives, some Egyptians also gained nicknames that were recorded on their personal monuments, often in the form of "So-and-so called 'Such-and-such'". Many of these nicknames were probably terms of endearment or pet names, or perhaps even common epithets referring to their nationality in the case of foreigners. Sometimes nicknames may have served another use, though. Egyptians believed that a person's true name could be used magically to work either good or ill against them. If no one knew a person's true name, they would be magically unassailable; an expression of ultimate magical power was to say of that person, "Not even his mother knows his true name".

This importance in a name was reflected in the story of Isis obtaining Ra's secret name. None of the other gods knew Ra's true name, as he was the all-powerful creator. Isis, according to the story, knew that obtaining his secret name was the key to his power. When Ra finally shared it with her under great duress – interestingly, that name is not spelled out in the Turin Papyrus! –

he instructed her to share it only with her son Horus. (Scholars conclude that, since the ruling king represented Horus on earth, the story was meant to imply that the king also knew Ra's secret name.) Similarly, in another story Isis magically cured a child's scorpion sting by invoking the scorpion's name.

Another belief regarding a person's name was that continuing to speak it after their death would ensure that their spirit lived on. Pessimistic literature from the Middle Kingdom expressed this by observing that the monuments of great sages like Imhotep and Hordjedef (a son of Khufu) had all crumbled, but their written works were still known and thus their names lived on. On the flip side, to erase a person's name was to consign them to oblivion. Chances are, vindictive Egyptians throughout ancient society may have tried to obliterate the names of their enemies, but our best examples of this actually come from kings' records. After Tutankhamun died, then his aged vizier Aye four years later, their successor Horemhab set about erasing every name associated with the Amarna legacy. Akhenaton, Tutankhamun and even Aye's names were hacked out of monuments, and to this day many temple reliefs in Thebes depict a king with Tutankhamun's unmistakable features but bear the name of Horemhab instead. Obviously Horemhab's vendetta turned out to be for naught, as Akhenaton and Tutankhamun are two of the most famous names associated with Egypt today. This turnabout would certainly have delighted Tutankhamun's most loyal subjects, one of whom secretly inscribed the king's titles in an out-of-the-way seam on a sculpture whose front inscription was usurped. Their act of defiance in preserving Tutankhamun's name – and with it, his memory – can still be seen on the statue today.

The last component of a person's identity was their shadow. Because the sun casts shadows, a person's shadow was seen as having come from Ra. In life, a person's shadow was "attached" to them, but like the *ba* and *ka* it separated from its owner upon death. Shadows apparently had some ability to travel, but they could also be eaten; one of the divine judges addressed in the Forty-Two Declarations of Innocence was "Eater of Shadows".

*Clerestory windows illuminate the approach
to one of the inner precincts at the temple of
Osiris at Abydos. Photo by Krys Garnett*

Abodes of the Gods

Today a church is often referred to as a "house of God", but it is also a place where its faithful congregate. In addition to the actual hall of worship, many churches also have community centers and gymnasiums that serve as meeting places for parishioners or even for the general public. Church grounds host not only worship services, but also seasonal festivals, study groups, and in some communities even town meetings. The underlying premise is that while the buildings have been dedicated to God (or the gods, in the case of a Hindu mandir), their function is to serve the people. Any who are faithful can enter the "house of the Lord", provided they observe proper respect.

Ancient Egyptian temples, however, operated in a totally different manner. A temple was indeed the "house [or mansion] of the god", but a deity's list of invited guests was considered quite exclusive. In many ways, temples were to gods and goddesses what a provincial manor would have been to nobility: an actual place of private residence that needed to be staffed and maintained. Like a country estate, a temple's outer precincts housed priests and other servants, livestock for food offerings, workshops and storehouses. Beyond these grounds lay the temple buildings themselves, considered more restricted territory and best-known today for their immense columned halls. These areas might correspond to the front parlors and reception areas of a mansion, where visitors would be allowed. Deep within each temple lay the actual shrines of the deities it housed, corresponding to the mansion's private quarters. In theory, the only person fit to enter the innermost room of the god or goddess's earthly 'home' was the king, or else his chosen representative – i.e., the high priest.

    Daily services occurred primarily at the break of dawn, at midday and at sunset. In preparation, the priests would purify themselves at the temple's sacred lake, then enter in procession followed by a coterie of singers, musicians and offering bearers. They would file past the columned halls, into the darkened recesses of the inner precincts, and stop outside the room housing the god's actual shrine (called a *naos* in Greek). While the vast array of freshly prepared offerings would be arranged on altars to the accompaniment of hymns and music, the high priest would enter the sanctuary room. He would recite certain statements to accompany each action as he broke the seal on the naos door; took the statue out; censed it with incense; washed it and changed its clothes; then presented it with a tray holding a sample of the bountiful offerings arrayed just outside.

    At the conclusion of the service, these offerings would be presented in turn to those blessed dead who had commissioned statues to be placed within the temple, so as to partake in the gods' bounty. Finally the food would be eaten by the priests and other temple servants. At the sunset service, the high priest would

The sacred lake, or **Isheru***, at Karnak; steps leading to the water's edge can still be seen. Photo by Krys Garnett*

replace the god's statue within its naos and seal its doors with string and a stamped clay seal, to await the dawning of the next day.

If a god's temple home was off-limits to his or her lay believers, then how did they worship? One way was through periodic festivals, during which the statues of local gods would be carefully loaded onto boat-shaped shrines and carried on the shoulders of priests through the streets of town. At various points throughout the processional route, citizens could present offerings to the enshrined god's statue – which was still curtained from view – to be blessed, or else to present questions for the god to answer. Correlating ancient accounts with practices still observed in rural Egypt today, it is thought that a deity's response to a question came when his or her barque shrine pitched forward or backward suddenly. The late Egyptologist Serge Sauneron described a small-town funeral in Upper Egypt in the 1950's where something similar happened. The casket of a family patriarch suddenly overburdened its pall-bearers twice, each time as it neared the home of a relative whom, as it was discovered, had murdered the old man!

The Red Chapel at Karnak was a way station for the barque shrine of Amun during festivals. Photo by Krys Garnett

In addition to the frequent feast days, Egyptians could also worship within their own homes. We still do not know what kind of shrines, if any, that the poorest Egyptians might have kept in their dwellings, which were probably simple mud-brick huts. But the remains of two villages that housed royal tomb workers and their families have offered a wealth of clues. Both at Deir el-Medina and Kahun, remains have been found of stone offering stands and wall-set niches in the front rooms of houses. These wall niches once held memorial tablets and ancestor busts, and in a few instances carved figurines of deities. Taken together, these artifacts suggest that private worship services mirrored temple services, on a much smaller and more simplified scale. While temple statues would frequently be fashioned of stone or gold (considered the flesh of the gods) and inlaid with semiprecious stones, in private homes they would be made of cheaper materials such as wood or pottery. Interestingly, statues and other images of the gods were infrequently pictured during the Old Kingdom, but became more common during the Middle Kingdom and afterward; indeed, the village of Kahun dates from the Middle Kingdom and Deir el-Medina from the New Kingdom. Perhaps the practice of worshiping gods and goddesses in one's own home became more frequent as religion was 'democratized' after the

This stone shrine—called a naos *in Greek—holds an image of Khepri, the scarab form of the sun god. From the Nubian Museum at Aswan. Photo by Krys Garnett*

collapse of the Old Kingdom. But we would need to find more evidence to know for sure.

Evidently, then, an Egyptian god or goddess could inhabit any effigy He or She wished, from a cast gold oracle statue to a humble artisan's wooden figurine, or even none at all. So why such an outpouring of man-power and materials toward grandiose state temples, then? What purpose did these massive estates serve?

Understanding the answer requires a little bit of imagination and perspective. For most of us Americans, thinking back to the dawn of our society means only going back about two hundred and thirty years; beyond that, our respective origins lie across the seas in Europe, Africa or Asia. Judeo-Christianity and Islam hold that all of humanity originated from the first couple in the Garden of Eden, considered to be in the Middle East (or Missouri, according to the Mormons). Only Native Americans – like native Europeans, Africans or Asians – can potentially look at their birthplace and say that their people have *always* been there. The same was true of the ancient Egyptians. To them,

Egypt as they knew it had existed since the dawn of time. Their land emerged when the gods created it, and each town, city or village's temple represented that place where Creation began. Indeed, the columned (or Hypostyle) halls of temples were meant to represent vegetation surrounding the Primeval Mound, and some temples' outermost mud-brick walls were shaped in wave patterns evoking the waters of Nun. Beginning from these outer precincts, one could symbolically walk from the realm of chaos toward the original center of ordered creation, finally reaching the place where the Creator first stood on firm ground at *Zep Tepi*, represented by the innermost sanctuary. An inscription of Hatshepsut's refers to Amun's temple at Karnak, saying, "for I know that this place is heaven on earth." Each temple was a model of the cosmos itself, and its daily rituals were an engine of *ma'at* that kept the universe running smoothly.

Even though most rank-and-file Egyptians could never set foot inside their home temple's inner sanctum, they probably looked upon these shrines with some sense pride as their gods' and goddesses' chosen places on earth. It is easy to imagine, then, the horror many of them would have felt to hear that their local temples were shut down during instances such as the Intermediate Periods and the Amarna revolution; or worse still, to see them sacked by the invading Assyrians and Persians and their precious metal statues melted down. (In fact, the scant handful of surviving gold statues of deities have come mostly from caches buried well before the Late Period.) Social upheaval such as this probably had a profound effect on the Egyptians' collective psyche. Did they feel as though the gods abandoned the country and its temples? We know from Petosiris' records that at least some people were determined to rebuild new homes for their deities. But at what point did they decide, as a society, that their gods no longer needed earthly mansions in order to function? Or did they decide this at all before the onset of Christianity? This we may never know. Still, these late Egyptians' hard-earned theological conclusions have surely paved the way for our modern ideas of how gods and people connect.

The pylons of Medinet Habu arising from the surrounding hills evoke the Primeval Mound emerging from the waters of chaos. Photo by Krys Garnett

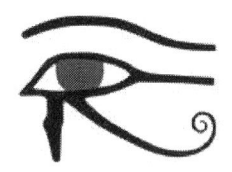

Who's Who of the Egyptian Gods

Egyptian religious texts contain the names of scores of deities, ranging from ephemeral beings who only receive mention in one or two contexts to powerful creator gods who protected the state. All of them were referred to in their native language as *netjer* (also written *neter*), or *netjeru* in plural. It is important to remember that the Egyptian pantheon did not remain fixed; the gods, like creation itself, were constantly changing and adding new dimensions or attributes. While some gods developed a national following long before written history, others remained fairly local even into recorded times. This "hometown" worship may help to explain why the Egyptians had several different, seemingly conflicting creation accounts, and why some gods and goddesses seem to swap parents or spouses. These local "flavors" are also another possible reason for the varied aspects of Horus and Seth, as we will soon explore.

The Egyptian gods and goddesses still resonate with us today because their stories and unique characters strike upon chords within us. They reveal a little about who we are, who we aspire to be, and sometimes what we fear. In getting to know them, we often get to know a little more about ourselves. In the pages that follow are some of the best-known, most popular and influential Netjeru to come from Egypt to us in the present day. They are grouped by their major mythological families and centers of worship.

Heliopolis

'Ennead' is a Greek word referring to a founding family of gods; the Egyptian word was *pesdjet*, which basically means "The Nine". As a number, nine signified abundance, being written by the plural sign (three strokes) times three. The 'Nine' of Heliopolis included Ra, Shu, Tefnut, Nut, Geb, Osiris, Isis, Nephthys and Seth; but because these latter four also figure in another myth cycle and religious center, they have their own grouping. The goddess Ma'at is included here because of her close relation to Ra.

Ra

Netjer A'ah – Great God

Neb Pet – Lord of the Sky

Neb Pesdjet – Lord of the Nine

Wa en Nun – Sole One of Nun

Spellings and meaning: His name is often spelled 'Re', but the hieroglyphic arm-sign in his name is generally rendered as an 'a' – hence the preferred spelling, *Ra*. The name simply means "sun".

Character: Ra is the quintessential sun god. His main center of worship, considered his earthly 'home', was Iunu (pronounced Yoo-NOO). Called Heliopolis, or "City of the Sun" in Greek, its ruins lie just north of modern Cairo. Fairly early in the Old Kingdom, Ra took on the attributes of Atum, a creator god whose name means either "completion" or "undifferentiated". In the Heliopolitan Myth of Creation, Ra-Atum emerged from the primeval waters of Nun in self-creation and set in motion the rest of existence. Ubiquitous as the sunlight he embodied, Ra had as many as seventy-five known manifestations. In the daily sun cycle he had three in particular: at dawn, he took the form of Khepri, seen as a child or scarab beetle. Scarabs were powerful symbols of the sun, thought to push the sun across the sky just as they rolled balls of dung across the ground in nature. They were also thought to embody Ra's power of self-creation as they emerged, seemingly of their own accord, from a ball of dung. At noon, representing the height of his powers, he took on the familiar falcon-headed form as Ra or Ra-Horakhety. At evening he reverted to Atum the primeval Creator, pictured as an old man. (This cycle of child at morning, adult at noon and old man at evening was probably the inspiration for the Riddle of the Sphinx.) Ra's travels across the sky were also commonly pictured as taking place in a type of boat called a barque, reflecting the earthly Egyptians' use of river vessels.

Over the course of pharaonic history Ra syncretized, or linked with, several other deities to create composites. In the Old Kingdom he connected with Horus, falcon god of the sun, sky and of kingship, to become Ra-Horakhety or "Ra-Horus of the Horizon". In the Middle Kingdom he combined with Sobek and also Khnum; in the New Kingdom, Ra combined with Amun to form Amun-Ra. His most eloquent combination comes from funerary texts, however. At the deepest point of Ra's nightly journey through the Underworld, he merged with the god Osiris. The Lord of Creation and the Lord of the Dead became one, said to "speak with one mouth", manifesting new life and the promise of a new beginning. A famous depiction of this moment comes from the tomb of Nefertari: "Here is Ra resting in Osiris; here is Osiris in Ra."

Many Egyptians throughout the country's ancient history worshiped Ra or one of his combinants as Lord of the gods. As Atum, he was regarded as the first to establish order or *ma'at* through his own creation. Together with his divine host, Ra defended order against the forces of chaos in the underworld every night. The Egyptians had a way of metaphorically expressing humanity's connection with him: according to his monologue in the Coffin Texts, human beings sprang from the tears of Ra.

Ma'at

Spellings and meaning: An idiomatic word, *ma'at* (pronounced "MAH-aht") generally translates to "truth, order, how things ought to be." Occasionally the word is also spelled 'ma'et'.

Character: As a concept, *ma'at* was the governing principle of a balanced and righteous world. As a goddess who embodied this concept, Ma'at was the daughter of Ra. Because he was the creator of an ordered world and arbiter of its justice, *ma'at* – as Ma'at – issued from him. She was always pictured with an ostrich feather emblem on her head; on the scales that weighed hearts of the deceased, she appeared as either a goddess icon with the feather or as the feather itself. This symbolism conveyed the sense that a righteous heart is light as a feather, whereas an unrighteous heart would be burdened with the weight of transgressions and regret. Images of Ma'at were also presented by ruling kings at the shrines of other gods as part of formal services, to symbolize the king's upholding of order (*ma'at*) through just rule. Many kings adopted the title "Beloved of Ma'at" to highlight themselves as good kings who ruled according to Her principles.

Ma'at generally had no consort and no divine children, although because of her presence in judgment of the deceased she worked closely with Thoth, who recorded the names of the innocent. Ma'at was also invoked in earthly Egyptian courts in order to insure that a fair and equitable ruling was given. Some scholars have argued that Ma'at had no actual centers of worship, being an embodied concept; but more than a few ancient priests and administrators held titles relating to sacred cattle and other temple assets belonging to the goddess.

Shu

Meaning: *Shu* means "void" or "emptiness".

Character: In the Heliopolitan creation story, after Ra-Atum came into being he created the elements of air and moisture, personified as Shu and Tefnut. How he went about creating them might seem scandalous to modern observers, but was perfectly natural to the pragmatic Egyptians. Having no partner to create offspring with, ancient texts say of Atum: "my fist became my spouse...I copulated with my hand...I sneezed out Shu...I spat out Tefnut." (In some accounts his hand actually took on the identity of a goddess, Iusa'as or "Increases As She Comes".) From himself he created male and female, and the rest of nature could then take its course. What's lost in translation, though, are the puns in this unusual story. 'Shu' sounds similar to the Egyptian word for "sneeze", *yshysh*, (which resembles the noise most of us make when we sneeze) and may also be an ancient Egyptian euphemism for ejaculating. Likewise, 'Tefnut' is similar to their word for spitting. Today, we groan whenever we hear a pun of this caliber, but to the ancients such similar-sounding words were never coincidence. Instead, they often suggested a hidden meaning.

Shu manifested as sunlit atmosphere. As the son of the sun god, he was also considered a prince of the Ennead. Together with Tefnut, Shu was referred to in the Pyramid Texts as one of "Atum's Twins". He was most often pictured holding aloft his own daughter, the sky goddess Nut, high above his son Geb who formed the earth. By doing this, Shu assisted his father Ra in the work of creation, allowing a living space and air for all the living creatures yet to be. Much later during the Aton revolution, Shu was incorporated as an aspect of Aton. It is thought that the Amarna-style art, which often showed the royal family wearing streamers blowing in the wind, was trying to capture the idea of Shu as the dynamic "breath of life" that came from Aton.

Tefnut

Spellings and meaning: Sometimes spelled 'Tefnet', *Tefnut* refers to moisture.

Character: While Shu formed the atmosphere of this world, Tefnut was thought to form the atmosphere of the underworld, or Duat. Tefnut, who presided over moisture and dew, was pictured as a lion-headed woman. Lions stalked the desert fringes of civilization throughout pharaonic history, so it is easy to imagine a lioness drinking at a desert pool inspiring terrified Egyptians' awe. Tefnut was also one of several goddesses who bore the title Eye of Ra. According to later-era accounts, Ra-Atum sent Tefnut as his Eye to seek out dry land while they still drifted within Nun (in variations, Shu and Tenfut left together). While the Twins were gone, Ra regenerated his Eye; some say that Ma'at became his new eye. When Tefnut returned, she was infuriated to have been replaced. She took off into the deserts of Nubia, and the other gods, led by Thoth, had to entice her back home with music and dancing. This story, called the Myth of the Distant Goddess, had several variations and also tied into a similar myth called the Destruction of Mankind. In this latter story, the leonine Eye of Ra goddess (whose identity alternated depending on regional tradition) left Ra well after the world had been created and populated with mankind. The other gods had to work not simply to entice her home, but to keep her from destroying all of humanity!

Eventually Tefnut settled down long enough to have two children with Shu, Geb and Nut. She was never completely 'tamed', though; bearing the sun disc and cobra on her forehead, she remained Ra's Eye and thus his lethal enforcer.

Geb

Spellings and meaning: In the commonly-available books by E. A. Wallis Budge, this god's name is frequently mis-rendered as 'Seb' or 'Qeb', owing to the difficulty of deciphering the duck hieroglyph used in Egyptian. *Geb* is the correct spelling, however. Its meaning is still obscure.

Character: Shu and Tefnut got to work and in turn bore Geb and Nut, who formed the earth and sky. It is interesting to note that whereas Indo-European religions personify the earth as a mother figure, to the Egyptians the earth was male. The enveloping, embracing sky was a goddess in their eyes. Their language reflected this thought: *ta*, their word for earth, is a masculine noun while *pet*, or sky (sometimes liberally translated as 'heaven') is feminine. The Egyptians illustrated the world schematically with Geb lying down, forming the ground; Nut arching her body over him as the sky; and Shu holding her aloft with outstretched arms.

Geb was seen as the divine ancestral pharaoh, a foundation of Egypt as well as the earth and one of its highest judicial powers. He was invoked during kings' coronations, and the Pyramid Texts refer to him speaking in favor of the deceased king before Ra. The earth was called the "*Ba* of Geb", meaning his power physically manifested. He also presided over both vegetation and earthquakes. Geb's wife and children, however, would capture popular imagination much more vividly.

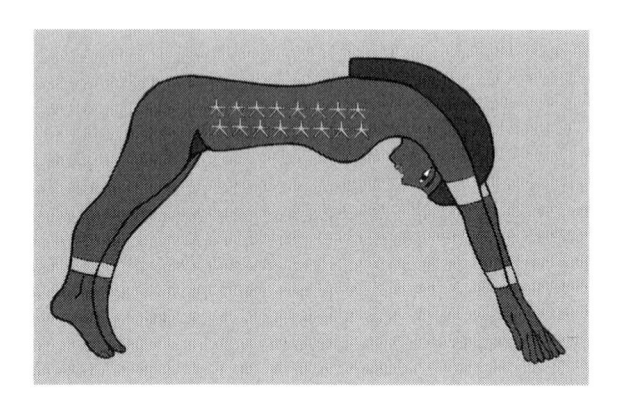

Nut

Netjeret A'ah – Great Goddess

Nebet Pet – Lady of the Sky

Mut Netjeru – Mother of the Gods

Kha Bauet – She of a Thousand Ba's

Spellings and meaning: Occasionally her name is spelled 'Niut' or 'Nuit', but the most common rendering is *Nut*. Its meaning is still obscure.

Character: Nut is most commonly depicted as a youthful, naked woman with her arms and legs out-stretched. She sometimes appeared clothed, however, as in the famous mural from Tutankhamun's tomb. The sexual connotation of her naked form was not accidental; in the Pyramid Texts, Nut was sometimes called "Owner of a Vulva". She was believed to swallow the sun god every evening, regenerating him in her womb and giving birth to him anew every morning. For this reason, some of the more detailed illustrations of Nut pictured the sun disc near her mouth, within her body and just outside of her pubic region. Later the schematic became more complex, with Nut pictured in twin form for the day and night. The sun god Ra traversed the outside of her diurnal body each day while the stars moved within her mirror underworld form. The cycle switched at sunset, with the stars being reborn into the night sky.

One of Nut's greatest powers was regeneration and renewal. Her womb was considered the source of rejuvenation and eternal life, so much that coffins were viewed as manifestations of her womb. Entire sections of the Pyramid Texts deal with spells to "Enter the Womb of Nut". It became customary to illustrate her stretched out on the underside of coffin and sarcophagus lids, so she would quite literally be over the body of the deceased. A common prayer in funerary literature read, "Oh mother Nut, put your arms over me and make me one of the Imperishable Stars that are in you." These circumpolar or Imperishable Stars were viewed as the *ba*-souls of the blessed dead; hence another title of Nut's was "She of a Thousand Ba's".

As an extension of her powers of rebirth, Nut was a mother goddess. While she was Ra's granddaughter genealogically, because she took him into her body and bore him anew, she became his mother; in some traditions, she also became his consort. She had four divine children with Geb, (five in Greco-Roman tradition), two of which became extremely powerful and popular deities. But motherhood was not Nut's only notable attribute. Some texts have her say that she was a great goddess while still in the womb of her own mother, Tefnut. Further, in her role as goddess of the sky, Nut acted as a protective boundary between creation and the primeval waters of Nun. Protection and the sustaining of life and order were certainly important roles, ones which Nut fulfilled daily.

Abydos

Our last four members of the Heliopolitan Ennead are key players in the Osirian myth cycle as well. The geographic center of Osiris' worship is without a doubt Abydos, or *Abju* in Egyptian. The holy family of Abydos included Osiris and Isis, their sister Nephthys, sons Horus and Anubis and daughter Serket. Also integral to their story is Seth, a patron deity to some but antagonist in the Osirian tradition.

Osiris

Khenti-Amentiu – Foremost of the Westerners

Un-Nefer – The Beatified (or Eternally Fresh)

Neb Abju – Lord of Abydos

Neb Djedu – Lord of Busiris

Spellings and meaning: Osiris is one of many gods known most commonly by their Greek name. His native name is difficult to transliterate; common spellings are 'Wesir' and 'Ausar'. A more user-friendly spelling would be *Osir* (pronounced "OH-seer"). The name seems to mean "to be established," or perhaps "copulates with the throne" – referring to Isis.

Character: Scholars consider Osiris to be a relatively young god; no present archaeological record of his worship dates before the Fifth Dynasty. However, references in the Pyramid

Texts and attributes that Osiris absorbed from two other deities, Andjedi and Khentiamentiu, suggest that Osiris may be older than current evidence places him. In any case, his worship centered in Djedu (Busiris in Greek), but especially in Abydos, a sacred town which was the burial ground for pharaohs of the First Dynasty. In fact, the tomb thought to be Osiris's in ancient times may have actually been the tomb of King Djer, the second pharaoh of Egypt.

According to legend Osiris, son of Nut and Geb, ruled Egypt during a golden age. He established civilization among humankind and taught them to farm. His brother Seth grew jealous, and plotted to kill Osiris. The most famous version of the murder comes down to us from Plutarch, the Greek author: Seth tricked Osiris into laying in a coffin during a party, whereupon he slammed the lid shut and drowned him in the Nile. Osiris's distraught widow Isis found the body and revived him with her magic long enough to conceive a son, Horus. Afterward Seth found the body again and hacked it into pieces, each one said to have been located in one of the different districts of Egypt. Anubis developed the art of mummification to finally restore Osiris' body and enable him to live on in the Duat. Variations of the story can be found in the Pyramid and Coffin Texts and in various hymns; in the Pyramid Texts Seth attacked Osiris and "cast him down" in Nedyt, a place-name that formed another pun alluding to the murder. Multifaceted and universal, Osiris's appeal went beyond his status as sovereign of Duat. As founder of agriculture, he was the Egyptian version of the Corn King, his fertility and vitality manifested in sprouting grain. He was an administrator of justice alongside Ra, and even took on Ra's solar aspects. In the Weighing of the Heart, it was Osiris who actually made the final decision of a person's righteousness while Anubis operated the scales. But his heinous and unjust demise also made him the everyman. All humans must die, and Osiris shared in that experience. The example of his resurrection provided hope for all people. To average Egyptians, Osiris was constantly present; through the plants that fed them, the civilization that supported them, and the hope of eternal reward for a life honestly lived.

Isis

Netjeret A'ah – Great Goddess

Nebet Pet – Lady of the Sky

Uret Hekau – Great of Magic

Mut Horu – Mother of Horus

Spellings and meaning: Meaning "throne", her name also presents challenges. 'Isis' comes down to us from the Greeks and Romans, and is still used by modern Pagans worldwide. Her Egyptian-language name is typically written as 'Aset' or 'Auset'.

Character: Sister-wife of Osiris and mother of Horus, Isis rose to become one of the most popular and enduring goddesses of Egypt. Her origins are uncertain, but she was worshiped well into the third century A.D., and temples were built to her in Greece and Rome. Very likely her influence spread to the limits of the Roman empire into modern Britain. Interestingly, though, temples built exclusively to her did not appear in Egypt until very late in pharaonic history. Her temple at Philae was the last pagan Egyptian sanctuary in operation, closing after Christianity became the official religion of the Roman Empire. But Isis's influence did not die: the image of Madonna and Child is thought to have been inspired by the ages-old image of Isis suckling her child Horus.

While she embodied queenly attributes and shared the title "Mistress [or Lady] of the Sky" with other prominent goddesses Nut and Hathor, Isis had appeal to the common person much as her husband Osiris did. Unexpectedly widowed, she was forced into hiding and had to raise their son Horus as a single mother. She used her wits, eloquence and skills in magic – one of her other titles was *Uret Hekau*, 'Great of Magic' – to prevail. In accounts of the Myth of Kingship dating from the Ramesside era, she even faced conflicting family loyalties as her son battled her brother and each appealed to her for support. Ultimately, though, she backed her son as the rightful victor. Above all else, Isis was a devoted mother.

Modern Pagans who have adopted worship of Isis often find a conflict within one of the ancient myths about her. According to a story found in Turin Papyrus 1993, she used an enchanted venomous serpent to coerce Ra into telling her and Horus his secret name; both Kemetics and other Pagans debate over whether to interpret Isis' actions as manipulative and conniving, or justified and even worth emulating. History provides valuable insight, however. The story of Isis and Ra's secret name dates from the Ramesside era, when many satirical works were being recorded. In fact, another story has been found in which Horus coerces a secret name from Nemty, a rival falcon god, in a similar manner. The Isis story's depiction of Ra as old and senile was probably also meant as parody. In addition, the story legitimized the pharaoh as inheritor of the knowledge of Ra's secret name, giving it a possible political motive. Finally, the Turin version also includes a manual and spells to cure poisonous bites and stings. Its practical use, then, should carry more weight than the story itself – just as Isis' abilities to heal were more valued by her worshipers than parodies of her clever tricks.

Nephthys

Spellings and meaning: Here again, 'Nephthys' (pronounced NEFF-this) comes from Greek. Frequent renderings are 'Nebet-het' and 'Nebet-hwt'...how does one say, 'hwt' anyway?! Her name means "Lady of the Shrine", and here is rendered *Nebet-hat*.

Character: Nephthys is the twin sister of Isis and sister-wife of Seth. Little is known about her. Most often she was pictured mourning Osiris along with Isis, or guarding the bodies of the deceased alongside her sister. Some scholars consider Nephthys to be a dark 'alter ego' of sorts to Isis. According to a late-era story, Nephthys devised a means to conceive a son, since Seth was reputedly sterile. She tricked Osiris into thinking she was Isis in the darkness, and the result of their tryst was Anubis. (Appropriately, one of Anubis's titles was "He who is over the secrets"!) Isis evidently never called her sister to task on the issue, and in many accounts even raised Anubis as her own.

Despite being married to Seth, Nephthys's loyalties lay with Osiris and Isis. She helped Isis collect the pieces of Osiris' body and restore him to life. In illustrations of the Book of the Dead, she stands beside Isis in support of the enthroned Osiris. Rituals com-memorating Osiris' death and resurrection called for two women to recite Lamentations as Isis and Nephthys. As one of the four guardians of the dead, she protected the feet of the deceased. Nephthys also had an association with weaving, and bandages used to wrap mummies were sometimes called the "tresses of Nephthys".

Seth

Neb Nubet – Lord of Gold-Town

Neb Deshret – Lord of the Desert

A'ah Pehty – Great of Strength

Sa Nut – Son of Nut

Spellings and meaning: The Greeks took the hard 't' sound in *Set* (or *Sut*) and softened it to a 'th'. Other variants of his name include 'Setech' and 'Sutekh', but these are actually Semitic in origin and were adopted by the Egyptians later. Translations are uncertain.

Character: Seth is, perhaps appropriately enough, one of the more problematic deities of the Egyptian pantheon. In Osirian legend he was the younger brother of Osiris – but archaeologically speaking, he is considered older. Worship of Seth dates back to the earliest recorded history, centering in the Delta but also in the mining outpost town of Nubet (modern Naqada) south of Abydos. He was a god of the sky, of storms and strength, guardian of desert routes and lord of its harsh wilderness. He was also an early god of kingship, and two early Dynastic kings wrote their names surmounted with Seth's unique animal form. Having a greyhound-like body, long squarish ears, a tapered snout and a forked tail, the Seth animal defies modern researchers' attempts at classification.

Seth was a powerful and prestigious deity, and he had adherents through the New Kingdom, Seti I being the most famous. Seti's dynasty came from the Delta town of Avaris, which had been rebuilt and officially re-dedicated to Seth some four hundred years before. Because Seth's aspect as a storm god – as opposed to the murderer of Osiris – dates from the earliest periods of Egyptian history, it's helpful to refer to it as his Archaic form.

He was a god of strength, but strength without temperance is dangerous. This must surely have been a conclusion of the Egyptians who wove Seth into the Osirian legend. Even in his Archaic form he was considered fearsome; the emblem of the 11th nome featured Seth's animal form on a pole, but by Dynastic times he was pictured with a dagger in his head. In the Pyramid Texts, he attacked his brother Horus among the stars. (Frequently Horus and Seth switch between being uncle and nephew and being brothers, even in the same literary work.) By murdering Osiris, Seth came to embody chaos, violence and usurpation. By the Ramesside era he was also associated with sexual deviancy; in the Chester Beatty I papyrus' account, Seth tried to humiliate Horus by sexually assaulting him. It is also interesting to note that while Seti's name was spelled on monuments with Seth's hieroglyph, in his tomb the spelling was changed to Isis's name (as *Isut*, a homonym,) to protect the dead king from Seth's violent aspect.

Some Kemetics claim that Seth's role as a god of evil is purely a Greek or Christian invention; this is not supported by records the Egyptians themselves left us. As might be expected of the unpredictable Lord of the Desert, Seth simply cannot be fit into an "either-or" framework. He was *both* a god of strength and patron of early kings, *and* a dangerous trickster who committed acts of chaos and treachery.

Horus

Netjer A'ah – Great God

Neb Pet – Lord of the Sky

Sa Iset – Son of Isis

Nedj-Her-Itef – Defender of his Father

Spellings and meaning: Frequently transliterated as 'Heru'; but given the number of names derived from this god's that are rendered "Har-" or "Hor-", a better spelling would be *Horu*. The name means "above" or "Far-Away One".

Character: Horus is another god with universal appeal, in part because he has more aspects than perhaps any other deity besides Ra. One aspect that remained consistent throughout pharaonic history was kingship; the pharaoh was looked upon as the earthly embodiment of Horus, and two of the king's official titles incorporated the name of Horus. Horus also acted as an opposite or counterpoint to Seth – in one theory Horus represented the day sky, Seth the night or stormy sky. The two were also depicted in heraldric motifs uniting Upper and Lower Egypt.

Worship of Horus underwent two revolutions of sorts during the Old Kingdom. The first came about when religious thinkers of Iunu (Heliopolis) combined Horus's kingly aspect with Ra. In the resulting 'reformat', Ra adopted the falcon-headed avatar of Ra-Horakhety, "Ra the Horus of the Horizon" and king of the gods. Horus became Hor-ur, or "Great Horus", more often translated as "Horus the Elder". Hor-ur was viewed as the son of Ra.

The second, far more profound, revolution of Horus's worship resulted from the rise of the Osirian legend. Just as Osiris's demise and resurrection democratized the afterlife for common folk, Horus's transformation into the son of Osiris made him accessible to the average worshiper. As Horu-pa-khered (Horus the Child) he protected children from illness, bites and stings; as Horu-iun-mutef (Horus, Pillar of His Mother) he supported his mother and provided the ideal example of caring for one's parents; and as Horu-nedj-her-itef (Horus, Avenger of His Father) he championed righteousness and proper inheritance. One of the most potent and well-known Egyptian amulets comes from Horus's role in the Osirian myth, also called the Myth of Kingship. The *udjat* eye (also spelled "wedjat") represents an eye lost by Horus in his battle with his uncle Seth. Magically restored to life, the Eye of Horus – not to be confused with the punishing Eye of Ra – symbolizes health, protection, respect for parents and the dead, and good triumphing over evil. If one considers the Osirian Myth of Kingship as the "Star Wars" of its day, then Horus is its Luke Skywalker.

At first the priests of Iunu tried to distinguish between Hor-ur and Horu-sa-Isut, but the more Archaic Hor-ur became somewhat eclipsed by Horus of the Myth of Kingship. Some scholars and Kemetics seem to fall into the same trap as the Old Kingdom priests of Iunu: on one hand, they insist 'Her-wer' and 'Her-sa-Aset' are two separate beings, but on the other hand they attempt to re-write mythology to incorporate both into the same story! It is far simpler and less mind-bending to look upon Horus as most Egyptians did; a god of such tremendous appeal, influence and flexibility that he transcended just one linear tradition.

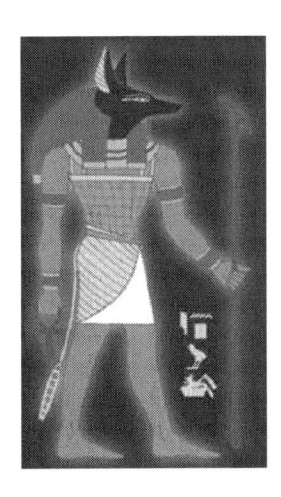

Anubis

Imi-ut – He in His Wrappings

Neb Ta-Djoser – Lord of the Sacred Land

Tepy Dju-ef – He Over His Mountain

Tepy Sesheta – He Over the Secrets

Spellings and meaning: As with other major Egyptian deities, the Greek form of his name, 'Anubis', is best known. Transliterations vary because the reed symbol in his native name has been rendered differently over the years – yielding 'Anpu', 'Inpu', and even 'Yinepu'. While it may have been spoken any or all of those ways at one time, for the Greeks to come up with "Anubis" they were probably hearing *Anepu* (AH-ne-poo). Its meaning is obscure, but may be a play on the word for "crown prince" or mimicking a puppy's bark.

Character: Anubis's worship is also fairly ancient. He may have originally been identified as Imiut, "He in His Wrappings"; or as Khentiamentiu, "Foremost of the Westerners", which was an Archaic jackal-headed deity of Abydos. The name eventually went to Osiris, but Anubis kept the identity as a jackal and funerary god. Some traditions hold him as son of Ra; in Osirian tradition he is Osiris's son through Nephthys, or alternately Isis. According to one story, Nephthys's husband Seth became enraged at her infidelity and tried to kill Anubis, but Isis took him as her own son and protected him. Anubis was certainly a loyal son, inventing the art of mummification to restore Osiris to life and going on to serve as operator of the scales before Osiris in the Hall of Two Truths, where souls of the dead were judged.

Popular throughout Egyptian history, in the Late Period Anubis took on roles in healing and even in love magic. His worship continued into the Greco-Roman era, when sculptures depicted him in centurion's armor. Today he is one of the most famous of all Egyptian deities.

His fame has brought him a number of misconceptions, however. Obviously, he was not a god of evil a' la "The Mummy Returns". Nor was he the personification of death; the Egyptians viewed death as simply a part of life and they had no equivalent of our Grim Reaper. Anubis's worship was not strictly related to funerary rites, as Hatshepsut built a chapel to him in her famous temple of Deir el-Bahari. Some scholars think he held a prominent role in initiations. He was also seen as a friendly ear and an advocate of truth: in the Middle Kingdom-era *Tale of the Eloquent Peasant*, for example, the title character threatens in exasperation that he will "appeal to Anubis" and commit suicide when no official will hear his grievances. The pharaoh himself then intervenes and restores justice for the slighted peasant. Undoubtedly the pharaoh, as with most Egyptians, would have wanted Anubis to speak well on his behalf before Osiris.

Serket

Spellings and meaning: Her Greek name is 'Selkis', from which many sources render 'Selket'. The Egyptians spelled it *Serket*, which comes from their word for "breathe".

Character: According to the Pyramid Texts, Serket is the daughter of Osiris and Isis. She in turn had a son, a lesser-known deity named Nehebkau or "Kas-Assigner". No centers of worship for her have been found, but the Pyramid Texts refer to a *Hat Serket* ("Shrine of Serket") in Qedem. Priests in her service specialized in healing magic. Healing scorpion stings was Serket's forte', so much so that her emblem was a scorpion. She also protected women in childbirth and nursing, and her control of magic was second only to Isis'. In the Books of the Underworld, Serket and Isis use magic to repel the evil serpent Apophis.

Serket is probably best known for the touching statue of her that guarded Tutankhamun's Canopic shrine. Her roles of protection continued from this life into the next, and she was one of the four guardian goddesses that safeguarded the deceased's body from harm. Paired with the Delta goddess Neith, she protected the head while Isis and Nephthys guarded the feet. She also paired with Qebehsenuef, one of the Four Sons of Horus whose funerary role was to protect the deceased's intestines. Canopic jars of Qebehsenuef typically carried a variation of the following spell: "Words spoken by Serket, 'I place my arms on that which is in me, I protect Qebehsenuef who is in me...'".

While her role may not have been as prominent as that of some of her divine colleagues', Serket's popularity as a friendly goddess of healing and protection seemed to have been widespread for much of Egypt's history.

Thebes

Thebes and its surrounding region in Middle Egypt, which includes the towns of Akhmim (modern Qift) and Khemnu (El-Ashmunein), are best known for the family triad of Amun, Mut and Khonsu. But several other gods had ties to the area, including Montu, Min, and Djehuty – better known by his Greek name, Thoth. The goddess Hathor, who had a major temple in nearby Denderah, was also mistress of a sacred valley situated across the river from Thebes. Further to the south in Esna lay a temple that was home to the creator god Khnum.

Montu at Karnak. Photo by Krys Garnett

Montu

Character: A falcon-headed god of war, Montu's center of worship was in the area just south of Thebes. Inscriptions refer to four temples to Montu in the towns of Thebes, Armant, Tod and Medamud, forming a rough square around the region. Four images of Montu representing each of these sacred places were painted on warships, wielding spears and crushing enemies of the state. Often invoked to fight alongside kings in battle, Montu became the royal patron and state god of the Eleventh Dynasty, made famous by kings named *Montuhotep* ("Montu is satisfied"). He merged with Ra to form Montu-Ra, who was considered at one time to be the southern counterpart of Ra-Atum. Later when Amun rose to prominence, he in turn merged with Montu to create the new aspect Amun-Montu.

Montu's consort was a lesser-known goddess named Raettawy, who was herself a 'female doublet' of Ra who wore a headdress similar to Hathor's. Montu's sacred animals were the falcon and the bull. He enjoyed a resurgence in the New Kingdom, as pharaohs who fought to expand an empire described themselves as fierce fighters who "raged like Montu". Later during the Greco-Roman Period, Montu's temple at Armant housed two sacred bulls, one white and one black, that were known as the "Buchis bulls".

King Amunhotep I offers to Min.
Photo by Krys Garnett

Min

Spelling: Originally scholars (especially Budge) translated his name as 'Amsu' or 'Imsu', but it has since been more accurately rendered as *Min*. The hieroglyph spelling his name is still more mysterious, perhaps representing an arrow's barb or a door bolt.

Character: Min is most famous – or perhaps infamous– for the statues and reliefs depicting him as a mummiform man wearing a bonnet with two tall plumes and gripping an impossibly erect phallus. (Victorian-era scholars considered his images downright scandalous, and often omitted the offending 'member' from copied illustrations.) His worship centered in the towns of Akhmim and Coptos (*Gebju*), and he also presided over the Eastern Desert. A 5,000 year-old stone Colossi of Min thought to bear his symbol was found in his temple at the edge of the Eastern Desert. He held a close link to Horus, often being identified with him as Min-Horus; but his lover was actually Isis. One of his titles was *Ka-mutef*, or "Bull of His Mother", an archetype of the god who impregnates his mother to perpetuate himself. Min also combined with Amun to form Amun-Min, a form of the divine creator whose virility produced all life.

Min was a god of fertility *par excellence*. A type of romaine lettuce, called Cos lettuce, was considered sacred to Min because it produces a milky semen-like sap when cut. During the growing season Min's cult statues were carried into agricultural fields to bless the crops, and the first sheaves of cut grain were offered to him at his harvest feast. Much of what we know of this Festival of Min comes from temple depictions commissioned by Ramses III. Greek travelers later described Min's religious festivals, in which his oracle statue was robed in red cloth and taken on procession. Similarly, the red ribbons trailing from Min's headdress (and sometimes Amun's as well) in classical images are thought by some to represent sexual potency. His feasts were celebrations of masculine strength and virility, including naked wrestling matches and climbing a pole – certainly a graphic representation of Min's divine 'member'.

Thoth

Netjer A'ah – Great God

Neb Ma'at – Lord of Ma'at

Neb Medu-Netjer – Lord of the Sacred Words

Neb Khemnu – Lord of Eight-Town

Spellings and meaning: Once again, 'Thoth' is the Greek spelling, but the Egyptian original – *Djehuty*, also spelled

'Tehuty' – hardly sounds similar. Its meaning is unknown; perhaps "He of Djehu", a town now lost to history.

Character: Djehuty's center of worship was Khemnu, called "Hermopolis" in Greek. He held many roles; moon god, lord of wisdom and mediator of the gods, inventor of writing and mathematics, and patron of scribes. Hieroglyphic writing was seen as the sacred words of the gods, the *medu netjer*, and before beginning a day's work scribes would offer water to Djehuty.

Djehuty most often took the form of a man with the head of an ibis, a grey heron-like wading bird that took long, measured strides as it hunted fish in ancient Nile marshes. His other animal avatar was a baboon; to the Egyptians, baboons' screeching calls at dawn were a secret language heralding the rising sun god. Djehuty's consorts are much less known; the lion goddess Nehmetawy was his wife in the Khemnu region, Seshat (who also presided over hieroglyphic writing) in others.

In the Hall of Two Truths, names of all the souls judged worthy by Osiris were recorded by Djehuty. He also presided over medical arts, which in ancient times included magic as well as practical remedies. It was Djehuty who restored Horus's *udjat* eye to health. As divine mediator and messenger, he also searched for the wayward Tefnut in one version of the legend of Destruction of Mankind.

One lesser-known role of Djehuty's, however, was ruler of Egypt in Ra's stead. According to the collection of myths gathered in the *Book of the Celestial Cow*, which includes Destruction of Mankind, dispensing with rebellious humans had left an aging Ra weary of earthly rule. So he took to the sky on the back of the Celestial Cow, leaving the office of pharaoh to a succession of gods, beginning with Djehuty. It was as acting pharaoh that he taught writing and the sciences to mankind. Quite possibly the line of pharaohs of the early 18th Dynasty who took the name *Djehutymose* – meaning "Born of Djehuty", better known by the Greek form 'Tuthmosis' – wished to emphasize this spiritual lineage. It was a way of linking their kingship back to Djehuty, and thus to Ra himself.

Seshat

Sefkhat Abwy - Seven-Pointed [or Horned] One

Spellings and meaning: Sometimes spelled 'Sechat', the name is a feminization of the word *sesh*, or 'scribe'; hence, it means "the female scribe" or "female writer".

Character: Called the "Foremost of the Library" who "reckons all things on earth", Seshat is the patroness of record-keeping, mathematics, astronomy and architecture. Together with Djehuty, she recorded the name and titles of each pharaoh as he was crowned, writing them upon the leaves of the sacred persea tree in Heliopolis. Seshat was invoked at a special groundbreaking ceremony known as the Stretching of the Cord, and she was believed to have built palaces for the other Gods in *Duat*. Royal tributes to temples and particularly spoils of war were pictured on temple reliefs being tallied up by the goddess. Seshat is often pictured holding a notched palm rib, representing an archaic way of marking time, and wearing a leopard skin robe that hearkened to ancient priestly roles associated with astronomy. Seshat is sometimes referred to as the consort of Djehuty, at other times as his counterpart.

Seshat's omission from the first edition of this book was an unfortunate oversight. Particularly today, when women find themselves increasingly edged out of technical professions by men, this goddess who presides over what we would now call STEM - science, technology, engineering and mathematics - could show us the way to a more balanced world of learning and discovery.

Amun

Neb Pet – Lord of the Sky

Neb Waset – Lord of Thebes

Neb Khemnu – Lord of Eight-Town

Ka-Mut-ef – Bull of His Mother

Spellings and meaning: The second vowel in his name is uncertain, yielding 'Amen', 'Amon' and *Amun*, used here. The name means "Hidden One".

Character: Amun's worship may once have been linked to Khemnu, the same religious center which honored Djehuty. Known as el-Ashmunein in modern Arabic, the city's name literally means "Eight-Town". This refers to their myth of creation, of which Amun played an essential part. The heart of Amun's domain, however, was Thebes, or *Waset* in Egyptian (meaning "City of the Scepter"). For all the glory and tribute that would later be dedicated to Amun, he is practically unknown before the Middle Kingdom. Very likely he held a small, local following until pharaohs who worshiped him came to power at the end of the First Intermediate Period.

The people of Khemnu and Thebes held a different view of creation from those of Heliopolis. Within the darkness of chaos before creation, their story explains, eight beings lay in a sort of dormant stasis; four male and four female, each a matched pair. Nu and Naunet formed the primeval waters, Heh and Hauhet the force of inundation, Kek and Kauket the darkness, and Amun and Amaunet hidden dynamic force. It was Amun and Amaunet's energy that broke the stasis and set forth the formation of the cosmos. Particulars of the story from there are difficult to unravel; in a Late Period version, Amun-Amaunet's creative force produced a cosmic egg that Djehuty placed in Khemnu to hatch, allowing the sun god to emerge.

In any case, Amun was held to be the source of all existence. The "Hidden One" of the beginning, his true nature was unknowable by mortals. He was greatly revered as a personal intercessor who heeded prayers and rewarded the just, being addressed in one stela as "lord of the silent, who comes at the voice of the poor". His adaptability led to several syncretized forms, including Amun-Min and Amun-Ra. By the Nineteenth dynasty, Amun and Ra combined with the creator god of Memphis, Ptah, to create a sort of trinity; Amun was the ultimate source, Ptah his form of creator, and Ra his visible manifestation. Amun still had counterparts, though. Aside from his female compliment Amaunet, Amun's wife was the goddess Mut, and their offspring the moon god Khonsu.

Mut

Netjeret A'ah – Great Goddess

Nebet Pet – Lady of the Sky

Nebet Tawy – Mistress of the Two Lands

Nebet Isheru – Mistress of the Sacred Lake

Character: Wife of Amun, Mut's name suggests one aspect of who she is: "mother". Her seemingly simple character belies her flexibility and enduring popularity, however. For a long time, scholars thought she played a passive role as Amun's consort in the myths and religious festivals of the Theban region;

but the recent work of Dr. Betsy Bryan in particular has shown that Mut had an active worship in her own right. Mut's temple in Karnak was most likely originally built by the female pharaoh Hatshepsut. Its features included a "porch of drunkenness", dedicated to a festival that combined Mut with Sakhmet. In the Feast of Drunkenness, celebrants drank red beer to appease Mut-Sakhmet in commemoration of the myth of Destruction of Mankind. Women ruled in other ways in the worship of Mut: depictions of festival rites in Hatshepsut's Red Chapel show almost half of the officiants as female, whereas most other representations of religious rites picture only males.

Mut was looked upon as the mother of the pharaoh and the embodiment of royal power; she shared motherly and protective roles with Isis, Hathor and even Bast. She was also worshiped by the Kushites of Nubia, modern Sudan, who ruled Egypt during the Twenty-fifth dynasty. One of Mut's titles was "Mistress of Isheru", which referred to the sacred artificial lake adjoining her temple. The last of its kind left in Egypt, conservation efforts are currently underway to restore the *isheru* lake to its original levels. Despite her nurturing qualities, though, she had a dangerous side. Aside from her association with Sakhmet as the Eye of Ra, at the end of the New Kingdom her temple also hosted the executions of criminals in the "Braziers of Mut".

A part of Mut's lore survived into the present era; at the turn of the century, local legend had it that if a single man ever ventured near the temple of Mut at night, he would encounter a beautiful woman. She would then turn into a lioness and attack the hapless bachelor!

Khonsu

Meaning: His name, which sometimes drops the -u as 'Khons', has been rendered as either "wanderer" or "The Traveler".

Character: A moon god, Khonsu was the child of Amun and Mut. In the Memphite region he could also stand in as the son of Ptah and Sakhmet. Khonsu was generally pictured as an oversized Egyptian baby, with a braided sidelock, swaddled body and a finger to his mouth, symbolizing youth. Occasionally he took other forms, such as a falcon-headed man. On his head he wore a crescent and lunar disc.

Brief passages in the Pyramid and Coffin Texts refer to Khonsu as a fearsome and angry deity who ate the hearts of the dead. In a baboon avatar, Khonsu was in charge of punishment and destiny. His title was "Keeper of the Books of the End of the Year", in which the names of all those would die in the next year were written. But he had a beneficent side as "Khonsu the Merciful", in which he could re-write a person's fate and ward off demons. This gentler side is reflected in a story from the Late Period, in which Rameses II sent an oracle statue of Khonsu to an allied country to heal a sick princess. The tale was written during the Persian occupation as a way of bolstering the native Egyptians' pride, but it suggests some of the friendlier aspects worshippers may have sought in Khonsu.

Khonsu's power to decide a person's fate for good or ill may have been alluded to in a statue group com-missioned by Tutankhamun. It shows him as a young adult, striding forward with Amun and Mut to either side, each putting an arm around him as his divine parents. This placed Tutankhamun in the role of Khonsu; suggesting that like the moon god, he too had the authority to determine his subjects' fate.

Many modern pagans try to equate various Egyptian goddesses with the moon, most commonly Isis and Hathor. Feminization of the moon is a completely non-native tradition. To the ancient Egyptians, the moon was decidedly male, either represented by Djehuty, Khonsu, or the much more obscure god Iah. As stated earlier, the sky was their goddess, the all-encompassing vessel in which the sun and moon were both carried and birthed each day.

Hathor

Nebet Pet – Lady of the Sky

Nebet Mafket – Lady of Turquoise

Nebet Amentet – Lady of the West

Sat Ra – Daughter of Ra

Spellings and meaning: The softer 'th' in the Greek name 'Hathor' comes from joining *Hat-Hor*, which means "Temple [or "House"] of Horu". Modern variants include "Het-hert" and the rather tongue-twisting "Hwt-hrw".

Character: Like Horus, who was her husband in most accounts, Hathor enjoyed widespread appeal, and chapels to her have been found across Egypt. Her well-preserved temple in Denderah has provided a wealth of information from its inscriptions about amulets, spells, ritual texts and holidays.

While Isis gets the most press in modern times as a mother goddess, in early Egyptian history Hathor was the preeminent mother deity. Daughter of Ra and wife of Horus – at other points the consort of Ra himself – she was also the guardian mother of the living pharaoh and a protectress of ordinary women and children. Milk was sacred to Hathor, and her animal avatar was a cow. In sculpture she was often pictured with a human face and cow's ears, giving her an almost elfin look. She eventually took on some of Nut's aspects as a sky goddess; later, as Isis grew in popularity, she and Hathor came to share many attributes. The crown of cow's horns framing a sun disk originally belonged to Hathor, but according to legend Isis gained them from her. A feast day was likely celebrated to commemorate the story.

Hathor was patroness of beauty, love (especially romantic), music, dancing and states of ecstasy. The sistrum, a type of rattle, and the *menit* necklace, which may have been shaken like a rattle, were her sacred instruments. She led people in drunken or altered states closer to the realm of gods and spirits. When a person died, she led them through parts of the perilous journey through the Duat, just as she did for Ra. She held many titles: Lady of the Sycamore and Lady of the West (in her funerary roles), Mistress of the Sky, Lady of Gold and Lady of Turquoise. She held great regenerative powers. In some of her temples excavators have found offering bowls painted blue with floral and fish motifs, to evoke both marshes teeming with new life and her sacred turquoise.

Hathor was universally popular, appearing frequently alongside the dwarf god Bes in paintings from the ruins of houses in the village of Deir el-Medina. Mirrors and sistrums commonly carried her image, and she was often invoked in love songs. She tended to syncretize with several goddesses, most notably Isis but also Nut, Bast and Sakhmet. In the *Book of the Celestial Cow*, Hathor was interpreted as the friendlier side of the lion-headed Sakhmet.

Khnum

Meaning: *Khnum* comes from a root verb meaning "to join" or "unite".

Character: The ram-headed creator god Khnum was considered ruler of the southern region of Elephantine near the First Cataract in the Nile. In drought years when the floods were poor, kings made offerings to Khnum as lord of the Inundation to ask for the waters' return. Besides controlling Nile floods,

Khnum's other specialty was humanity itself. A generally benevolent god, he was seen as the force behind the physical body and its workings. Khnum is often pictured working at a potter's wheel, on which he was believed to create human beings and their *ka*s. In his temple at Esna, an annual Festival of the Potter's Wheel was celebrated in honor of his creation of mankind. Celebrants chanted a hymn that was surprisingly anatomically detailed; describing Khnum's designing of the bloodstream, skeleton, respiratory system and reproduction. It described Khnum as supervising pregnancy and initiating labor. In other texts, he created not only Egyptians but also animals, foreigners, even the other gods. He also syncretized with Ra to form Khnum-Ra.

In the reliefs on Amunhotep III's "birth chapel", which presented him as conceived by Amun (in the guise of his father) with Queen Mutemwiya, Amun personally instructs Khnum to fashion Amunhotep and his *ka*, then place them within the queen's womb. This story was obviously composed well after the fact as a propoganda peice, but it leads one to wonder how many expectant Egyptian mothers such as Queen Mutemwiya prayed to Khnum to give them either a son or a daughter – then perhaps later invoked his name when their water broke and contractions began.

Memphis

Memphis is the Greek name for the capital city during the Old Kingdom, located just outside of modern Cairo. Once a fortified town called "White Walls", Memphis was also the seat of worship of another major divine triad; Ptah, Sakhmet and Nefertem. The ancient cemeteries outside of Memphis were called Rosetau, and their guardian deity was Sokar.

Ptah

Netjer A'ah – Great God

Neb Ma'at – Lord of Ma'at

Sedjem Nehit – Hearer of Prayers

Neb Ineb-Hadj – Lord of White-Walls

Character: Ptah's center of worship was Memphis, near modern Cairo. In fact, the name of his temple – *Hat Ka Ptah*, "Shrine of the *Ka* of Ptah" – was rendered to *Aiguptos* in Greek, which in turn gave us our word "Egypt".

In the Memphite creation story, Ptah came into existence first. His heart then prompted him to utter the names of the other gods, the earth, the sky, and so on, which then came into being. Scholars have frequently observed the similarity between this creation account and that of *Genesis*. While Ptah's is certainly one of the more intellectual versions of creation, it lacked the visual imagery of Atum's version or the drama of Amun's, and never seemed to gain the same popularity. Ptah did have wide acceptance, however, as patron of craftsmen and artists, and his high priest bore the title "Great Overseer of Craftsmen". Long considered a state god, Ptah eventually formed a sort of trinity with Ra and Amun during the late New Kingdom. His consort was the lion-headed goddess Sakhmet, and their son was the lotus god Nefertem. Eventually they gained another son, who was elevated from mortal ranks: the famous vizier and architect

Imhotep. Renowned for wisdom centuries after he designed the Step Pyramid, Imhotep was deified as a son of Ptah and Sakhmet.

Ptah was credited with devising the "Opening of the Mouth" ceremony, and he came to be closely linked with Osiris. His iconography was similar; Ptah was always pictured wrapped in a tight cloak or wrappings, like a mummy, with his arms extending outside and holding a scepter or set of scepters. Ptah also combined later with Sokar, who was guardian of the gateway of Rosetau that led from the realm of the living to the realm of the dead. But despite these associations, Ptah was not strictly a funerary god. His titles included "Lord of Ma'at" and "Benevolent of Face", as well as "Hearer of Prayers".

Sakhmet

Nebet Pet – Lady of the Sky

Netjeret A'ah – Great Goddess

Nebet Senedjet – Mistress of Fear

Irit en Ra – Eye of Ra

Spellings and meaning: Also known by the Greek form 'Sakhmis' and the alternate spelling 'Sekhmet', *Sakhmet* means "Mighty One". It comes from the root *sakhem*, meaning "power" or "might".

Character: Worshiped in Memphis alongside her husband Ptah, Sakhmet became extremely popular during the New Kingdom and afterward. Her appeal in the modern day has continued to grow; a 1999 *Time Magazine* article on feminism actually described this powerful goddess in a discussion on the history of women and society. In the Memphite school of thought, she gave birth to Nefertem, who embodied the primordial lotus blossom from which the sun god emerged. However, Sakhmet later merged with other goddesses, Mut and Hathor in particular, and as a combinant with Hathor she became re-interpreted as the daughter of Ra. Her similarities to Tefnut, another lion-headed goddess and daughter of Ra-Atum, may have also led to this attribution. As an agent of the sun god and his ready enforcer, Sakhmet wore a sun disc with the uraeus cobra atop her head.

Best-known today is Sakhmet's role as a warlike goddess. She took on the punishing role of Eye of Ra, who slaughtered humans for rebelling against the sun god. So ferocious was her bloodlust, though, that the other gods had to stop her before she annihilated all of humanity. To do this, they made a lake of red-colored beer. When Sakhmet encountered this lake, she mistook it for blood and drank the entire thing, passing out cold and forgetting her vengeance. (In other variants of the Destruction of Mankind, it was Tefnut or Bast who went on the rampage.) Two of her titles certainly reflected this reputation – "Lady of Pestilence" and "Mistress of Fear". But she was also a goddess of fortune, and was invoked to ensure a good harvest for the nation as well as personal prosperity. It is thought that a plague swept through Egypt at some point during the reign of Amunhotep III, prompting him to commission some seven hundred-thirty statues of Sakhmet, two for every day of the year. Many of these statues were moved to the temple of Mut at Karnak, reflecting these two goddess' close association during the New Kingdom.

Somewhat overlooked today, however, is Sakhmet's role as a goddess of healing. In fact, many of her priests were known to be surgeons. Just as she had the power to kill, Sakhmet also held the power to heal and protect. In the *Book of Gates*, Sakhmet and Horus guarded foreigners awaiting rebirth in the underworld. She was also invoked as mother of the king, and as the protector and even mother of young Horus.

Nefertem

Character: Also son of Ptah and Sakhmet, Nefertem represents the lotus (more accurately, the Egyptian blue lily) from which the sun emerged. Generally he is pictured as a man with a lotus flower on his head. More recently, the wooden sculpture of Tutankhamun as an infant emerging from a lily has been interpreted as an image of Nefertem. Along with his close ties to the sun god, Nefertem is also referred to a protector of unified

Egypt. In different locales, he swaps mothers; in Buto he is son of Wadjit, the cobra goddess, and in other instances his mother is the cat goddess Bast.

Sokar

Spellings and meaning: Also spelled 'Soker' and 'Sokaris', *Sokar*'s name has been translated as "Speeder", or perhaps a word related to sledging.

Character: Often portrayed as a man or as a mummy with a falcon's head, Sokar was associated with meteors and comets, to which the name "Speeder" may have referred. He was also the patron of metalworking, which linked him to Ptah. His most important roles, however, had to do with death and rebirth. Sokar was the lord of Rosetau, the ancient cemetery of Memphis which came to be viewed as a gateway to the Under-world. Transformative power and the ability to cross the worlds of the living and the dead seemed to have been Sokar's specialty. In the Book of Am-Duat, Ra had to travel into the Cavern of Sokar deep within Duat (the Underworld) in order to regenerate. Sokar tended to merge not only with Ptah, forming the composite Ptah-Sokar, but also Osiris to form the trinity Ptah-Sokar-Osiris.

As a god of the Underworld, Sokar was honored any time that tombs or canals were dug or fields were planted. A major planting festival was the Feast of Sokar, in which his statue was taken in procession through the cemetery and fresh ground was ceremonially hewn in the fields. Reflecting his close ties to Osiris, the Feast of Sokar was celebrated as part of the Osiris Mysteries.

Lower Egypt

Having once been an independent kingdom from Upper Egypt, the Delta, or Lower Egypt, maintained its own traditions and folklore. In the latter half of ancient Egypt's history, the Delta became the seat of power, and under the Ptolemies Greeks settled extensively in the region. They wrote about many of the deities they encountered there who called the Delta home: Neith the primeval mother, her son Sobek, and one of Egypt's most famous goddesses, Bast.

Neith

Netjeret A'ah – Great Goddess

Up-Waut – Opener of the Ways

Nebet Sau – Mistress of Sais

Nebet Djedet – Mistress of Mendes

Spellings and meaning: Again, 'Neith' is the more commonly-known form of *Nit*, pronounced "neet". A possible meaning of her name is "Terrifying One"; it may also refer to the Lower Egyptian crown, which she often wore.

Character: Neith's worship dates back to Predynastic times and her center of worship is in the Delta city of Sais, or *Sau* in Egyptian. Her emblem is a source of debate: some interpret the long ellipse with c-shaped ends to be a shuttle used in weaving. Others see it as a click beetle, an insect commonly found near water that was a symbol of rebirth before the scarab beetle gained prominence. Yet another interpretation of the Neith emblem is a carrying case or shield with two bows strapped behind it. Her role as a warrior goddess and "Mistress of the Bow" certainly supports the latter idea. Before the unification of Egypt she was a patroness of the Lower Egyptian king. In early Dynastic times her embodiment was the queen, until Hathor's popularity supplanted the role. Throughout the remainder of pharaonic history, Neith was a war goddess who shared the title "Opener of the Ways" with the wolf god Wepwawet. Images of both deities were carried into battle as standards by Egyptian troop divisions named after them. Her popularity peaked during the Late Period, specifically during the Twenty-sixth or "Saite" dynasty whose power was based in Sais.

Besides a warrior, Neith was also a primeval creator goddess. She conceived without a consort, "instituted giving birth where there had been no childbirth before", and bore Sobek, a crocodile god of the sun who was later syncretized with Ra. Neith was also attributed as the mother of Ra himself, Elder Horus and even Osiris. Of all ancient Egypt's bountiful pantheon, Neith would most appropriately be considered their archetypal Mother of Creation. In the Ramesside-era tale of the Contendings of Horus and Seth, which equally parodied both the Heliopolitan and Osirian traditions, the tribunal of gods very deferentially asked Neith for her wisdom as to who deserved the throne of Egypt! Later still, a Roman-era text explains that Neith created the world by uttering seven magic words.

Neith also held a funerary role as one of the four guardians of the dead. She protected the feet of the deceased with Serket, and paired with Duamutef to shelter the stomach. In New Kingdom underworld texts such as the *Book of Imy-Duat* ("What is in the Underworld") she was a guide for Ra's entourage of justified souls. The last noteworthy tale centering on Neith has a dark side, though. According to a Greco-Roman legend she spat into the waters of Nun, and her spittle formed into the serpent arch-fiend Apophis.

Sobek

Spellings and meaning: Related to the work *sebeq*, an Egyptian word having to do with keen senses and fortune, the crocodile god Sobek was also known as 'Suchos' in Greek. His name is also rendered 'Sebek' because scholars aren't sure of the original vowels used, but *Sobek* is a conventionally accepted spelling.

Character: Sobek's worship may have originated in the Delta, though his major cult centers include the Fayum Oasis; areas near Thebes, including the village of Deir-el Medina; and Kom Ombo further south. Appropriately, many of these areas are also thought to have been prime Nile crocodile habitats. Beginning around the reign of Amunhotep III, temples to Sobek actually bred and raised sacred crocodiles. Feeding and caring for them had to be an interesting priestly job!

The son of Neith, Sobek was a sun god. He embodied fertility, magical effectiveness, and powers associated with water. Just as crocodiles emerged from the river with wet, glistening scales, Sobek was imagined to have been born of Neith in the primordial waters of Nun to manifest the shining sun. During the Middle Kingdom he became associated with Ra to form the composite Sobek-Ra. Later he also linked with Khnum, a creator god, as well as Horus and eventually even Osiris. He was thought to have a celestial palace at the sky's horizon.

Perhaps reflecting his mother's warlike nature, Sobek also embodied predatory instincts and the sun's destructive aspects. Later in history, he came to be associated with Seth. Around the same time, however, another story evolved in which he drew the Four Sons of Horus out of the Nile in a net. Sobek's seemingly contradictory traits illustrate how adeptly Egyptian thought could reconcile opposing ideas without reducing them to a simplistic "either-or" formula.

Bast

Spellings and meaning: Common variants of her name are 'Baset', 'Bast', and *Bastet*, which may be closest to the Egyptian pronunciation. The vase symbol spelling her name alludes to perfume, and some scholars translate it as "She of the Perfume [or Ointment] Jar".

Character: Bast is easily the most famous Egyptian deity alongside Anubis. Her center of worship, located in the eastern Delta, was called 'Pi-Baset' by the Hebrews and 'Bubastis' by the Greeks. Unfortunately, because of the poorer state of preservation of many sites in the Nile Delta, tracing Bast's earliest history is difficult. She was mentioned in the Pyramid Texts, though, and she was not always portrayed in the form of a house cat. In fact, until the Late Period Bast actually took the form of a dangerous lioness! Along with Tefnut and Sakhmet, she sometimes bore the title of "Eye of Ra", acting as the sun god's enforcer and protecting the king against his enemies. Bast's popularity burgeoned during the Late and Greco-Roman periods, however, and much of what we know of her today comes from this era.

In regions where her worship was predominant, Bast was seen as both the daughter and consort of Ra-Atum. She had to be persuaded to return to Ra after raging in the desert wilderness as part of the Myth of the Distant Goddess. In other variations, Bast's role was taken by Tefnut, Sakhmet, Mut or Hathor. Together, Ra-Atum and Bast had a son, a lesser-known lion god named Mihos (or Mahes). In the Memphite tradition, Bast sometimes replaced Sakhmet as wife of Ptah and mother of Nefertem. Love, pleasure, music and perfumes were Bast's domain, as well as the hunt, hence the Greeks equating her with Artemis. The Greeks also described feasts of Bast that amounted to city-wide, orgiastic frenzies. Herodotus described women in festive processions drinking wine, dancing, cajoling onlookers and even pulling up their dresses to reveal their private parts!

According to Diodorus, a Roman in Bubastis was actually lynched for killing a housecat, Bast's sacred animal. The irony is that perhaps thousands of cats were ritually killed and mummified by priests of the Late and Greco-Roman Periods, who then sold them to wor-shipers who couldn't afford votive statues of Bastet. In those final centuries of ancient Egyptian history, animal cults became widely popular and an entire industry of mummified animal votives sprang up. Cats were one of the most popular, along with ibises dedicated to the god Djehuty.

Finally, a more obscure myth related in a healing spell describes a poisoned cat that Ra saves, which may have been the goddess Bast. Another spell meant to avoid becoming sick with the plague instructs the user to state that they are the 'son of Bast'.

Miscellaneous

Our last group of deities have no home areas, with the exception of course being Aton. Bes and Tawret could be found everywhere, however, while Ammut was seen almost exclusively in funerary contexts. Last on our list is the Egyptian arch-fiend Apophis.

Aton

Spellings and meaning: Rendered as 'Aten', 'Iten' and *Aton*, the name means "Disc"; as in, the visible disc of the sun.

Character: While Aton will always be associated with the Amarna revolution, he was referred to as an aspect of the sun god as far back as the Pyramid Texts. As the sun's "Disc", Aton was his physical manifestation that provided light of day. So naturally, the pharaohs of the late Eighteenth Dynasty who sought to emphasize solar worship over Amun's more abstract theology made use of this form of Ra. It was Akhenaton who actually gave Aton an independent identity.

Akhenaton effectively took the existing trend of henotheism, which concentrated worship on Amun, and transposed it. Aton became literally the new 'face' of the divine Creator, who provided for all beings and guaranteed the order of the cosmos. Modern scholars and readers alike have been struck by the universality and poetry of the Hymn to Aton, which was likely composed by Akhenaton himself. His ancient subjects, however, did not find a satisfactory answer to the questions of life after death within the new Aton theology. Its emphasis on daylight and life, almost to the exclusion of death and the nocturnal realm, left too much ambiguity in their minds.

Aton's worship as sole supreme god ended with Akhenaton's death. Under Tutankhamun, Atonism seemed to enjoy a peaceful coexistence with traditional theology; but with his passing, Aton reverted back to his old form as the disc-aspect of the dominant sun god.

Bes and Tawret

Spellings: *Tawret*'s name includes several variants – "Tauret", "Tawaret" and the Greek form "Thoeris". She is also sometimes known by another name, Ipi.

Character: Both Bes and Tawret are composite creatures. Bes is usually seen as a bow-legged dwarf with a lion's head and mane, or else with a mane and caricatured human face. Sometimes he is shown as a full lion, but his signature mark in all of these forms is his extended tongue. Tawret appears as a pregnant hippopotamus standing upright with human breasts and belly, lion paws and a crocodile tail. Sometimes she holds a rearing cobra in her teeth, or has her tongue extended like Bes. She is often shown wielding a pair of knives, and occasionally so is Bes. Frightening as those images may seem, though, the Egyptians understood these two blade-wielding hybrid beings to be their armed defenders. In fact, Bes and Tawret are often depicted resting a hand on the hieroglyph *sa*, or 'protection'. Whether alone or as a team, they protected all Egyptians regardless of rank or class from evil forces that threatened them during vulnerable periods; especially as they were being born, going through childhood and when they were sleeping. Even as mortal Egyptians slept through the hours of the night, Bes and Tawret also protected the sun god while he traversed the perilous regions of the Underworld. He too, underwent birth each morning, and needed Bes and Tawret's vigilance to emerge safely at daybreak.

Bes served another function as a god of entertainment. Dancing and singing were his domain; he can be seen in some carved reliefs dancing and holding a tambourine. In this respect he overlapped somewhat with Hathor, who favored music and ecstasy.

While some gods and goddesses served lofty functions for the state or claimed sanctuaries staffed by elite priests, Bes and Tawret could be found every-where. Their images were carved on headrests, head-boards and footboards of beds, on chairs, wands, jewelry and amulets. Their representations have been found in the tombs of pharaohs and the ruins of workers' homes. It is significant to note that figurines of these two deities have been found in Akhet-Aton; its citizens may have willingly given up worship of old gods such as Amun in favor of the sun disc Aton, but they refused to abandon their two most intimate guardians who watched over them each night.

Ammut

Character: *Ammut* (sometimes spelled 'Ammit') is also a composite animal, but she lacks the ubiquitous roles that Bes and Tawret held. Her title was "Devourer of Souls", and she waited by the scales as the deceased were judged in the Hall of Two Truths. Having the back end of a hippo, front half and mane of a lion and head of a crocodile, Ammut certainly presented a fearsome profile. Should an unlucky Egyptian's heart outweigh the feather of Truth, proving that their evil deeds outweighed their goodness, Ammut would gobble up their *ka*, condemning them to wander as ghosts. If a person was judged as good, though, Ammut was harmless. Not only would she quietly watch the righteous pass on to Osiris' kingdom as completed spirits, but she was also thought to hold affection for them. Perhaps reflecting the hopes of his loved ones, an inscription on a piece of Tutankhamun's furniture describes him as "beloved of Ammut".

The Evil One-- Apophis

Spellings: *A'apep* is more commonly known by the Greek form of his name, 'Apophis'. In the Old Kingdom, he was referred to by the name 'Rerek'. In modern culture, Apophis is the name of a character from *Stargate SG-1* and the designation of a dangerous asteroid expected to brush past the earth on April 13, 2029.

Character: Apophis was the ultimate incarnation of evil; in some passages from Underworld texts he was simply called 'the Evil One'. Taking the form of a massive snake, he embodied chaos, destruction and non-existence. His birthplace was in the waters of Nun, or pre-Creation, and in one story he formed when the creator goddess Neith spat into the Nun. Each night as Ra's sun barque crossed through the Underworld, Apophis would attack the boat in an attempt to swallow it up, with Ra still in it. The other gods would have to band together to defeat him; even Seth was needed for the task. While Seth's evil tendencies were somewhat on-again, off-again, Apophis was completely wicked. The *Book of Gates* and *Book of Caverns* describe him swallowing up Underworld Nile water in order to beach the sun barque on a sandbar, sucking up denizens of the Underworld along with the water. Serket and Isis must use chords and harpoons to restrain Apophis, and Seth spears him to force out the water and hapless beings that had been swallowed. In the pre-dawn hours, Ra finally defeats Apophis in a battle beneath a persea tree, in which Ra takes the form of a tomcat. Representations of this struggle are painted in tombs and on papyrus copies of the *Book of the Dead*, but ancient artists were always careful to picture Apophis already pinned with spears and knives so as to render his image harmless. Citizens sometimes pictured themselves spearing Apophis, reflecting their wish to be counted as allies of goodness and servants of Ra in the afterlife.

Occasionally, Apophis was pictured as a donkey instead of a serpent. While donkeys were used as pack animals, they also had an association with evil in some regions – but usually with Seth. Late in Egyptian history, Underworld texts and illustrated vignettes switched Seth's role from one of assistance against

Apophis to standing trial as an enemy of Osiris. Ironically, the ancient god of strength who boasted in the Underworld texts that he alone possessed enough strength to defeat the Evil One, eventually came to share attributes with Apophis himself.

Conclusion

Thus concludes our survey of major gods and goddesses. We've met majestic lords of the sun and earth; mistresses of the heavens and rulers of the Underworld; patrons of arts and science; tricksters and guardians; and sweet, nurturing mothers who could also be bloodthirsty enforcers. We've also come to know their world a little better, and understand how the gods' and goddesses' fortunes rose and fell with their people's. But the past is only a foundation. Now that we have set the final stones of it into place, the time has come to build a brand-new edifice, one that incorporates our knowledge of the past with our needs of the present and our hopes for the future. Three millennia of the ancient Egyptians' accomplishments have helped to bring humanity to where we are today. Now it is our turn to continue their legacy.

Part Two-- Practice Today: Ancient Wisdom, Modern Lives

By looking at the history of Egyptian religion, we have caught a glimpse of its vibrant past and gained a greater appreciation of its roots. But the faith is evolving yet again, taking the new form of Egyptian Paganism. This time, to understand Egyptian religion no longer means fixing our attention on a distant place and time. The focus of our interest is now close at hand: for it is *us*.

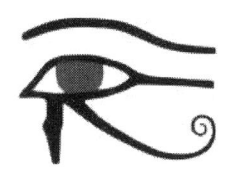

Building And Using Your Own Sacred Space

Some years ago I read through a do-it-yourself book on "altar magic". I was curious to explore its interpretation of altar spaces and how to use them, especially compared to my own experiences with building Buddhist and Egyptian altars. Unfortunately, this particular book (the title of which I have lost) seemed to go in totally the wrong direction. After invoking the ideas of psychologist Karl Jung and author Joseph Campbell (of Hero With a Thousand Faces and The Power of Myth fame) to assert that building altar spaces is a part of human nature, the book then proceeded to offer a series of laundry lists on objects, colors, deities and general spells that a person could cobble together in order to perform magic. This approach misses the point entirely. An altar is not something set up simply to perform a spell or even a series of spells; while rites that could be considered 'magic' might be enacted at either a temporary or a permanent altar, the main purpose of an altar is to provide a special space for spiritual devotion. An altar is an installation wherein worship takes place. That worship can be in the form of prayer, meditation, or other activities. An altar is a spiritual place, not a mere magical tool.

Style of Worship: East versus West

Of course, much more than just that one short book I read

through has been written in recent years about not only how to build your own altar, but also how to conduct 'authentic' rituals – be they Egyptian/ Kemetic services, or any other kind of Pagan rite. Some sources of 'advice' are better than others, but all of them seem to skip an important beginning step. Even the most carefully researched Egyptian altar will miss something if it does not reflect the style of worship used by the ancient Egyptians.

In order to better understand their style of worship, we must first examine our own frame of reference and contrast it with that of other religions. Most of us who are interested in Egyptian faith come from a Judeo-Christian background, and that religious background can still affect our frame of reference. The Judeo-Christian-Islamic family of religions all follow a similar method of worship, in that they primarily use a sacred space outside of members' homes and direct their worship to a completely abstract deity. Indeed, even though the Catholic church has often been singled out for its continued use of statuary, and the Eastern Orthodox church uses icons of Jesus, the Madonna and saints, neither tradition permits physical representations of the Deity Himself for worship. It is precisely this reason, this unfamiliarity with physical representations and use of personal sacred space, that has given rise to our current proliferation of literature attempting to explain how to build an altar and conduct a ritual. We, as Westerners, have forgotten how to use these forms of religious expression and are grasping for a means of rediscovering them. But in the Eastern Hemisphere, these same basic practices have not only been in use for centuries, but continue to thrive today. They are our best living model for the spirit and principle of worship as the Egyptians themselves would have practiced.

Two major Eastern religions, Hinduism and Buddhism, use elements that function in much the same way as their Egyptian counterparts. These three elements are: *icons* of the entity being worshiped, usually statues or pictorial representations; *personal shrines* to house those icons, that serve as a sacred space in an adherent's home; and *personal rituals* that make practical use of those shrines. The identities of the deities, the artistic style and languages may all be different, but the purpose of these elements remains the same between all three respective religions. Let's examine each element more closely:

Icons - The traditional Western assumption is that a physical object of worship, derogatorily called an 'idol', actually *is* the entity being worshiped. Hindus are quick to point out, however, that an enshrined statue is simply a vessel which the deity can inhabit in order to interact with worshipers. These icons are treated with respect because they serve as direct links to the beings they represent. This was the same reason for which the Egyptian priests cared daily for enshrined statues of their gods.

In order for a statue to become a sacred link, generally it is consecrated; Hinduism and Buddhism both have special consecration ceremonies that mirror the Egyptians' Opening of the Mouth rite. In fact, the Buddhist version is called "The Opening of the Eyes". In the Hindu version, the ritual culminates in a statue's eyes being uncovered and a mirror being held before the deity's face. All of these rites serve the same purpose of calling forth the entity represented and allowing it to manifest within its icon.

Personal shrines - Because Judeo-Christian-Islamic worship is completely abstract in its thinking, setting aside a physical space in the home for worship is not considered necessary. By contrast, the use of an icon as a tool of worship essentially demands its own space. And while a church, synagogue or mosque generally negates the need for a private shrine, temples in Eastern religion do not. If anything, a shrine in a private home reflects the function of a temple on a smaller scale.

Likewise, we know from Egyptian archaeological sites such as Amarna, the village of Kahun and Deir el-Medina that many residents kept family shrines in their homes. These could be simple wall niches or elaborate garden shrines, depending on the family's wealth and status. The same is true in modern Eastern religion. Wealthy Hindu or Buddhist households will reserve an entire room of their home specifically for their shrine. Some Buddhists will save up thousands of dollars for a *butsudan* ("Buddha-home") cabinet the size of a small entertainment center. Other shrines are much more humble. But regardless of size or intricacy, both modern *butsudan*s and their ancient Egyptian counterparts serve the same function: as a sacred space outside of the usual bustle of daily life wherein the third element of worship, ritual, can occur.

Personal Rituals - Obviously, this is an act of worship that involves the repetition of set steps. But the length, complexity and intent are often varied and flexible. The basic Hindu ceremony is called *puja*, from Sanskrit for "to honor", and can last several minutes or be carried out over the course of several days! But a common element shared by both Hinduism and Egyptian religion is the giving of offerings through ritual. Even the types of offerings given – water, light (through candles), incense and food – are the same in Hinduism and Buddhism as they are in Egyptian religion.

The giving of food, water and other drink in ritual can be another source of confusion to Westerners. A literal-minded person might question why sustenance is being offered to an entity that cannot actually consume it. But just as the deity or being in question is inhabiting the icon spiritually, the *spirit* or essence of the food and drink offerings is taken by its recipient. Another common question is what to do with the food or drink after it is offered; but here again, Eastern religions and even historical records from the Egyptians themselves provide the answer. In Hinduism, food is called "enjoyment" as it is offered and "blessings" after the ritual is completed and the food is eaten. Similarly, writings from the temple of Horus at Edfu inform us that "one lives on the provisions of the deities... There is no ill or misfortune for those who live on His goods..." Clearly, then, food and drinks are consumed by the worshipers after being offered during ritual. In this way, the act of offering food becomes a blessing to the worshiper.

The three basic components of Eastern-style worship – icons, personal shrines, and personal rituals – mirror what we know of Egyptian religious practices, and offer a perspective not to be found in intellectual Western thinking. These modern counterparts are just as vital to our understanding of Egyptian worship as its historical framework, but for a different reason. Egypt's history gives us the benefit of hindsight, and understanding *why* their religion evolved as it did. If we are to practice their religion anew, however, these present-day comparisons will not only tell us more about *how*, but also *where*, by keeping us looking in the right direction: forward. This focus is crucial if we are to avoid a major obstacle of Reconstructionist faiths.

The Most Common Pitfall in Reconstructionism

Tameran Wicca generally makes use of modern sabbat and esbat formats developed within mainstream Wicca over the last sixty years. But Kemetic Reconstructionism bases its rituals on ancient texts. The temptation in using these prototypes from antiquity is to claim that modern derivations of them are 'authentic', meaning that they are just like what the ancient Egyptians themselves performed. In truth, this is impossible because even scholars do not have a complete picture of what 'authentic' ceremonies looked, sounded or acted like. Parts of the Egyptian language still elude a definitive translation, and one author's interpretation often differs from another's. Texts inscribed on temple and royal tomb walls frequently have gaps (called *lacunae* in academic jargon) from damage incurred over the centuries. Finally, in the case of tomb literature such as the Pyramid Texts, we have reasonably complete sections of ritual text translated but no clear idea of what order to put the sections in. James Allen's recent translation of the Pyramid Texts proposes a set sequence for them, but no doubt his choice of order is still open to debate in scholarly circles.

In addition to the uncertainties of language, we also have only theory to go on when it comes to how ancient Egyptian temple music was played, how the hymns were sung and what some of the cooked food offerings were. Given what we lack in terms of this "practical application" knowledge, then, anyone who claims to have 'recreated' pharaonic Egyptian rites just as the ancients themselves performed them is boasting perfect clairvoyance in addition to knowledge that not even experienced scholars have. Such claims of recapturing the past are unfounded, unnecessary and dangerous, but unfortunately they also represent the most frequently-sprung trap in all Reconstructionist faiths.

What gives a ritual power and efficacy is not the fact, or indeed fallacy, that 'the ancients did it just like this'. In order to have legitimacy, a religious rite must have *faith* behind it. Research and knowledge are our allies in building new expressions of worship, but without faith they cannot help us. While it is human nature to place our trust in something asserted to be effective since antiquity – even a famous chapter of the Egyptian Book of the Dead claims that its original copy was found centuries before by a sage – true belief will always hold more weight than supposed age. Keep in mind, there was a time when even the rites that came to be recorded as the Pyramid Texts were brand-new.

Building a Shrine that Works for You

Once someone discovers a connection with certain Egyptian Gods or Goddesses, their initial questions are usually twofold. How do I pray to Them? is frequently their first inquiry, one whose deeply personal answer will vary from person to person. Some possible approaches will be outlined later in this chapter and in the next. Beginners' usual second question is, How do I build a shrine to Them? The solution to this puzzle is also unique to each individual. Each altar or shrine is a reflection of the person (or family) using it, and no two shrines will be alike, even if they are built by the same person in the same house. But being a physical space that incorporates physical objects, a shrine also reflects the circumstances of its owner's environment and resources. Constructing one requires a little hands-on advice in order to work well.

The first factor any shrine project must address is its user's home surroundings. Consider your living arrangements; do you live in a house with parents or other family members? Are you a college student, sharing a dorm room with one or two roommates, or do you have a private room? Do you live in an apartment? How much space do you have in your home? What kind of pets do you have, if any? All of these considerations will have a direct effect on what kind of altar you will be able to build. Some newcomers to Egyptian faith still share a house with family members of a different faith who might not approve of 'graven images' under their roof. In such an instance, privacy is definitely an issue; keeping a shrine in a closed cabinet will suffice if family members aren't too nosy. Otherwise, a 'pocket shrine' that can be kept hidden or even carried on your person might be your best option. These are becoming somewhat popular, and some users post pictures and descriptions of their pocket shrines online. A cabinet or pocket shrine could also prove useful if you have dorm roommates who might not respect your personal space or religious practices.

Sometimes you can have a residence to yourself, or share it with others who wouldn't mind having an altar in their home, but space is at a premium. I ran into this problem when setting up a *butsudan* in my efficiency apartment years ago. In building that altar, I learned that despite the grand visions we can often create in our minds, we ultimately must stick with what is available to us. Placing an altar on top of a dresser is certainly acceptable, though you will probably have to rearrange a few other things in the room in order to clear off that precious bit of real estate. Despite the temptation it might present, though, building a shrine in the bathroom is *not* recommended – and yes, unfortunately I know of people who have done this... In Egyptian religion particularly, concepts of purity would be completely negated by building an altar in the bathroom. Pets are another consideration. Cats in particular like to explore high places, and as I learned the hard way, our feline friends will not think twice about hopping onto the middle of an altar and knocking over an incense tray filled with ash!

Once you have 'staked out' an area for your altar that is private, secure, and pet- (or child-) proof, the next obvious concern is what objects to place in it. Aside from icons, which have already been defined, altar objects can generally be grouped into two categories: *functional* and *symbolic*. Functional items are tools used as part of a ritual. Symbolic items are not used, but hold a particular meaning or aesthetic value. Let's start with the functional elements you will need:

Icon - Clearly, the icon or icons are the crux of your altar. These are the vessels through which your Gods will interact with you, so they should be chosen with care. Statuettes of the more popular Egyptian deities can be found in novelty or metaphysical supply stores, online or in trading company catalogs. Some Egyptian practitioners also sculpt custom figurines for sale. Not all pre-made resin statues are alike, however. Some are copies of famous artifacts, such as Anubis reclining in jackal form on a golden dais, Serket standing with her arms outstretched, or Horus in falcon form wearing the double crown. Others, such as Anubis candle holders, skeleton-faced figurines and figures of Egyptian deities in Greek-style robes, are pure flights of modern fancy. Taking the time to look through books on Egyptian art and familiarize yourself with classical representations of the gods will help you pick out statues that speak to you.

In the event sculptural icons are not an option, a search through references on Egyptian art will prove especially useful as a source of icon material. Books are still your best place to begin, as most images of Egyptian deities found online lack accurate reference information such as who is the deity pictured, where was the original piece found, and so on. Web images also tend to be low-resolution, and print notoriously badly. Nowadays scanners and printers are more easily accessible; with a little card stock (which is more durable than printer paper) and a trip to an office supply store to get it laminated, you can have your own personal icon that comes from an ancient original. Note, however, that for copyright reasons you should never sell or distribute images taken from printed books or from an artist or owner's website. Aside from being illegal, that would also be artistically dishonest and thus upset *ma'at*. Put simply, it's wrong.

Once you have acquired icons for your altar space, you may want to formally consecrate them. To do so, you will need to assemble a few other functional altar tools and refer to the Opening of the Mouth Rite in the next chapter.

Water and Milk Cups - Water cups are essential for offering rites. Milk is known as an offering from the Opening of the Mouth ritual, and was also regarded as sacred to Hathor in particular. The basic rite given at the end of this chapter includes a milk offering. For those who have lactose allergies, soy, almond or coconut milk will service equally well.

Generally, water and milk cups should be small in order to fit into a limited space. Ceramic is the best material to use; Japanese tea and sake sets are an excellent, and very handsome, source for offering cups. You can also look online in Buddhist supply sites for inexpensive offering tableware. Other possibilities include Asian-style condiment dishes (originally meant to hold soy sauce), which can be found at either Asian grocery stores or sometimes in the cookware sections of major retailers.

Candles - Either one or two candles will suffice, depending on your altar arrangement. Shorter votive or tealight candles placed in votive holders will function better than tapers, which even without their holders are often taller than most icon statues. Tapers also tend to drip, risking the possibility of wax dripping onto your icons and even damaging them. Votive holders can be either metal, glass or stone, but if you use two it is best to get a matched pair. Simple designs are preferable to something ornate that will distract attention away from your icons. Keep on the lookout for interesting possibil-ities: for example, at a museum gift shop I found two alabaster votive holders made in Egypt, and the warm glow they emit is positively homey.

Although I prefer white as the best candle color, we have no hard and fast rules about color because the Egyptians did not have paraffin wax or dyes in the array of colors we do today. In pharaonic times, either oil lamps or torches of twisted linen charged with animal fat were used. These were sometimes dyed, but the colors available then were mostly restricted to madder red, yellow or green. Thus, 'candle magic' as we know it today would be an anachronism in an Egyptian context.

Finally, in dorm rooms or other settings where flame candles are prohibited, battery-powered "flameless" tealights are now becoming more widely available.

Incense and Incense Burner - Incense has become so popular that today packs of "Happy Home" incense can be found in gas stations and discount stores. However, not all incense is created equal, and some kinds can actually cause problems when you burn them.

The most commonly available type of incense, found in brands such as Nag Champa and Happy Home, comes coated on thin sticks. These tend to put off a noticeable amount of smoke when burned, and their heavy oil-based scents linger in the air. People with respiratory allergies can actually have reactions to these kinds of "dipped" incense (referring to how they are made). Cone incense produces similar problems. By far the better alternative is stick incense from Japan, which is made using a different process and leaves no "core" behind when burned. Shoyeido, a popular brand, can be found online and sometimes at health food stores. Online Buddhist supply stores also offer "less smoke" brands such as Takara. These put off less smoke and have a light, sweet fragrance. Frankincense and sandal-wood fragrances are especially useful in an Egyptian context, but don't be afraid to experiment; some worshipers of Bast, for example, have observed that She has an affinity for floral scents.

Packs of Shoyeido incense come with a tiny holder made to let the incense stick burn upright. If you use an upright burner, make sure to have something underneath to catch the ashes that will accumulate. An alternative is a soapstone incense burner with holes in the lid for burning sticks; these can be found in the craft sections of major retail stores. Some Buddhist supply stores also offer incense trays meant to hold a stick burning horizontally. These can be a useful option, but you will also need a bed of "starter ash" to lay the burning sticks of incense upon. The more you use your incense burner, the more ash will accumulate. Don't leave it where it can be tipped over, and be alert when cleaning your altar. Nothing will make you curse yourself faster than accidentally spilling an incense burner filled with light, powdery ash.

One final note of caution must be made for the ambitious souls who find resin incenses such as frankincense and myrrh. Burned on charcoal disks – which *must* be placed in a heat-resistant container such as soapstone or abalone shell for safety reasons – resin incense is the closest we can get to the kind used in ancient Egypt. However, pharaonic homes and temples lacked smoke detectors. Resin incense puts off a tremendous amount of smoke, and *will* set off your smoke alarm. Speaking from personal experience, resin incense is best saved for outdoor rituals.

Offering Plate - Thankfully, we finish with another simple altar implement. This will be the dish on which food offerings are placed. Some practitioners use bowls, but plates better accommodate differently-sized and shaped offerings. It does not have to be a full-sized dinner plate. Keep in mind, when the ancients cooked daily offering meals for temple services, only a representative sample was actually placed in front of the icon.

This altar setup includes a water cup, several food dishes, a candle, incense burner and other ritual objects arrayed before the icon statue. Author's photo.

Families probably did the same in front of their shrines, so a simple, ceramic plate that can fit on your altar will work nicely. If your altar space is small, even a dish for soy sauce will do; a pack of M&M's, cookies or small fruit will fit in a soy dish.

As for types of food offerings, these will vary from person to person. Candies and sweets are probably the most popular, followed by fruit and bread. Meat offerings are acceptable, but do not leave them (or any other cooked offerings) out for long. Whatever you do offer, it is best to choose something that you eat yourself – that's the whole point of making the offering.

These five types of functional altar implements are the most basic essentials. As you pursue your practice further, you may acquire or make other functional implements such as a sistrum to incorporate sound into your rituals, natron salt for purification, oil for anointing, and so on. Any altar items that are not used in the steps of a ritual can be considered *symbolic*. A shrine may have all of these, or none. To survey a few:

Flower vase - Eastern religions frequently include fresh flowers as offerings, and the Egyptians were passionately fond of floral arrangements. Records from Ramses III tell us that the temple of Amun presented almost two *million* bouquets over the course of three years! If you live in an area that has wildflowers or gardens, include a few on your altar, especially at holidays. Just watch out – campus and city gardens often impose fines on would-be harvesters for picking public flowers.

Greenery - An alternative to fresh-picked flowers is either live indoor plants, or silk ones. In some Eastern religions, greenery has a special meaning. In the Egyptian language, the word "flourish" came from their word for "green". As with candles, you can use either one piece of greenery, or two as a matched pair.

Cabinet and *icon pedestal* - If you need to keep your shrine private, or would prefer to keep it in its own space, a small cabinet could be your best bet. Cabinets already assembled can be expensive; some Buddhist supply stores carry *butsudan* cabinets in varying prices that can house your Egyptian icons. If you're mechanically inclined, you can get a ready-to-assemble cabinet at hardware retailers, or build one yourself. Craft stores sometimes have materials you can use, but you may also have to get creative. I made a *butsudan* out of a wooden wine box, and I also knew a woman who made one out of an old dynamite box!

As you arrange your altar, you may wish to elevate one or several of your icons. Craft stores sell wooden trays in varying sizes that can be painted and turned over to make a useful dais or pedestal.

Altar cloth - Not every altar will need one, but some are completed by the right drop cloth. Print or color are up to the shrine builder's tastes, but cotton cloth works best – preferably something washable, as spills of incense ash, food and drinks are inevitable.

Your Shrine as a Work of Art

While an altar may serve a function, it will certainly be more enjoyable to use if it looks attractive. This point is often lost upon 'magical' altars. A well-arranged shrine can truly be a work of art; nowhere was this better illustrated than by one of my college art professors, who was famous for assigning his mixed-media classes to build shrines around otherwise mundane subjects. Even if you cannot draw a stick figure, you can still create a small masterpiece in your personal shrine by using a few basic design principles in its arrangement.

Notice that some altar items have been suggested above as pairs; while this is not mandatory, when items are mirrored they create *symmetry*. Placing one candle or greenery vase on either side of an altar, for example, creates repetition and a sense of equilibrium. The Egyptians loved symmetry in their art and architecture, which also played upon their concept of duality. Using the principle of symmetry in your arrangement can give it a stately and dignified effect.

Single items can be used in tandem to create *balance*. Instead of mirroring two of the same object, you can establish balance by matching two (or more) different items with a similar shape, size, color or visual sense of 'weight'. For example, you can place a small offering dish to one side at the front of your altar, and at the opposite side place a round soapstone incense burner. If your water and milk saucers do not come from the same set, you can still achieve balance by choosing two of a similar size and shape. The goal is to have them create a sense of harmony when they are placed side-by-side. To test the balance and symmetry of your altar arrangement, take a step back and look at it. How does it 'feel' when you take in the overall appearance? Are too many objects to one side or the other? Does the whole shrine feel as if it 'leans' in a particular direction? Test out different arrangements until your altar feels balanced.

  I have seen several Pagan or magical altars that were solemn, balanced affairs, but they lacked the last and most important design principle: a *focal point*. This is the part of a composition to which your eyes find themselves gravitating. In drawing or painting, the focal point can be almost anything, but in an altar arrangement the focal point is naturally going to be the object of veneration. Without this focus, little separates an altar

Notice the use of symmetry, balance, and repetition. Can you tell where the focal point is? Author's photo.

space from any other prized collection of articles on display. Different options can help ensure that your icons command attention as the focal point of your altar. One is the element of *contrast*; if the icon is the most detailed or intricate item on your altar, or the only thing appearing in a certain color, the differences will be eye-catching. Another very simple trick is to center your icon(s), and to slightly elevate them on a small pedestal or dais. If you have greenery or other items that are taller than your icon, you can still direct attention toward it by centering it between the matched pairs. This way, the symmetrical elements will appear to radiate outward from the focal point. Not only does this help your shrine 'work' artistically, but it also evokes the idea that the Gods stand at the center of Creation just as They did on the First Occasion.

Now that you have your shrine put together and it feels right to you, it is ready to be used. The final authority on how to use your own personal space is you. What follows in the final section of this chapter and throughout the next are prayers, rites and spells that draw from original sources, but can be adapted to fit your own needs. We'll start with a basic offering rite that can be done anytime, for any occasion.

Iru: The Basic Ritual

The Egyptians had several words for ritual actions, but one of the most common was *iru*, which literally meant "things done". Below is a simple and flexible *Iru* rite for everyday use. For those interested in the source materials, refer to the "Offering" and "Morning Ritual" sections from the texts of King Unis in James Allen's The Ancient Egyptian Pyramid Texts.

Basic *Iru*

Light the candle to start. Use this as a quiet moment, to signal your mind and body that it is time to slow down and relax.

Pour water into the water cup. Say: "Take these, Your cool waters that are the Inundation."

Pour milk into the milk cup. Say: "Milk, milk, may You taste it in Your shrine."

Light incense. Say: "I give You incense, I give You incense, great of purity."

Place food offering. Say: "Take this, Your bread on which gods live."

Reversion of Offerings. Holding open your hands to the offerings, say: "Turn Yourself to these, Your offerings; receive them from me."

Silent Prayer. This can be whatever you need it to be; quiet time for reflection or meditation, requests for things needed or for guidance, and so on. You can use the prayers found in the next chapter or your own. This time is between you and your Gods.

Closing. Place your palms together and bow your head (this is known as *gassho* in Buddhism). Or, raise your hands, palms forward, to shoulder height and bow your head (this is a gesture of adoration called 'henu' by Egyptian Pagans). Say: "In-un-Ma'a [Truly it is]."

This *Iru* rite can take as long or short a time as needed, and the steps are easy to remember. If you lack an offering item such as milk or incense, simply skip over that step until the next time. As we will explore in upcoming chapters, the basic elements of this service occur again as part of longer and more involved ceremonies.

Another gesture of respect is to rest your hands face-down in front of your thighs, as depicted in this colossal statue fragment from Thebes. Photo by Krys Garnett

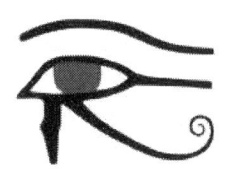

Prayers, Rites and Spells

Ultimately, when it comes to invoking and praying to our chosen deities, each of us remains our own best compass. We human beings are creatures of habit, however; having a few prayers and short rituals or spells written down for reference, even recital and memorization, can be a source of comfort when we aren't feeling at our most eloquent. Several of the works that follow have been adapted from academic translations, in which case the sources are given before each selection. Most of the adaptation has been to clarify the English wording where necessary, or to address very obscure references from the original text whose precise meanings have been lost through time. In some cases, excerpts from several similar ancient writings have been put together to form a larger whole. Other selections presented here are new, however, having been inspired by the ancient literature but written to reflect a modern audience. If these in turn inspire you to write your own prayers, you may want to keep a journal for them near your shrine.

Prayers for Various Occasions

The first two prayers are drawn from various devotional inscriptions from the village of Deir el-Medina, translated by Miriam Lichtheim in <u>Ancient Egyptian Literature, vol. II: The New Kingdom</u>. The latter two are original works.

A Basic Prayer:

May You grant life, prosperity and health,
Alertness, favors and affection;
May my eyes see You every day,
As one righteous who sets You in their heart!

Supply my needs of bread and drink,
And guard my mouth in speaking!
Come to me and give me counsel,
Make me heedful of Your wisdom.

When one appeals to You, You come from afar;
Lend Your ear to the lonely and the poor!
May You give breath to those who are wretched,
And bread to those who have none.
Guardian of the weak, may You set the oppressed free,
And let Your blessings surpass all wealth!

Prayer of Contrition:

I place not my share under the strong arm of a man,
For my Lord /Lady is my protector.
_____ who knows compassion,
Who hearkens to one who calls Him /Her.
Though the servant is disposed to do evil,
The God(dess) is disposed to forgive.
The God(dess) spends not a whole day in anger;
His /Her wrath passes in a moment, none remains.
His /Her breath comes back to us in mercy, returns upon

His /Her breeze.

May Your *ka* be kind, may You forgive,

It shall not happen again.

A Blessing of Ra:

Hear us, o Ra, Great Lord of Iunu,

And place your arms in blessing around _____.

Let _____ rejoice in Your bounty, and

Their heart(s) take joy in Your kindness.

Tell Up-Waut to open His ways for _____,

And may You protect with Your strong arm of compassion.

For You are the All-Lord, the Lord of Ma'at,

Holy and splendid is Your name:

Khepri at dawn, Atum at dusk,

Ra-Horakhety as You rule the Nine!

Blessing Before Meals:

"Osiris, Great God, the Beatified; You are Lord of Grain and Lord of Ma'at.

We thank You for Your gifts of bread, civilization and justice. We ask for Your blessing as we share this food and fellowship, and may we always build positively upon the gifts which You have given us."

In-un-Ma'a (Truly It Is)

Ritual Purification

The subject of ritual purity is a figurative bait on the pitfall in Reconstructionism. The Kemetic Orthodox in particular has generated much controversy with its requirements for ritual purity, which includes forbidding those with open wounds or women who are menstruating from performing rituals. Ancient records provide somewhat scanty references to menstruation and ritual purity, although a letter from a certain Lady Ir at Kahun village suggests that she *went into* the local temple, rather than stayed away, to perform a 'monthly purification'. Regarding issues such as these, a modern approach is probably the most practical.

As for proscribed foods, ancient accounts varied because taboos differed according to locale. We do know, however, that certain freshwater fish were considered sacred to Osiris and pork was said to be abhorred by Isis (but was enjoyed by Seth). If you intend to work with either Osiris or Isis, you may want to avoid eating these foods before doing so.

For everyday *Iru* observances, keep it simple. Make sure you aren't hot and sweaty, and consider changing clothes to get comfortable, especially if you have been outside in rain, snow or summer heat. Wash your hands – in fact, in modern Shinto this is a common pre-ritual lustration – and you may want to brush your teeth. Let the process of getting clean, cool and comfortable help you to relax and reflect.

The consecration rites listed below are not considered 'everyday' activities, so a more formal purification would be appropriate for these. Take a shower, or a fragrant bath if you prefer, and make sure that you are clean-shaven wherever you habitually shave. Change into your ritual garb if you have any; this will be covered in more detail in the following chapter. Use this purification before you begin your actual ceremony. You will need some natron salt and a bowl of water. In a pinch, a sink with a faucet will work just as well. The rite is adapted from Rosalie David's translation of the daily ritual at Abydos, found in Appendix A of <u>Religion and Magic in Ancient Egypt</u>.

Basic Purification Rite:

Lustration. Dip your hands in the bowl of water, or place them under running water at a comfortable temperature. Say: "These cool waters are upon my hands. They purify me as Tefnut purifies me."

Cleansing with natron. Natron is rather gritty and salty, so instead of chewing it, you may want to mix it in a cup of water for a mouth rinse, or else put it on your toothbrush. Before using it, say: "My natron is that of Horus, my natron is that of Djehuty, my natron is that of the gods."

After rinsing your mouth, say: "I am pure. I am pure. I am pure. I am pure."

Statement of purity. As you approach your sacred space, say: "I have come before You, o Gods, to perform this rite. I have not come to do what is not to be done, for I have cast out all evils that pertain to me."

Consecration Rites

While conducting a formal consecration is not absolutely essential just to use an icon or a shrine, if you feel it necessary for your own practice, the Opening of the Mouth and Temple Consecration ceremonies listed here are useful references. Both of these have been taken from the Pyramid Texts in James Allen's translation, listed above and in the bibliography.

Many Egyptology books refer to the Opening of the Mouth rite in a funerary context because it was performed on mummies before burial. However, as we saw in "Egyptian Concepts of the Soul", this rite was meant to open various spiritual vessels including, but not exclusively, the bodies of loved ones. To perform an Opening of the Mouth in a traditional style, you'll need to fashion a model adze. If you're artistically inclined, you could try carving one from balsa wood. If making your own adze tool is not an option, use a ceremonial knife or *athame* to gently touch the mouth of your icon. In addition to the standard offerings used in *Iru*, you will also need a black and a white cup (representing the Eyes of Horus); natron, a recipe for which is given in the next chapter; and oil. You can use either an essential oil from a metaphysical supply store, or make your own Egyptian-style unguent using another recipe to be found in the next chapter.

The Opening of the Mouth:

Libation. Pour the water offering. Say: "Take these, Your cool waters that are the Inundation, that they may cool Your heart. Come, _____, you have been invoked." Repeat three more times: "Come, you have been invoked."

Incense. Light the incense and say: "I give you incense, I give you incense, great of purity. Let its scent reach you and purify you."

Cleansing the Mouth. Place a dish of natron salt on the altar. Say: "This is your natron of Horus, this is your natron of Djehuty. This is your own natron among the gods. You are purified with it. Your mouth is clean as a calf's on the day it is born."

Pour the milk offering next. Say: "Milk, milk that parts your mouth, may you taste it in your shrines. That of Horus, that of Seth, that of the two gods reconciled, milk."

Opening the Mouth and Eyes. Carefully touch your icon's face with the implement. Say: "I have fixed your jaws spread for you. Let me part your mouth for you."

Next, hold up the cups. Say: "Here are your two Eyes of Horus, black and white; lift them to your face, and illuminate it."

Anointing. Using your pinkie finger, gently anoint the forehead of your icon with oil. Say: "Ointment, ointment, from the forehead of Ra; I shall put it on you and it shall transfigure you."

Offering and reversion. Place your food offerings. Say: "At peace for you is Ra in the sky. Peace be given for you, peace be what you see, peace be what you hear, peace be before you, peace be behind you, peace be your lot. Ra, may your dawn be for this god. As every good and pure offering is for you, so let it be for Him/Her."

Consecration of a Formal Shrine or Temple

Temples in Egypt all had names. Even the individual pyramids had names; in fact, the name of Pepi I's pyramid, *Men-nefer Pepi*, has come down to us via Greek as *Memphis*. Home shrines generally do not require a formal christening. But if you wish to establish a community worship space for a coven or congrega-tion, or perhaps if you've moved into a new home that you plan to stay in for some time and you want to formally dedicate your shrine space, you can recite this consecration text. You can also incorporate it into an Opening of the Mouth rite or an extended *Iru* service. If you choose not to name your shrine, simply say "shrine" in each blank instead a name.

Consecration Rite: (*adapted from Pepi I's spell PT601*)

"Oh, Great Ennead in Iunu! May may you make this _____ be firm for eternity as the name of Atum, Foremost of the Great Ennead is firm.

As the name of Shu, Lord of Upper Menset in Iunu is sound, so shall this _____ be sound likewise for eternity.

As the name of Tefnut, Mistress of Lower Menset in Iunu is sound, so shall this _____ be sound likewise for eternity.

As the name of Geb at the earth's ba is sound, so shall this _____ be sound likewise for eternity.

As the name of Nut is sound in the Shrine of Shenit in Iunu, so shall this _____ be sound likewise for eternity.

As the name of Osiris is sound in Ta-Ur, so shall this _____ be sound likewise for eternity.

As the name of Isis is sound in Philae, so shall this _____ be sound likewise for eternity.

As the name of Seth is sound in Ombos, so shall this _____ be sound likewise for eternity.

As the name of Horus is sound in Pe's Seal-Ring, so shall this _____ be sound likewise for eternity.

As the name of Ra is sound at the *Akhet*-horizon, so shall this _____ be sound likewise for eternity.

As the name of Horus-Eyes-Forward remains sound at Khem, so shall this _____ be sound likewise for eternity.

As the name of Wadjit is sound in Dep, so shall this _____ be sound likewise for eternity."

Protective Spells

All of us have felt fear at some point in our day-to-day lives. When we sense something intangible that causes us to be afraid, we share an instinct of self-preservation with the most ancient of Egyptian people and beyond. So universal is our need for protection against threatening forces, both seen and unseen, that among the Pyramid Texts were protective spells against just such beings. As their literature evolved, so did the Egyptians' spells against evil and their invocations for divine protection; but our common motivation for using them continues today.

Below are three such invocations. The first is adapted from the Pyramid Texts, using the same source as above. The second invocation is taken directly from The Great Goddesses of Egypt by Barbara Lesko, which has an extensive chapter on Isis. The last selection is inspired by the Book of the Dead, using both the Egyptian language (corrected from Budge's hieroglyphic translation) and English. It was composed to ward off a psychic attack, and has come in handy on other occasions since then.

Repulsion of Negative Forces: (*adapted from Pepi I's spell PT 534*)

Go back, go far away! Let Horus respect me and Seth protect me.

Go back, go far away! Let Osiris respect me and the Ferryman protect me.

Go back, go far away! Let Isis respect me and Nephthys protect me.

Be far away! Let Horus, Looking Forward, respect me and Djehuty protect me.

Go back, be far away! Let those of the night respect me and those in old age protect me.

Invoking Isis: (*quoted from Papyrus Ebers*)

"O Isis, Great of Magic, Heal me,

Release me from all things bad and evil!"

Casting Out Evil:

Dua Ra im Osir, Dua Osir im Ra.

Khefty-ek kher; Mosu Badesh nen un senu.

Im ren en Ra, hui-en-i Sebiu.

Hail Ra in Osiris, Hail Osiris in Ra.

Thine enemy has fallen; The Children of Rebellion shall not rise.

In the name of Ra, I have smote the Evil One.

The Offering Formula

Veneration of *akhu*, or ancestors and blessed dead, was an integral practice in ancient Egypt that has been incorporated into Egyptian Paganism. Some Kemetics even have separate *akhu* shrines for their deceased loved ones. Whether you choose to build a dedicated shrine to your loved ones or simply honor them in your heart, one way you can do so is to recite the traditional Offering Formula. Also called the Voice Offering, as it was originally a spoken prayer, its purpose is to feed the spirits, or *ka's*, of the deceased in lieu of physical offerings. Variations of the Offering Formula were carved on memorial tablets, coffins and statues throughout the pharaonic era. (Incidentally, silently reciting this Formula is a fascinating thing to do in museum exhibits.)

How to Read Egyptian Hieroglyphs by Mark Collier and Bill Manley gives an excellent breakdown of the Offering Formula, complete with the original Egyptian-language version. As their book also explains, calling someone "the Osiris" was a customary way of saying "the late" or "the departed".

"Peret kheru ta, heneket, khau kau apedu, khut nebet noferet wabet ankhet netjer im, en ka en Osir _____, ma'a kheru."

"A voice offering of bread, beer, a thousand of beef and fowl, and every good and pure thing on which a god lives, for the ka of the Osiris _____, true of voice."

Forms of Meditation

In our modern culture, meditation has gained a tremendous amount of both popularity and misconceptions. Meditation as a form of silent reflection during prayer has been part of both Western and Eastern religion since time immemorial. However, silent seated meditation in order to contemplate emptiness comes to us from Buddhist Asia. This kind of meditation is called *zazen* in Japanese, and in fact the name *Zen* Buddhism comes from the *zazen* technique. It was first popularized in America by the Beat movement of the 1950's, and has since been co-opted into various forms of New Age and Pagan practice. For this reason, meditation deserves addressing here, particularly how it relates to Egyptian practice.

Contrary to claims made otherwise, the ancient Egyptians did not practice meditation as a means of formal introspection or contemplating emptiness. They probably meditated through prayer, just as their ancient Hebrew, Greek, and later Christian neighbors did. Greco-Roman magical papyrii do describe what are essentially scrying techniques – probably another import from Greece – that could induce an altered state of consciousness. Often the objective of these scrying sessions was to receive a vision or contact a deity, much like in modern Pagan practices.

Visualization, or guided imagery, is another meditative technique used today in a New Age or Pagan context. It also has parallels in Buddhism, where practitioners visualize and contemplate a particular Buddha or Bodhisattva, or reflect upon certain concepts and scenarios. However, here again we have no record that the Egyptians practiced something similar. This does not mean that a modern Egyptian Pagan could not employ visualization or *zazen* into their practice; it simply means that in this context they are borrowed and entirely new techniques, having no ancient Egyptian precedents.

One form of meditation used in Buddhism may have parallels in Egyptian religion, but ironically it is a form not widely understood in the West. *Meditative chanting* involves the slow, steady, rhythmic intonation of phrases or passages of text, often in very archaic forms of language. The Nichiren school of Buddhism makes extensive use of meditative chanting, along with instruments such as drums to accompany their chanting and keep tempo. (According to one Nichiren minister, other schools often call them "the noisy Buddhists"!) The objective of the rhythmic chanting is to induce an altered state of consciousness for meditation. A variety of clues suggest that the ancient Egyptians may have used rhythmic chanting as part of their worship services, particularly in temples. Ancient hymns sometimes used repetition and alliteration, which could have produced a rhythmic pattern when read aloud. Sistrums, sacred to Hathor as mistress of ecstasy, were often used in accompaniment to hymns and were thought to induce altered states of mind. Thanks to the ancient author Apuleius, we even know a rhythm used by sistrum players that consisted of three beats followed by a pause. The Egyptians certainly made use of archaic language in their state and religious texts, which often did not reflect the spoken language of the time. So very conceivably, they could have chanted their hymns as a form of meditation, with their instruments keeping a steady rhythm.

However, before you try your skills at meditative chanting, you need to be aware of how this powerful technique is often misused. Because repetitive chanting induces an altered state of consciousness, it can be employed as a thought-stopping technique. It comes as no coincidence that mind control cults commonly use high-speed chanting to dull members' critical faculties. Chanting can create not only a hypnotic state, but also a euphoric 'high' when someone chants so fast that they hyperventilate. More rarely, some people have reported adverse physical or mental symptoms from relaxation-induced anxiety (RIA). Having first been introduced to chanting meditation by a manipulative cult, I had to learn the hard way how best to use this practice. There is a good way and a bad way to chant.

If you wish to try meditative chanting in any context, the cardinal rule is *go slow*. Using an instrument, such as a bell, drum or sistrum, is an ideal way to maintain an even tempo. Go too fast and you will literally feel light-headed and numb. Chanting for too long will also cause this sensation (or just give you a headache). When you finish chanting, do something to "shake it off" or clear your head. Definitely do NOT try to read or listen to something – or someone – complicated after chanting. Any state of meditation can be easy to fall in love with; but as with all things, meditation has its time and place.

Chanting ancient hymns in (an approximation of) the Egyptian language would require intensive study. An easier alternative would be to locate English translations in Egyptology books and develop your own rhythm for reciting them. Another possibility is to create your own equivalent of a mantra using the native names and titles of deities given in "Who's Who of the Egyptian Gods". Simply add *Dua*, which means "hail to" or "adoration of", at the beginning of the name and title of your chosen deity. An example would be:

Dua Osir, Neb Abdju – "Hail to Osiris, Lord of Abydos".

You can create your own to suit your personal practice. As stated elsewhere in this book, knowledge is empowerment: whatever chants or mantras you incorporate into your practice, make sure they are something you understand and feel comfortable using. Understanding their meaning will empower both you as the user and the words as your tools.

Divination

Probably the best-known form of modern divination is tarot cards. Modern tarot was developed from the late 18th-century writings of Antoine Court de Gebelin, a Swiss Freemason. Gebelin claimed that tarot was descended from secret Egyptian books containing mysteries of Isis and Thoth, and that the word 'tarot' came from Egyptian words meaning 'royal road', i.e. to wisdom. However, his assertions came some forty years *before* the Rosetta Stone was finally translated by Champollion, so they are woefully inaccurate. Modern tarot, which is related to playing cards, has no precedent in ancient Egyptian practices. Other forms of divination were used or adopted by the Egyptians, however, some of which are already familiar to us.

A few of their divination techniques were surprisingly simple. One way that is well-attested in ancient records was to consult a deity's icon statue. Usually this was done during festivals, when the icon was carried through its city or village in a portable shrine on the shoulders of priests. Ancient literature is often a bit cryptic in describing how exactly the gods answered questions, but most likely their answers manifested through the shrine's movement as the priests carried it. Potsherds have been found in Deir el-Medina and elsewhere that have questions written on them which could have been answered with a simple yes or no: "Is this meat good?" "Will I make foreman?" "Will I marry so-and-so?" These were probably presented before the god or goddess' icon for an answer. Adapting this technique might actually provide an alternative use for tarot cards; using your own icons, you could present a question and then draw from a deck of tarot cards placed in front of the icons, interpreting your answer based on the card drawn. Other possibilities might also present themselves.

Another simple technique, for which we unfortunately do not have any surviving literature available, is casting sticks or knucklebones. We know this was done, not just in divination but also as a precursor to playing dice for Egyptian board games such as Senet (modern reproductions of which can be found online). Some Kemetic groups practice divination using four Senet throwing sticks, but their techniques and interpretations are entirely modern and regarded as trade secrets.

One popular form of Egyptian divination endures today, and that is dream interpretation. Many of us already know the Biblical story of Joseph interpreting the pharaoh's dreams to foretell seven years of plenty and seven years of drought, thus avoiding famine. Interpreting dreams as omens was a common practice throughout Egyptian history, and entire manuals were written on the subject. One that survives today almost echoes modern dream dictionaries; it lists dream imagery in the format of, "If a man sees XYZ", then whether this image is good or bad, as well as why. The dream manual even includes a separate section for devotees of Seth, suggesting that images might mean something different for those followers. Unfortunately, the text breaks off before listing any Seth-oriented symbolism.

Toward the end of ancient Egyptian history, scrying techniques appeared in Demotic and Greek papyrii. Instructions given for scrying tended to run on the elaborate side; a practitioner had to seek out a dark room or a cave, set up a special offering table, burn certain kinds of incense and recite lengthy spells. Strangest of all, these manuals frequently called for a young boy to lay on four special bricks and stare into the bowl of water and oil until the god being invoked (most frequently Anubis) finally appeared. 'Magic bricks' are known from pharaonic times for various other purposes, but having a young boy act as a 'spotter' may be a Greek addition.

In our present era, the Kemetic Orthodox tradition has adopted ritual possession into their practices for the purposes of divination and consulting deities. This draws from a combination of Wiccan channeling techniques ("drawing down the sun" or moon) and particularly voudon ritual possession; indeed, the originator of the Kemetic Orthodox also practices a form of Haitian voudon. However, the only ancient Egyptian source that specifically describes possession by a deity comes from the late New Kingdom tale "Report of Wenamun", in which a young Phoenician boy is spontaneously possessed by a local god in order to demand the return of stolen goods. The location of this event suggests it may have been considered a 'foreign' practice. Nowhere else in classical Egyptian literature are gods described as speaking through the possession of individuals. This is one area in which ancient Egyptian religion does not behave identically to other African Traditional Religions.

Unfortunately, today misinformation far outweighs reliable information on Egyptian divination techniques. Those with an interest in doing Egyptian-style divinations certainly face challenges in that regard, but a combination of research and your own intuition will serve you well. To get started, refer to the bibliography at the end of this book for some excellent modern archaeological sources.

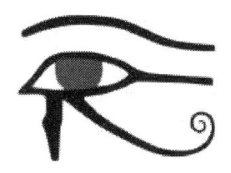

Do-It-Yourself Egyptian

As you delve into the history, beliefs and practices of the ancient Egyptians, sooner or later you will find yourself wanting to try your hand at some 'practical knowledge'. Even archaeologists catch the do-it-yourself bug, having conducted experiments on everything from baking Egyptian sourdough bread to carving limestone with Bronze Age tools. Carving a backyard obelisk probably doesn't rank very high on most Egyptian Pagans' to-do lists, but successfully making your own ritual natron and oils or even cooking your own Egyptian-inspired cuisine can be quite the rewarding venture. The benefits can sometimes be more than spiritual; especially given the current movement toward "green" products that lack harmful chemicals, foods and beauty products based on ancient recipes are seeing increasing demand in health food stores and online specialty retailers.

Natron

The ancients harvested natron from naturally occurring deposits, such as the one now called Wadi el-Natrun ("Valley of Natron") west of the Nile Delta. Chemically speaking, natron is made up of sodium bicarbonate, sodium carbonate and salt. Natron is best known as the dehydrating agent in mummification, wherein bodies were covered with natron and left on a slanted table to dessicate over the course of several weeks. A side-effect of the process was that natron raised the acidity of body tissues, inhibiting bacterial growth.

Egyptians found tremendously more use for natron than just as an embalming agent, though. As we saw from the ritual purifications, natron was used as a precursor to tooth paste. It was also used as a body scrub, which might seem odd until one considers our modern interest in 'detoxifying' salt scrubs and bath salts. Natron was offered to deities and to ancestors, and was traded as a commodity. It was used to make pigments, sprinkled in lamp oil to reduce smoke, and used as a flux in metalworking. Some medicinal remedies also included natron among their ingredients. The list of ancient applications could go on and on.

Naturally occurring natron is fairly rare, and today its use has largely been replaced by sodium bicarbonate, better known as baking soda, and soda ash (sodium carbonate). Fortunately, its constituent ingredients are easily obtainable, and you probably have one or two of them in your home already. Egyptian Pagans have devised different methods of making homemade natron, the basics of which follow:

Homemade Natron, version 1: You will need roughly equal parts table salt and baking soda. Regular iodized salt will work fine, though you can also experiment with various sea salts. Rock salt does not work well, as the crystals are too large and resist dissolving. This dissolving is exactly what you need the mixture to do. Mix the two dry ingredients together in a bowl, preferably ceramic, and add water. You want enough to just barely submerge the mixture, slightly less than if you were cooking rice. Stir it gently to make sure the water has saturated all parts of the mixture. Now comes the part that requires patience: place the bowl somewhere warm so that it can set undisturbed for several days. Depending on the size of your batch, it may take up to a week to dry completely. As it dries, some of the natron mixture will wick up the sides of the bowl, forming thin sheets. The rest will harden, so when it finishes drying your next step is to pulverize it. How fine a mixture you want is up to you. A stone or ceramic mortar and pestle would be the ideal container in which to mix, dry and pound the natron. Short of that, however, a regular ceramic bowl and wooden spoon will certainly suffice.

Variation: Obviously, letting the water evaporate naturally to yield natron takes time, and this technique won't do if you need it for a ritual the next day. A variant of the recipe is to simply mix the ingredients in a saucepan, add water and cook it down until the water has evaporated completely. Use medium heat, observe proper cooking precautions and don't leave the mixture unattended.

Another possible variation: The third constituent compound in natron is soda ash, which used to be called washing soda because it was used in laundry before the advent of modern detergents. In fact, you can still find Arm&Hammer Washing Soda in the laundry sections of some groceries and drugstores. Soda ash is still used to set dyes and adjust the pH levels in pools. However, the compound is also caustic, can irritate the lungs if inhaled, and can cause stomach pain and vomiting if too much is swallowed. Caution is definitely advised.

An online ceramics forum described a way to make your own soda ash using none other than baking soda. In fact, the method given is the same as our recipe variation above, except that no salt is included. So, if you choose to add the extra step of boiling down some soda ash to mix with salt and baking soda, you certainly can. But considering that modern soda ash is extracted both from baking soda and from table salt – our other two natron ingredients – this added step is purely discretionary.

Ancient Egyptian rituals often called for natron from different areas, which may have contained varied trace minerals or even colors. You can experiment with your own additives, but make sure that if your natron is to be used for ritual purification that you use edible coloring or flavoring agents.

Ritual and Practical Uses: Natron is an integral part of purifying and consecration rites. By extension, you can also use it to spiritually 'cleanse' items that need to be purified. When moving into a new home or apartment, sprinkle natron at the threshold or in doorways. You can also use natron to mark spiritual boundaries. To put such a protective boundary around your home, tie four cloth bundles of natron and place one at each of the four cardinal points inside your dwelling. As a practical use, adding a bit of natron to your toothpaste will act as a polishing agent. It has an obvious salty taste, but some people have observed that using it made their teeth look a little brighter.

Perfumed Oils

Living in a dry desert climate, the Egyptians knew the value of a good lotion. Most of their unguents used a base of either rendered animal fats, or vegetable oils such as moringa (a type of tree native to Africa and Asia), sesame or linseed. Olives were introduced to Egypt relatively late, not appearing before the New Kingdom, so consequently olive oil was not often used in pharaonic times. To perfume their oils, they added herbs and flowers, boiled the mixture, cooled and strained it before adding more flowers and herbs and then repeating the laborious process. Their hard work paid off, as Egyptian perfumes were renowned as the best in the Mediterranean world.

Traces of perfumed oils were found in stone jars in Tutankhamun's tomb. Sadly, modern chemical analyses of their contents have not been allowed to date. Excavators in the 1920's did notice a coconut smell to these remnants of unguent, which were dried out but not rancid. While coconut was nowhere in the ancient ingredients, and the unguent's present aroma is probably a result of 'seasoning' over three millennia, it does provide an excellent springboard for concocting a modern version with easily obtainable – and usable – ingredients.

To make your own Egyptian-style unguents, you will need a small enamel or stainless steel saucepan. It helps if you can dedicate one specifically for this purpose, so you won't have to raid your cooking utensils each time you make a batch of perfume. For your finished product, find containers that can be sealed, such as small glass jars with lids. The ancients, lacking glass, preferred stone containers; if you use soapstone for your unguent dishes, be aware that the oils will absorb into this highly porous material. You will also need a jar of coconut oil. This can be found at health food stores, Asian grocers and in the international cuisine section of regular grocers. Scenting agents will vary by recipe; for a full complement you will want to have essential oils of sandalwood, frankincense, spikenard (more on this ingredient below), and either myrrh oil or myrrh resin. If you have access to pine or cedar wood in your area, a few beads of these resins can also be used.

Fragrance #1, Sandalwood Oil: We'll start off with a good all-around fragrance using essential oils of sandalwood and frankincense. First, dollop out two to three heaping tablespoons' worth of coconut oil into your saucepan. Put it on a low heat. Notice that at room temperature, the oil is solid; but as it starts to warm, it quickly becomes a clear liquid. In fact, the warmth of your fingers is enough to soften coconut oil, which is what makes it so useful for solid perfumes. Once your coconut oil is completely melted, add several drops each of the frankincense and sandalwood oils. In a liquid state, the smell will be stronger, so don't worry if it seems too 'overpowering'. The aroma will become more subtle as the perfume cools.

After you've stirred the oil a bit to make sure the scent has incorporated throughout, turn off the heat and get your perfume jar (or jars) ready. Carefully pour the mixture into the jars, then let them set for a few hours, preferably overnight. Wait until after the oil has cooled and re-solidified enough to keep from spilling before you cap each jar. You'll know the oil has set when its surface is opaque white or off-white throughout.

When you're ready to use your unguent, just open the jar and press your fingers into its contents. The oil will start to melt and become liquid again at the touch, and you can use it just as you would any other ritual oils. In fact, coconut oil's receptivity to warmth has a downside when used in outdoor rituals; it melts quickly in warmer months, so transporting it in a securely sealed container is a must.

Fragrance #2, Myrrh Oil: You can sometimes use resins to scent your oils, but it helps to have kinds that will melt fairly easily. Myrrh resin is much more receptive, for example, than frankincense, which is why frankincense oil is preferred for perfume making. Pine resin has a medium level of ease, as it will melt but requires slightly higher heat. It also tends to bead on the surface of saucepans and is tough to remove, which is why you might want to use a different vessel from your best cookware!

To make myrrh-scented unguent, get one 'teardrop' of myrrh and melt it as far as it will go on a medium heat. (Some of it will in all likelihood be stubborn and resist melting; leave it alone until after the perfume-making part is done.) For a unique twist, melt some pine or cedar resin before adding the myrrh. Once you have your resins reduced to a mostly liquid state, lower the heat and add your coconut oil. Stirring to incorporate the ingredients is important. As before, pour the mixture into your jars or containers to set. You may want to use a steel mesh sieve to strain out the bits of unmelted myrrh. One possible use for these remnants is to let them cool and save them for burning outdoors on a charcoal disc.

Resins will color the oil a tan or golden hue. Some kitchen chemists have also warned that resins, if not properly melted, will interfere with the consistency of the perfume; probably the best way to work through these issues is through trial and error. You may end up developing your own recipes in the process.

Fragrance #3, Royal Spikenard: True spikenard is fairly expensive, as a single vial of essential oil can easily run to $25 or more. In the ancient Near East, this root was a commodity afforded by royalty and nobility, as it grows only in the Himalayas and went through countless middlemen on the ancient trade routes. The precious 'nard' oil a woman used to anoint Jesus' feet in a Biblical story was probably made using spikenard root. Chemical analysts in the 1920's determined that spikenard was also one of the ingredients in Tutankhamun's unguents, hence our name for this fragrance, "Royal Spikenard."

Begin as above by melting your coconut oil. When it is fully melted, add a few drops of spikenard oil and a few drops of frankincense. Mix well and pour into containers to cool as with the recipes above. Because of its unique ingredient, this oil is best saved for special occasions, such as New Year's celebrations.

You can also experiment with other essential oils to create your own unique fragrance. Recall that devotees of Bast report Her having an affinity for floral scents; given that oils used in Her ancient temples were perfumed with flowers such as white water lilies, imported spices like cinnamon and cardamom, and sweet wines, these adherents' shared gnosis is borne out by research. Try your own mixes of floral scents and see what works for you. For further reading on the subject, <u>An Ancient Egyptian Herbal</u> and <u>Sacred Luxuries: Fragrance, Aromatherapy and Cosmetics in Ancient </u>Egypt by Lise Manniche contain a wealth of information.

Practical Uses: Besides ritual anointing, Egyptian-style unguent also soothes and moisturizes sunburns. For some people with sensitive skin, it can even be applied as an alternative to store-bought deodorants. Nowadays, more people are growing conscious of the potentially harmful chemicals in cosmetics that absorb readily into the skin; coconut oil has the advantage of being a non-toxic 'carrier' oil that can safely dilute essential oils. Any Pagan who's mistakenly used straight cinnamon oil for ritual anointing can probably appreciate those properties...!

Ritual Clothing (or, Egyptian Street Gear)

Garbing, or re-creating 'period' clothing, is a hobby shared by many Pagan and non-Pagan enthusiasts alike. Accuracy of materials and garments can quickly become a contentious issue, however. In the case of ancient garb, one book states that cotton was one of the main textiles used in ancient times. In actuality cotton plants, which originated in India, and cotton fabric did not reach Egypt until the Late Period. Cotton was known to the Roman world, but it was considered a luxury material until a much more recent innovation – the cotton gin, patented in 1794 – made it easier to separate cotton fiber from its tough, clingy seeds. One of many social changes brought about by this invention was that cotton became much more efficient and profitable to harvest, ultimately replacing flax, the staple textile crop that was used since pharaonic times to make linen.

If you wanted to be completely historically accurate in creating garb for Egyptian rituals, you would need to use linen fabric. However, the role reversal between linen and cotton has become so complete that linen fabric is now expensive and hard to find. Cotton has become to us what linen was to the ancient Egyptians: inexpensive and easy to work, and for our purposes here, ritually pure. (While the Egyptians did make some use of wool, it harbored insects and therefore was prohibited in temples and burials.) In truth, however, even a synthetic material such as rayon can be used to make ritual clothing. What ultimately destroys a vestment's validity are misplaced notions about its antiquity or importance, not the materials from which it is made.

To make your own Egyptian-style clothing, you will need either a willing friend or accomplice who can sew, or else be able to sew yourself. A sewing machine will certainly reduce the length of time it takes to make a single garment, but Egyptian patterns are straight-forward enough that they can be sewn by hand quite easily. If you've never sewn before, there's always a first time to learn; but practice making a few quilt squares or joining scraps of fabric to "get the hang of it" before trying to sew your own clothing.

Garment #1, The Basic Kilt: In ancient times, kilts were generally worn by men. The hem usually stopped either above their ankles or at their knees. Women typically did not wear kilts. This custom is reversed in our modern equivalent, the skirt.

It's always better to start out with more material than you need for a project, so that you don't under-estimate and run short midway through assembly. For a basic kilt, start with two to two-and-a-half yards of material. When you buy fabric, it usually comes folded in half on the bolt. When you're ready to measure for your kilt, unfold the material and lay it flat, preferably somewhere clean that offers you plenty of space to spread out your work. For this project, it helps to orient your material longways (see figure 1).

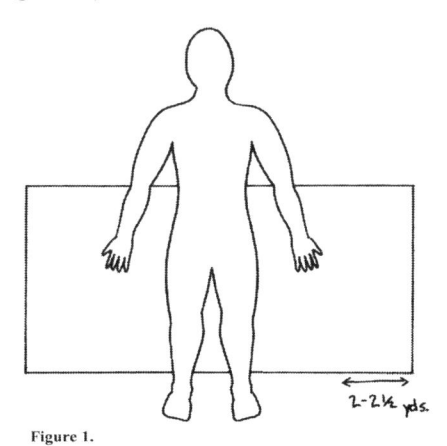

Figure 1.

Measure from your waist down to where you want the kilt to stop on your leg. Starting from the top edge of the material, measure that same distance on the fabric and mark it. *Important*: When you cut the material, *do not* cut on this same line! Add another inch or so and then cut it. You will need the extra fabric to fold over and make your hem.

Your next measurement will be how wide to make the kilt. This will actually be wider than your waist measurement; remember, you won't always be standing or sitting still in it. The kilt needs to be wide enough to accommodate a comfortable stride. You may need to have an extra pair of hands to help you wrap the material around your waist, then take a step and mark where the fabric meets at the bottom (see figure 2). Again, cut at least an inch away from that line, to make room for your hems.

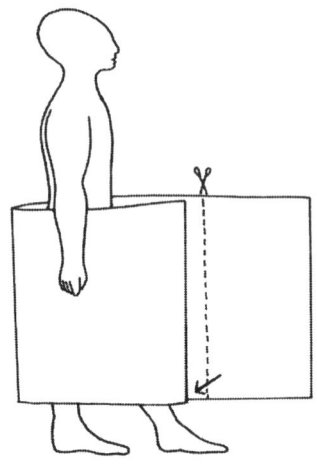

Figure 2.

The sewing, at least in principle, is very simple. Just keep in mind the cardinal rule that most beginners – and sometimes even a few of us experienced folks – forget: always turn your work inside-out to sew, keeping all your hems and seams facing the same direction. Sew the two ends together to close the kilt, then hem the bottom. Remember that to make a hem, you fold the cut edge of the material completely under to keep it from fraying. For the top of the kilt, you have a couple of options. One is to measure a length of elastic to form a waistband, or cord to form a draw-string, and fold your top hem over it. Sew carefully at the bottom edge of the hem to enclose the elastic or drawstring. (Make sure to sew your elastic together at the ends beforehand.) Another alternative is to leave several inches open at the top of your closing seam; then hem all the edges left exposed. This leaves you with two "tails" that you can tie together. When you're done, turn it right side out. *Voila!* You have a Egyptian-style kilt.

Garment #2, The Tunic: The most common garment in ancient Egypt is rather unflatteringly called the 'bag tunic'. It was unisex, being worn by men and women. It was also versatile; it could be worn ankle-length with a sash, or with a fringed shawl draped over it, or short in combination with a kilt. It could be long-sleeved or short-sleeved, and its simple design is echoed today by modern garments. In the long form, it can resemble either the *galabaya* worn by modern Egyptians, or a plain muumuu. In its shorter form, a bag tunic bears some resemblance to a t-shirt. Some fashions really don't die.

How much material you'll need for a tunic will depend on how long you want it, as well as how roomy you need it to be. Three to four yards should comfortably cover most people. As before, unfold your material on a clean work space. This time, however, you want to vertically orient the material (see figure 3) and fold it over. Hold the material at its fold to the top of your shoulders and let it hang down. Mark the bottom where you want it to stop, allow for your hem and cut as before. Next, hold the fabric (still folded) across your body. Start with one long edge of it at the middle of your side and go across to the middle of your other side, but then add some extra "wiggle room" so you can move around in the finished garment. Mark the stopping point and cut down the length of the material. Using a yardstick or other guide will be extremely helpful; don't try to "freehand" your cutting until you're experienced at it.

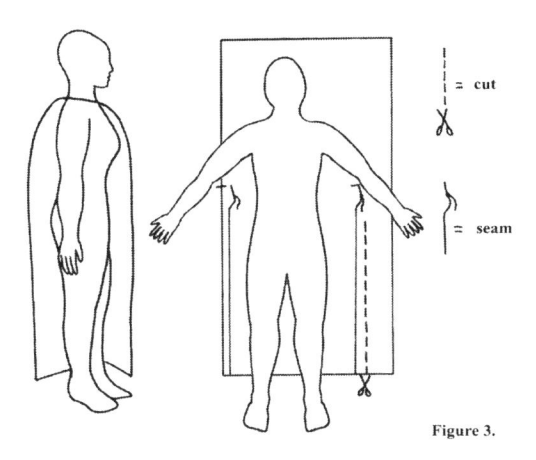

Figure 3.

Once you've gotten the basic body of the garment cut to size, pin the edges of the fabric in place so they don't move. You will also want to pin or mark where to stop the seam on either side to allow for your sleeves. Be sure to allow plenty of room for your arms to move; more than you think you will need is my general rule.

Now you need to cut a neck hole. A common mistake (that even I have made) is to cut the hole too wide, which for women will have the obvious dis-advantage of allowing people to see your bra straps. But those wily Egyptians had a handy pattern for neck holes that allowed enough room for someone to fit their head through a tunic while still covering their shoulders, and today it is called a *keyhole neck*. (See figure 4.) Find the center of the body along the top fold, carefully cut a half-circle out of it, then cut a slit down no more than three inches from the bottom edge of the circle on one side. (See figure 5.) This slit will mark the front of your tunic. Don't make the cut too deep, unless you plan on showing off some cleavage.

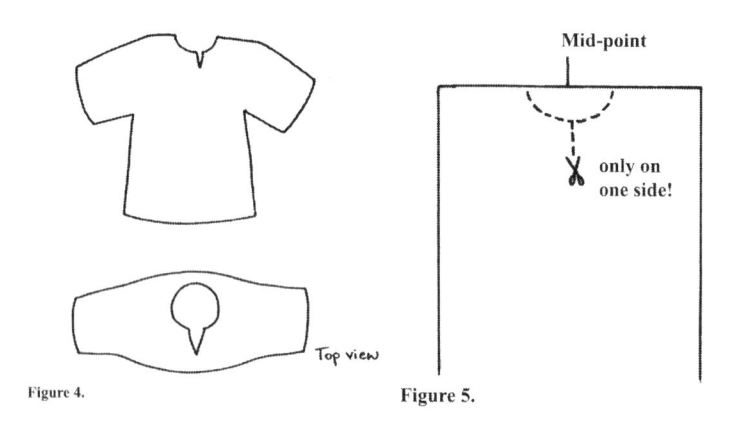

Figure 4.

Figure 5.

All that remains now is to cut your sleeves, sew everything together and hem the edges. Sleeves are the easy part. Use some of the extra material you cut away from the body of your tunic and fold it over width-wise, matching the size of your arm openings and cutting to fit (see figure 6). If you want longer sleeves, you may need extra material, so plan accordingly. As always, leave extra room for seams before you cut. All that remains now is to sew the sides of the tunic closed, sew the sleeves to the body, and hem all of your edges. Round hems can be challenging at first; two sanity-saving tips are to fold a wide enough hem to handle easily, and make tiny cuts into the fabric to accommodate the curve (see figure 7).

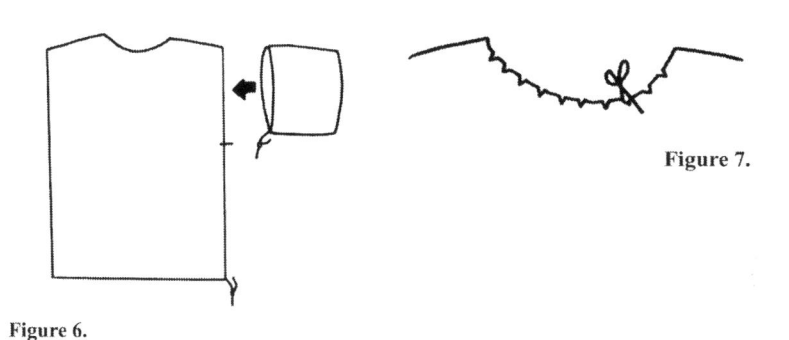

Figure 7.

Figure 6.

Garment #3, The Tube Dress: This was exclusively a woman's garment in ancient times. Even during the New Kingdom when well-to-do women of Egyptian society wore flowing, translucent tunics and shawls, goddesses were always pictured wearing a tube dress. Patterns painted onto these dresses on wall reliefs suggest that tube dresses were sometimes decorated with a netted covering of beads. In fact, a tube dress made of bead netting was found in an Old Kingdom burial and is now on display in the Museum of Fine Arts in Boston.

The pattern for this garment is simple, at least in principle. It consists of a body, much like a bag tunic except fully open at the top, which stops right at the bust line. In ancient times people didn't shy away from the sight of exposed breasts, consequently the straps connected to the top of the tube dress didn't always cover them. Today, however, we have to take modesty into account. (Although, if you're creative with patterns, you could theoretically make a tube dress that could accommodate breastfeeding.) Once you've measured and cut a sheath for the body of the dress, you will next need to measure two long rectangles for straps, making them broad enough to cover your bust on either side and long enough to fold over your shoulders and meet the top of the dress in back (see figure 8). Simply sew the connecting seams and hem the edges to complete the dress.

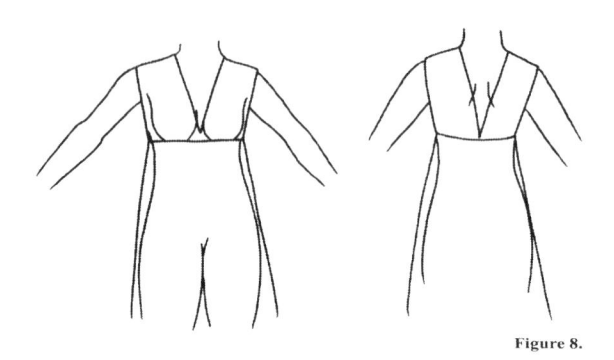

Figure 8.

Important caveats: This type of dress may be easy to make or difficult, depending on your body shape. Whenever you are making clothes, it is essential to see how they will lay on your body, which is impossible to tell with the material laid flat on a table. Another adaptation you may have to incorporate into either a tunic or tube dress is slits up the sides to allow for ease of movement. This can be accomplished by simply not sewing all the way down the side seams, and instead hemming the bottom edges. (Remember, a 'seam' joins two parts of material together; a 'hem' is done to an edge to strengthen it and keep it from fraying.)

Accessories - Generally, women tied their dresses with narrow sashes whereas men (especially during the New Kingdom) wrapped broad sashes around their waists so that the ends hung down in front like an apron. Fringed cloth scarves are considered feminine apparel today, but they can still be legitimately 'co-opted' into Egyptian garb. Sandals are another obvious accessory, but keep in mind that Egyptian texts describe putting on woven rush sandals (the "white sandals" of Merikara's

Instructions), rather than leather sandals, to attend temple services. For a modern alternative, synthetic-material sandals are probably your best bet.

Of course, virtually every metaphysical or alternative store carries some variety of *ankh* pendant, which has become the default jewelry for Egyptian Pagans (myself included). Ironically, *ankh*s were not worn as pendants or amulets at all in ancient times. Nor were they used as ritual wands; I've heard Pagans rattle off elaborate explanations about *ankh* wands with solid centers representing one thing or another, and none of these claims are supported by fact. You can wear whatever jewelry you wish with your Egyptian garb – even they borrowed foreign jewelry motifs – as long as it has personal significance. You shouldn't need a convoluted explanation in order to wear anything.

Colors - Another area of modern convolution lies in the color, or lack thereof, of garb. One of the reasons why the Egyptians usually pictured themselves wearing white is because linen fibers resist dying, making white more practical. But that does not mean that they had no colored fabric; ancient accounts describe some icons of deities, Min in particular, being robed in red or purple. While they lacked the means to dye designs into their fabric, embroidery was known to them. An elaborately embroidered tunic, which some scholars believe may have been ceremonial garb, was found amongst Tutankhamun's wardrobe. Its colors have long since faded, but were once a veritable tapestry of green, red, blue and yellow.

So what does this mean for the modern Egyptian Pagan? If you are a solitary practitioner, it means that you can wear any color or combination of colors you wish in your garb. If anything, the most 'un-Egyptian' ensemble would be mostly black, the Goth scheme so unfortunately associated with Egypt in our pop culture today. If you practice as part of a group, the members officiating as clergy would be historically correct to wear all white. They would also be correct in not wearing any jewelry, as ancient priests did not wear obvious trappings of fashion. However, regular participants should not be restricted to wearing all-white. The ancient Egyptians loved color, and had they been able to print or dye patterns into cloth, then many of them probably would have worn loud and festive prints for their celebrations. Indeed, the one ancient occasion that called for everyone to wear plain, all-white attire out of custom and not necessity was at funerals.

Egyptian Style-Cuisine

Unfortunately, the Egyptians left us with no cookbooks – at least, none that we have yet found. The closest to ancient Egyptian recipes we have come from Ptolemaic times, and a few of these can be found in <u>An Ancient Egyptian Herbal</u>. What little we know of pharaonic cooking has been pieced together from paintings of offerings, mentions of food items in writing, and a few actual foodstuffs left in tombs. These have included dates and figs, shredded vegetables covered in some type of dressing, salted meats, breads of various kinds, dry beans, watermelon seeds, honey and seasonings. Bread was the staple food throughout pharaonic history. Though they do not seem to have eaten as much meat as we do today, many Egyptians were well-fed and fat Egyptians were not unusual, especially in middle and upper classes.

Modern Egyptian cuisine bears influences from Mediterranean cooking and from the Ottoman Empire, which occupied the country from the 16th to the 19th century. Many Greek and Lebanese restaurants offer a bean dish called *Fuol Medames* (spellings vary) that is considered the 'national dish' of Egypt; something similar may have been served under a different name in ancient times. Felafel, another common menu item in modern Mediterranean cuisine that is made from chick peas, may also have had ancient antecedents. Records from Deir el-Medina include a letter from a man to his wife, asking her to make more bean bread for him because he had given all of his to hungry coworkers. It's easy to imagine this royal tomb worker toting a basket of his wife's particular recipe with him to the Valley of the Kings, then having it gobbled up by comrades who agreed what a good cook she was.

Chances are, however, that you might have encountered a culinary gift of the Nile in a most unlikely place. Cumin is native to Egypt, and its use as a seasoning spread to the North African Moors, who in turn brought their cooking to Spain. The Spanish in their turn brought this seasoning with them to the New World, where cumin – called 'comino' in Spanish – is a major flavoring in Mexican cuisine. Cilantro and its seeds, better known as coriander, were also used by the Egyptians and later carried along trade routes in much the same way. Odd as it might seem, our fajitas wouldn't taste the same without a few seasonings once used by the pharaoh's cooks.

To find another modern seasoning used by the ancient Egyptians, we must turn eastward again. Fenugreek seeds were found in Tutankhamun's tomb, and today fenugreek seasoning is most prominently used in Indian cuisine. As a seasoning, fenugreek can be somewhat hard to find unless you look in Asian or Middle Eastern groceries. If you find it as whole dry seeds, you will need to pulverize them in a small coffee grinder in order to use them. The flavor given by fenugreek is rich and earthy, and goes best with lamb or beef.

Many vegetables and seasonings familiar to us were also common in pharaonic kitchens. Garlic and onion, staples in our modern cooking, were also Egyptian staples as well. Workers and farmers often ate onions with their bread and beans. Okra, now a defining ingredient in New Orleans gumbo, comes from Africa and was eaten in ancient Egypt as it continues to be in modern Egypt. Juniper berries, which can be found in grocery-store spice aisles today, were also used for seasoning in pharaonic times. For sweeteners, the Egyptians used honey and fruit juices, particularly date juice. They extracted another natural sweetener from carob beans; in fact, their word for "sweet", *nedjem*, was spelled with a pictogram of a carob bean pod. Today carob and date syrup are still used in Middle Eastern cooking, and carob beans are used as a chocolate substitute in vegan cooking and doggie treats.

Does all of this discussion about seasonings and food have you hungry yet? Then it's time to try our hand at a couple of Egyptian-inspired recipes.

Egyptian-Seasoned Beef Roast

You will need:

1 large pack of beef stew meat, or

small beef roast

Minced garlic

1 chopped onion

Onion powder (NOT onion salt)

Garlic powder (again, different from garlic salt)

Cumin powder

Coriander, powdered

Fenugreek, powdered

Worcestershire sauce

1/2 cup canola or vegetable oil

    Ideally, this recipe is done in a crock pot or slow-cooker overnight. Just put your stew meat in the crock pot with a little oil, or cut up the beef roast if you will be using one of those. (Some cooks argue that you get a more tender result starting with a sirloin roast instead of pre-cut stew meat.) Alternatively, season your roast well with all of your powdered seasonings and Worcestershire's, then brown it whole in a skillet with the oil. Make sure to season and brown all sides, and handle it carefully with a spatula or tongs; poking holes in the seared meat will allow the juices to drain out. The purpose of browning a roast is to keep all those juices inside so the meat stays moist and tender.

    Once you have the meat and oil in the crock pot, add the minced garlic and chopped onion. Then cover the meat with a generous dusting of each seasoning. I use roughly equal amounts of each seasoning, but each cook develops their own unique ratios of spices. Remember, by using actual garlic and onion powder instead of seasoned salts, you get the true flavor of those seasonings without loading down your dish with an unhealthy amount of salt. If you're cooking for folks who have hypertension, they will appreciate you for it.

Many slow-cooker recipes state not to add water, but if you add enough water to just barely submerge the meat, you can be reasonably assured the end result won't be too dry. In fact, the resulting gravy makes a handy soup stock, or can be poured over rice. Just be careful not to wash all the seasonings off the meat as you pour in the water. That done, set the cooker on 'low', or for six to eight hours if the cooker has a timer, and let it cook. You'll know the roast is well on its way when you can smell the aroma permeating your house.

If you don't have a crock pot, you can use a deep skillet instead. First cut up the roast if you will be using one, and season the meat generously. Oil and preheat the skillet; when a drop of Worcestershire sizzles on the skillet, it's ready. At the same time, though, try not to let the skillet preheat too long, or the oil with oxidize and turn brown. Put in the meat, garlic and onion, taking care not to spatter yourself with hot oil. Brown the meat on all sides, add another healthy dusting of seasonings and Worcestershire's, then reduce the heat and let it finish cooking on low-medium heat. (On a dial numbered one through ten, put it at 'four' or 'five'.) Keep turning the chunks over with a spatula or meat fork so they don't stick. The roast should be done in about ten minutes.

Voila! You now have a tasty main course seasoned with Egyptian spices of cumin, coriander and fenugreek, which will give it a unique and enjoyable flavor. The Worcestershire will provide it an additional zest, in place of the wine-based sauces used in Alexandrian recipes. I have served this at local functions, to rave reviews. Try it for your next gathering, but don't count on taking any leftovers home.

"Festival" Bread

You will need:

6 cups flour

1/2 cup warm water (no more than 115 degrees Fahrenheit)

2 cups milk

2 tbsp. sugar or honey

1 tbsp. butter

1 pack dry yeast

1 container of honey

1 pack chopped almonds

1 pack dried, chopped dates

The ancient Egyptians made yeast bread, but they did not understand precisely how the yeast worked as a rising agent. They would simply leave a bowl of wet flour or batter outside for a few days, where it would collect natural airborne yeast spores and begin to bubble. Nowadays packs of store-bought yeast make the work quicker, not to mention a bit more sanitary. Start by putting the pack of yeast into a small bowl with the warm water. A good rule of thumb is to check if it's warm to the touch, but not hot; any higher than 115 degrees will kill the yeast. Add either the sugar or some honey and let it "proof", or bubble. (If the yeast in your pack is dead, you won't get any effervescence.) While the yeast is proofing, warm the milk and butter in a saucepan until the butter has melted down. Let it cool down to roughly 110 degrees (again, where it feels warm but won't burn your finger if you test it,) and add it to the water and yeast mix.

Now you'll need a clear space to work, preferably a kitchen countertop or table. Grease a big mixing bowl with either cooking spray (the easiest route) or melted butter. Pour in about half of your flour, or three cups' worth, then add the milk and yeast mix. Then add your chopped almonds and dates. Start mixing to incorporate the ingredients. As you mix, start adding honey and stir it into the batter. Be generous; you'll know you have enough when the batter starts to turn a light golden color.

The toughest part about making bread is knowing when your dough is the right consistency. If it's too runny, keep adding more flour and mix it in until you have a batter that starts to pull away from the bowl as you stir it. You will also know it's the right consistency when it feels almost springy and tends to hold its shape, but is still moist.

When the dough has reached that point, cover the bowl with a towel and put it someplace warm, but not hot, so that it can rise. This should take about half an hour to an hour. When the dough has almost doubled in size, punch it down; not quite literally, but flour your hand and then deflate the dough ball so you can work it one more time. For this second round you'll turn the dough onto a floured cutting board and flatten it with a rolling pin. Coating the board and pin with flour will keep the dough from sticking to them quite as much. After you've rolled the dough to about an inch thick, cut it into sections to match the length of your bread tins and roll these into tubular loaf shapes that will fit. (If you've gotten to this point and don't have any bread tins, don't panic; just roll your whole dough batch into a loaf shape and put it on a greased cookie sheet or baking pan.) The dough now needs to rise one final time, which will give the bread its airy, spongy texture. A convenient place for this is on the stove top while you preheat your oven to 400 degrees.

After another half-hour or so, the dough should have risen to almost the size of a finished loaf. Once in the oven, it will rise just a bit more before the cooking temperature kills off the yeast. If your dough has been sluggish in rising, or if it's cold in your home, one possible option is to not preheat your oven; just give the bread dough half an hour to rise normally, then put it in the oven and turn it on. The warmth of the oven as it climbs to temperature will give the yeast one last burst of activity before finally cooking it.

Give the bread about forty minutes to cook. If you're making smaller loaves, subtract about ten minutes. When it's done, it should slip right out of the tin, but be sure to wear oven mitts or use potholders when handling the hot bread tins.

Making bread from scratch is rather time-consuming, but the end result using this recipe tastes decadent. It won't require any honey or jam; just a few slices with butter is all you need. It makes an excellent food offering for special occasions – hence the name for it here – as well as dessert, party snacks and Christmas gifts.

If you want to prepare a full ancient Egyptian-style banquet, serve the beef roast with some *fuol medames* or some felafel; a salad of romaine (Cos) lettuce, cucumbers and onions drizzled with olive or sesame oil; slices of melon or canteloupe; some festival bread; and dates or figs for dessert. Wash it down with beer or red wine; or if you must forego the alcohol, serve water or your favorite fruit juice. In a word, *yum*.

Sistrums

After seeing an original sistrum in the *Tutankhamun and the Golden Age of the Pharaohs* exhibit, I had to try making one just so I would know what it sounded like when used. And truly, the only way to really understand what sistrums sound like is to either acquire or make one and try it for yourself. You can actually find Ethiopian-made sistrums for sale online, which often have handles made from spent 50-caliber shell casings. You can also make your own using common household and hobby materials, which is how I made my first three.

You will need:

1 metal wreath hanger

1 dowel rod, one inch in diameter

1 sheet of craft aluminum OR

about 6 metal washers

1 thin wire hanger, uncoated

small nails

notebook wire

heavy-duty scissors

wire cutters (or pliers)

hammer

heavy-duty phillips-head screwdriver

block of wood, or some other sturdy surface that you can afford to damage

Optional: gold paint

To start off, if you would like to paint the handle of your sistrum, paint the dowel rod gold and leave it to dry. Most decorative wreath hangers are gold-colored, so a gold-painted handle will match nicely.

The square part of the wreath hanger, which ordinarily would go over a door, will form the bottom of your sistrum's metal frame. But it will need a hole in the bottom so it can be attached to the end of handle. The simplest way to accomplish this is to find a small block of wood (carving blocks sold at hobby stores work well for this) that will fit inside this square shape and solidly brace it while you pound a hole in it using the hammer and phillips-head screwdriver. While this isn't the most elegant – or quiet – method, it usually works. (If the door hanger is especially thick, you may be better off finding a power drill.) Driving a screwdriver tip through the metal on one side will create some flanging on the opposite side, however. By starting from the outside of the wreath hanger top (see figure 9), despite the rather tricky angle, you will make sure the resulting flanges face inward and don't prevent the finished sistrum frame from matching flush with the handle.

Figure 9.　　　　　　Figure 10.　　　　　　Figure 11.

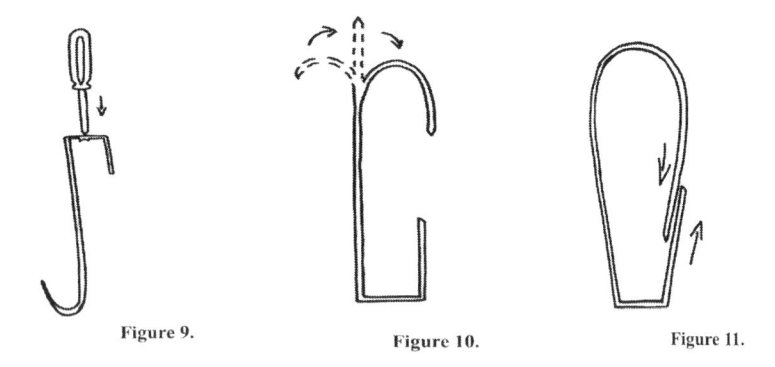

It may be difficult at this stage to see how this wreath hanger will form a sistrum, so it's time to start shaping. Begin by straightening out the bottom curve (see figure 10) which is easily done by hand. Next, use the hammer and screwdriver to punch two more holes in the wreath hanger, one about two-and-a-half inches up from the square bottom and the next about two inches above the first. At this point, which side has the flanges becomes less of an issue, so work from whichever side is easiest for you to maneuver. Then, bend the wreath hanger the rest of the way to form an arched top. The very end, which would have held a wreath before it was straightened, should overlap with the first end, which in its former life would have hung over the back side of a door (see figure 11). Tuck this top end inside of the bottom end so the shape will stay closed.

Now you simply have to make matching holes on the other side of the sistrum frame. Try to line them up so that the crossbars, which you will make next, will be level. Depending on how the wreath hanger is made, it may have a hole near the bottom end already. If not, you may have to move the two ends around temporarily in order to punch holes through both and match them up.

For the crossbars, take the wire cutters and cut two lengths of hanger wire that will span the width of the sistrum frame, leaving enough room to bend the ends up or down (see figure 12). If you can't find wire cutters, use a pair of pliers to

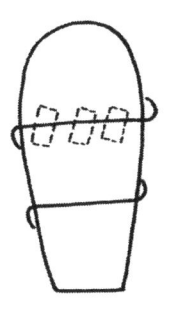

Figure 12.

bend the metal back-and-forth in one spot until it breaks. Thread the two lengths through one side of the frame, but not the other just yet. Now you need to make the jangles. These can be cut fairly easily from a small sheet of lightweight craft aluminum or copper; you may want to flatten them out using the hammer and wood block, since scissors tend to bend the metal slightly. Use the hammer and screwdriver to poke a hole in the center of each jangle. Alternatively, you can just use metal washers. This will produce a different sound, but is just as interesting. (If you can find tambourine jingles, those create a great sound with less work.) Thread three apiece on your crossbars, then thread the free ends through the holes on other side of the sistrum frame. Bend the remaining lengths, which should be about half an inch on either side, back against the sistrum frame in order to keep them in place. Now all that remains is to attach the frame to its handle.

This part is tricky. To make life easier, start a hole in the top end of your dowel rod using the hammer and a nail; tap it in about a third of the way, then pull it out. Now you can line up the hole in the bottom of your sistrum frame with the hole in the dowel, and hammer the nail in the rest of the way. Work slowly and carefully; at this point it's easy to miss and hit your fingers with the hammer, which is no fun!

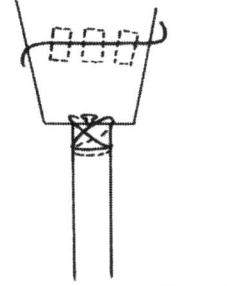

Figure 13.

At this point, the frame is attached, but not as tightly as it needs in order to be used. This is where the notebook wire comes in. But first, take a steak knife or serrated knife and score a ring around the dowel about a half-inch below the bottom of the sistrum frame. Make it deep enough to loop one end of the notebook wire around tightly and twist it closed. Then just loop the rest of the wire length around handle and frame, especially around the nail on the inside of the frame, then back down and around again in a figure-eight pattern (see figure 13). Keep it tight, so it will hold the frame steady. Twist the final end around a segment of the figure-eight to secure it.

An optional finishing touch would be to use some colored ribbon to wrap around the wire, in order to conceal it and cover any sharp edges. Another possibility would be to use some craft wood to form a brace around the junction between handle and frame; you can paint it with Egyptian floral patterns, or with the face of Hathor, patroness of the instrument. Now that you have your sistrum done, try it out! If you have friends that like to host drumming circles, sistrums form a unique accompaniment. If you're playing solo, try using the rhythm described by Apuleius as three beats followed by a pause, then three beats again and another pause, and so on. Be creative, and most of all, have fun with your very own hand-made instrument.

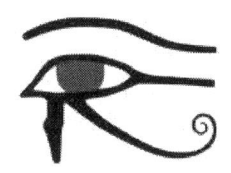

The Egyptian Liturgical Year

Before we delve any further, I'm going to take us on a proverbial side road. If you happen to remain skeptical about the effects of climate change, then you may not agree with our short detour, but don't skip ahead - you could still find it useful.

Since the first edition of this book was initially published, we have experienced five of the top ten 'hottest years on record', according to results published on climate.org. In the temperate latitudes of our world, spring is now coming earlier and autumn arriving later in the year. Considering these changes, it makes no sense to read aloud Mabon ritual introductions that describe frost tingeing the Goddess' breath while coveners stand listening in 80° F heat (which I have done); or to praise the melting snow at Imbolc where no winter snow ever fell (likewise, I have witnessed this firsthand). If Paganism and especially Wicca celebrate the rhythm of the seasons, then we need to re-examine and adapt our festivals to reflect our current climate conditions - particularly when they do not match the Victorian-era northern temperate climate of England and Ireland, upon which much existing Sabbat literature is based. For those of us old enough to remember cold autumn and winter months, this traditional literature still rings familiar, but for younger generations - some of them likely reading this book for the first time - those 'transplanted' interpretations of the Wheel of the Year will seem more artificial and irrelevant as warming trends continue. If our Pagan traditions are to continue, they must remain relevant to our lives.

That said, the Egyptian calendar offers a marvelous potential resource for new ideas to weave into Sabbat rituals and meanings. Ancient Egyptian society was agrarian, like many European pre-Christian societies. But the desert Egyptian climate saw temperature ranges not too dissimilar to southern latitudes of the United States and parts of Australia - and as the effects of climate change continue to unfold, more areas could routinely feel as hot and dry as Egypt. The ancient Egyptians based their insights into the divine upon different natural phenomena than the ones we see disappearing before our eyes. Their wisdom coupled with our creativity could provide us with the means to adapt and move forward in a world marked by unprecedented environmental changes. To better understand how the Egyptians marked time, let's begin with a short recap of their seasons, then move upward to their view of the heavens.

Egyptian Reckoning of Time

As mentioned in "Seasons of the River", the Egyptians began their agricultural year with the start of the annual Nile flood. The floods actually did not occur all at once. The river level rose first in the southernmost part of the country, then gradually increased down-stream to the delta over the course of two months. The Inundation did begin with remarkable regularity year after year, though, and at some point early in their history the Egyptians noticed that its occurrence coincided with the movement of certain stars. So the real key to understanding their measurement of time lies in the observable movement of the stars.

The Egyptians closely watched the heavens. In fact, some scholars now theorize that the earliest Egyptians may have worshiped certain deities as stars. This is certainly supported by their veneration of the star goddess Sopdut (or Sopdet), who came to be seen as an aspect of Isis. Today we know the star Sopdut as Sirius, the Dog Star, visible to the immediate lower left of the constellation Orion – whom the Egyptians identified with Osiris. In pharaonic times, Sirius rose just before dawn on the same day that the Inundation typically began. (The technical term for a star rising above the horizon prior to dawn is its *heliacal* rising.) Thus one of the Egyptian names for New Year's was *Peret Sopdut*, the "Emergence of Sopdut".

Observing further, the Egyptians noticed that a new star or group of stars heliacally rose every ten days. Their Greek visitors called these stars the Decans. Over the course of a year, there appeared thirty-six Decans; hence, the Egyptians further divided their calendar into thirty-six weeks of ten days each, yielding 360 days. But they knew that it took 365 days for Sirius/Sopdut to begin a new cycle, so they added five extra "Days Upon the Year", known in Greek as the Epagomenal Days.

What the Egyptians did not know, however, was that a full solar year is 365 1/4 days. This was probably because, while they used a 24-hour day, they did not have very precise means of measuring individual hours and therefore could not determine that a full year contains an extra six hours. This meant that every four years, their calendar grew out of synch with natural markers by a whole day. In fact, the exact dates and events only matched up precisely once every 1,456 years! The Ptolemies tried to institute a Leap Year to adjust the calendar, but met with resistance from the native population; it was not until Roman times that the calendar was permanently reformed to add a Leap Year. This reformed calendar is still used today by the Coptic Orthodox Church, and a similar one is used by the Ethiopian Orthodox Church.

But despite the Leap Year discrepancy, the Egyptian calendar was actually more reliable than Greek and Roman calendars. In fact, the prior to the reforms of Julius Caesar, the Romans used a ten-month calendar with variable 'intercalary months' that were essentially determined by politicians. The more mathematically regular Egyptian calendar was later used in the Middle Ages by the astronomer Copernicus to build tables charting planetary motion. A similar calendar, using ten-day weeks and thirty-six week years, was briefly adopted by the French Republic following the Revolution but failed to gain lasting popularity.

Equivalent Dates

So, in order to match equivalent dates from the Egyptian calendar with ours, we simply have to determine the heliacal rising of Sirius, right? Not exactly. While the Earth keeps a regular cycle as it orbits the sun, our sun is itself moving with the rest of the Milky Way galaxy; so the movements of constellations, and thus the position of stars such as Sirius, go through their own cycle called *precession* which lasts roughly 25,800 years. This is why astrologers recently proposed adding another constellation, Ophiuchus, to the Zodiac between Scorpio and Sagittarius to account for precessional shift. (So far the idea hasn't gained much support.) This same phenomenon of precession has pushed back the date of Sirius' heliacal rising over Egypt from July 18th during New Kingdom times to July 25th today. (This topic is further explained, complete with 'analog graphics', in the YouTube *Kemetic How-to Guide* episode "The Egyptian Calendar".)

But here's another 'wrinkle in time': while today Sirius emerges over Egypt on July 25th, for places further west that date occurs even later. Sirius rises before dawn around August 3rd in the central United States, which is when the Kemetic Orthodox (based in Joliet, Illinois) marks their New Year's. Sirius rises a few days later over the West Coast, which is home to the Kemetic Temple of San Jose, so they begin their liturgical year anywhere from August 4th to August 7th. Meanwhile, a different Reconstructionist group, Amentet Neferet, begins their liturgical year in late June, the Sirius cycle notwithstanding. This situation with differing Kemetic calendars parallels the differences between Roman Catholic and Eastern Orthodox Christian calendars; speaking of which, the Coptic Orthodox Church uses a calendar based on the ancient Egyptian one - but because of influence from native agricultural seasons, their year begins on August 29th. With all of these conflicting points of reference, where should a newcomer to Egyptian Paganism begin?

The answer depends on how you plan to celebrate your holidays. Tameran Wiccans might prefer starting at August 1st and using their Lammas Sabbat to observe the Egyptian New

Year. Some of the subsequent Egyptian holidays will roughly coincide with other Wiccan Sabbats, give or take a couple of weeks; however, certain observances, such as the Wagy Feast and Hab Sed, don't match with any of the Sabbats and the Imbolc Sabbat lacks any obvious Egyptian parallel. Adaptations can still be done, but they involve a little bit of extrapolation.

Beginning in mid-July lacks the obvious advantage of synchronizing with Sirius' modern heliacal emergence – assuming that one has the time and adequate visibility to watch for it to rise in the early morning hours – but it does allow for Egyptian dates to synch with our modern calendar dates rather painlessly. The subsequent holidays do not always match up with Wiccan Sabbats, but in some cases they match with secular holidays. This could prove advantageous if you want to host a gathering and have time off from work to celebrate and then recover. Another consideration is the frequency of holidays; some Egyptian observances are only two or three weeks apart, suggesting a liturgical season not unlike the Christian seasons of Lent and Advent. Fitting holidays to the Quarter and Cross-Quarter format of the Wiccan year can potentially disrupt that rhythm. There are advantages and disadvantages to both systems.

The Egyptian Calendar Year

For our purposes, we'll start our calendar with July 18th. This date tends to work rather handily in conjunction with the astrological Cairo Calendar, which will be discussed later in this chapter. Below is a breakdown of the Egyptian calendar year, with corresponding modern dates. During the Old and much of the Middle Kingdom, months were referred to simply as "Akhet I", "Akhet II," and so on. The month names listed here were developed during the New Kingdom, but did not begin to see common usage until the Late Period. The Greek equivalent names listed are used today by Tameran and Hellenistic groups.

Modern Date - Egyptian Month (*Greek Name*):

Season of Akhet (Inundation)

July 18 - August 16 – Djehutet (*Thoth*)
August 17 - September 15 – Pa'en-Opet (*Paopi*)
September 16 - October 16 – Hat-Hor (*Hathor*)
October 17 - November 14 – Ka-Hor-Ka (*Khoiakh*)

Season of Peret (Emergence)

November 15 - December 15 – Ta-ib (*Tybi*)
December 16 - January 13 – Makhir (*Mechir*)
January 14 - February 12 – Pa'en-Amunhotepu (*Panemot*)
February 13 - March 15 – Pa'en-Renenut (*Parmuti*)

Season of Shomu (Summer)

March 16 - April 13 – Pa-Khonsu (*Pachons*)
April 14 - May 13 – Pa'en-Inet (*Payni*)
May 14 - June 12 – Apip (*Epipi*)
June 13 - July 12 – Mosu-Ra (*Mesore*)

July 13-17 – Heriu Ronpet (Days Upon the Year) (*Epagomenal Days*)

Egyptian months were based on the lunar cycle and commenced with each new moon, not unlike the Jewish months still do today. But because the moon's cycle is not in perfect synch with the annual solar cycle, every three or four years the calendar gains an extra month. In Egypt this extra lunar month was added at the beginning of the new year and celebrated during the Djehutet Festival, honoring Thoth (Djehuty). This extra lunar month was also called Djehutet, perhaps in parallel to the extra Jewish month of Adar I, which follows the usual month of Adar.

Periodic festivals were also held based on the major phases of the moon. One of our sources of information about these lunar festivals is from memorial stelae commissioned by private citizens, who hoped to receive offerings on the New Moon Feast, the Half-Moon Feast and the Full Moon Feast. The moon's waxing and waning states were compared to Horus' Sound, or *Udjat*, Eye being torn apart by Seth (the waning phase) and then restored to completion (waxing and the full moon). For a Tameran system, these lunar observances can be adapted to the Esbats. If you want to track current phases of the moon in order to observe such occasions, the *Old Farmer's Almanac* remains a highly informative source; it also includes monthly positions of stars, including Sirius. You can also check online at almanac.com, and as with everything else nowadays, "there's an app for that".

The Egyptian Religious Year

Below is a list of some of the major Egyptian holidays. This calendar would not have held true for all parts of the country, as some occasions were tied to local mythological lore and probably had regional variants. Other festivals, however, had national appeal and are attested in various ancient sources.

Heriu Ronpet - *Days Upon the Year*
Epagomenal Days 1-5 - July 13-17

Each intercalary day was considered the birthday of one of the children of Nut: Osiris (July 13th), Horus (14th), Seth (15th), Isis (16th) and Nephthys (17th). Horus' inclusion was probably a conflation of his Elder Horus aspect as Isis and Osiris' brother instead of their son. Seth's birthday was considered an unlucky day, and some records suggest people avoided doing important business then.

Litanies to Sakhmet were read during the Days Upon the Year in order to ensure good luck and rich harvests, as Sakhmet was the decider of fortune. Priests may have also performed divinations to forecast events for the upcoming year.

Upet Ronpet (or **Wep Ronpet**) - *"Opening of the Year", Egyptian New Year's*
Djehutet 1 - July 18

New Year's was considered the birthday of Ra and the anniversary of *Zep Tepi*, the First Occasion. Temples throughout the country would bring their icon statues out of the shrines and into sunlit courtyards, to be 'recharged' and re-consecrated through the Opening of the Mouth ceremony. Another important temple rite was the Subduing of Apophis, in which effigies of state enemies were burned or smashed before the icons of the gods while hymns or special liturgies called the Execration Texts were read.

For the general public, New Year's was a time to celebrate the return of the Inundation and new beginnings. Curiously, modern Egyptians throw flowers into the Nile during the national holiday *Wafaa el-Nil* (Flooding of the Nile), and Copts throw symbolic 'martyr's fingers' into the river. These modern practices parallel an ancient tradition of throwing flowers or writing ink into the river to honor Osiris or Djehuty.

Tameran equivalent: While mainstream Wiccans often observe their New Year at Samhain (October 31), using August 1 as the Egyptian New Year date coincides with Lammas (or 'Lughnasadh'). Thus a logical Tameran adaptation would be to observe Lammas as the 'Opening of the Year', rather than as the first harvest.

Hab Wagy and Hab Djehutet - *Supply Feast* and *Feast of Djehuty*

Djehutet 17 and 19 - August 3 and 5

The Wagy Feast was one of many occasions to make offerings to the deceased. The memorial stela of brothers Suti and Hor mention receiving flower garlands for the Wagy Feast, suggesting that relatives decorated the markers of deceased loved ones with flowers. Relatives also made physical offerings of food and drink, hence the name "Supply Feast". The Djehutet Feast, described above, was celebrated two days later, and the two festivals may have combined in ancient times.

As the Wagy-Djehutet occurs just over two weeks after New Year's, it has no Tameran equivalent.

Hab Nefer en Opet - *Beautiful Feast of the Residence*

Pa'en Opet 15-26 - August 31-September 11

Opet was a Theban festival that Hatshepsut greatly expanded, if not instituted. The 'Opet', or Residence, refers to the god Amun's shrine in Luxor, a southern district of Thebes. At the time of the Opet observance, Amun-Ra needed rejuvenating; so in a grand procession, his icon traveled from the Karnak temple precincts to Luxor, home of his aspect as 'Amun-em-Opet' (Amun-in-His-Residence) which was related to fertility and renewal. The pharaoh himself (or herself, for Hatshepsut) took part in the procession, which also included soldiers, dignitaries, dancers and musicians, as well as throngs of local citizens. The icons of Mut and Khonsu joined Amun-Ra for the roughly two-mile trip, which made frequent overnight stops at special 'barque shrines' where commoners could petition the gods directly. Once underway again, the spectacle must have resembled modern Mardi Gras or Carnival parades.

Inside the shrine of the Southern Residence, the pharaoh conducted rites before Amun-Ra and Amun-em-Opet that both rejuvenated Amun and imbued the king with Amun's divine power. Thus recharged, Amun-Ra and his entourage made the return trip to Karnak amidst further adulation from the crowds. There were evidently local variations on the Opet around the Theban region; for example, at Deir el-Medina the villagers paraded a statue of the deified king Amunhotep I, patron founder of the community, instead of Amun.

Modern and Tameran equivalents: Today, most holidays are not celebrated for almost two weeks as the original Opet and many other festivals were. However, in the United States and Canada, August 31 often falls during Labor Day weekend; this would be an appropriate time to celebrate the rejuvenation of not just the gods, but also their work-weary devotees. In a Tameran system, Opet would fall about two weeks later, close enough to Mabon (September 21) to be transposed fairly easily. Instead of observing second harvest and the onset of colder weather – which in southern regions of the United States does not occur for at least another month – a Tameran Mabon can mark Amun's, or another Egyptian deity's, annual renewal.

Khenut Hat-Hor - *Sailing (or Navigation) of Hathor*
Hat-Hor 30 - October 16

At her temple in Dendera, Hathor was celebrated throughout the month bearing her name with various small festivals that led to a culminating feast at month's end called the Navigation (or Sailing) of Hathor. She was said to "enter the sky" and people did good deeds in her name. Young girls would take part in the goddess' procession, dancing and shaking sistrums or holding hand mirrors. (Earlier in the month of Hathor, festival processions included objects such as stone or wooden phallic symbols.) At other points in the year and in other parts of Egypt, goddesses such as Mut and Wadjyt also had "Navigation" feasts, as did some male gods such as Ptah, suggesting a recurring theme.

Modern and Tameran equivalents: Since the first edition of this book was originally published, we have held a live-streamed Sailing of Hathor feast during the month of October; however, its close proximity to the Osiris Mysteries and Samhain sometimes makes observing the holiday difficult. (One can get 'burned out' celebrating too many feast days.) But, for those seeking Goddess-specific observances, Hathor has plenty to offer. Mabon falls during the month of Hat-Hor, so observing the Sailing of Hathor then could provide a 'girl power' alternative to the Opet theme.

Khoiakh or **Hab Haker** - *Haker Feast*
(also called 'The Osiris Mysteries')
Ka-Hor-Ka 25-30 - November 10-14

During the Egyptian month of Ka-Hor-Ka the Nile floodwaters finally receded, marking the start of the planting season. Planting was associated with death because seeds, like the dead, had to be buried in order to sprout to new life. Festivals throughout Egypt incorporated the themes of tilling the earth and the journey to the Underworld, such as the Feast of Sokar, which honored the chthonic Lord of Rosetau. But Egypt's festival of the dead *par excellence* was the Haker Feast of Osiris, celebrated at his center of worship in Abydos. Each year, pilgrims from all over the country converged to commemorate Osiris' death and resurrection through processions and re-enactments of what may have been an early passion play.

The parades were led by a masked priest or standard-bearer representing the wolf god Wepwawet, "Opener of the Ways", considered the son of Osiris. The icon statue of Osiris followed in his portable *Neshmet* boat-shrine, into the desert cemeteries which were lined with tablets, statues and cenotaphs of people who hoped to participate spiritually in the 'Great Procession'. Osiris' icon was taken to a tomb shrine, probably the tomb of the First-Dynasty King Djer, where priests performed funerary and other secret rites throughout the night culminating in the raising of a 'Djed' pillar symbolizing the backbone of Osiris. Meanwhile, citizens participated in a mock trial of Osiris' enemies, who were then 'executed' at the riverbank. Finally Osiris, restored from death to eternal life, made a triumphant return to the temple amidst rejoicing crowds.

Modern and Tameran equivalents: The Haker Feast, with its emphasis on commemorating the dead, has similarities with modern festivals of the dead such as All Souls' Day and Samhain. Shifting the date of observance to Halloween, or October 31, would allow for a fairly seamless blending of holidays. (In fact, the Cairo Calendar lists a "Feast of Osiris in Abydos" on Ka-Hor-Ka 10, which is even closer to Halloween.) In a Tameran context, using the Haker Feast of Osiris for Samhain would be a logical choice.

Hab Sed - *Sed Festival*
also **Coronation of the Sacred Falcon, Rebirth Feast of Neheb-Kau**
Ta'ib 1 - November 15

Following the sometimes somber mood of the Haker Feast, Egyptians ended on an upbeat note with celebrations of new life. One of these was the Rebirth Feast of Neheb-Kau, celebrating a lesser-known deity whose name means "*Ka'*s-Assigner" or "Gatherer of *Ka'*s". Other observances continued the Osirian theme by centering on the coronation of his son Horus. At Edfu, a live falcon was taken in a silent, solemn procession along with the icon statue of Horus for the Coronation of the Sacred Falcon. The two were carried by priests wearing falcon and jackal masks to represent the *Ba*'s of Nekhen and Pe respectively. The living falcon was ceremonially crowned, then allowed to live in a special aviary with other falcons who had been crowned in previous years as incarnations of Horus. The celebrations lasted for five days.

Less often, Egyptians celebrated the jubilee of a pharaoh who had ruled for thirty years. The Sed Festival, perhaps meaning "Tail", was meant to renew the king's vigor, and Egypt's by extension. If a king lived long enough to celebrate one Sed jubilee, every three years afterward he would celebrate another. Some pharaohs broke with this tradition, most notably Akhenaton, who made it an annual celebration toward the end of his seventeen-year reign. Celebrations at a Sed Festival involved a renewal or even re-enactment of the king's coronation, as well as ritual actions demonstrating his vigor such as running a circular course, jumping and dancing. Crowds attended some events, and musicians played traditional music. Like the Coronation of the Sacred Falcon, the Sed Festival began on the first day of Ta'ib, the start of the season of Emergence (*Peret*), and lasted for several days.

Modern and Tameran equivalents: Following so closely on the heels of the Haker Feast, the Sed and Coronation Feasts lack an equivalent Sabbat in a Tameran Wiccan system, unless one were to shift them a month later into Yule. Groups that are headed by a pharaoh-figure, such as the Kemetic Orthodox, have dispensed with the thirty-year tradition and celebrate annual Sed feasts centered around their group leader. An alternative observance would be to celebrate the *Hab Sed* of a historical king, as pharaohs' burial inscriptions expressed a common wish to celebrate "millions of *Sed* jubilees" into eternity.

Hab Nakhtiu - *Feast of Victory*
Makhir 21-25 - January 5-9

In the region of Edfu, another sacred drama was performed annually for the local populace as part of the Feast of Victory. An intensely cathartic ritual, the Feast of Victory recounted and dramatized Horus' victory over Seth, who took the form of a hippopotamus and was felled by Horus' harpoons. The Ptolemaic reliefs and inscriptions provide our most complete record of the passion play, as well as the related Legend of the Winged Disk, which was probably recited during the festival. In fact, the passion play was translated and arranged as a modern drama, which was performed at Padgate College in the United Kingdom in 1971. The modern actors faced certain limitations which the ancients evidently did not; at Edfu, a live hippo may have been sacrificed, cooked and distributed to the festival-goers in an act meant to absorb and neutralize Seth's powers.

Modern and Tameran equivalents: Using a July-based calendar, the Feast of Victory falls in early January and could be observed during modern New Year's (January 1) as an occasion to release negativity from the previous year. Using the August-based calendar, however, the date falls almost a month after Christmas. The Feast of Victory could be adapted into a Tameran system, but would involve taking the liberty of bumping it forward a month and observing it in December. But given that Yule Sabbat (in certain traditions) observes the birth of the sun god and eventual return of sunlight, celebrating the victory of Horus of Behdet – himself a solar deity – would make sense.

Hab Min - *Feast of Min*
Pa-Khonsu 1 - March 15

The start of the harvest was another cause for celebration in Egyptian society. The pharaoh would ceremoniously cut the first sheaf of grain amidst ritualized mourning, then offer it to Min, god of fertility. Min's icon, robed in red linen, was carried in procession amidst singing and dancing. Arrows were shot in the four directions (which was also done for many other observances), naked wrestling matches were held, and games involving climbing poles were played. Fertility and sexuality were celebrated in abundance.

Modern and Tameran equivalents: Using a July-based calendar, as the dates given above are, the Feast of Min occurs in mid-March. Using the August-based reference point, it falls at the end of the month. In either case, its most logical Tameran equivalent is Ostara, which is itself a fertility festival.

Hab Nefer en Pa'Inet - *Beautiful Feast of the Valley*
Pa'en Inet 15 - April 28

In Thebes, the Egyptian summertime saw one more festival honoring the blessed dead. But this festival centered on Hathor in her role as Mistress of the West, and was much more upbeat than the Haker Feast. For the Beautiful Feast of the Valley, Amun's icon traveled from Karnak west across the river to a nearby desert valley considered sacred to Hathor. Hatshepsut's famous Deir el-Bahari temple was built to accommodate this procession and Amun's stay in the desert. Meanwhile, families would travel across the river to the cemeteries and bring offerings to the tomb chapels of loved ones. Much beer and wine were drunk in honor of Hathor, as drunkenness was believed to bring people closer to the gods and blessed dead. Families spent the night in the tomb chapels and visited one another to pay their respects.

Echoes of this festival continue today in a local festival honoring a Muslim saint. Villagers parade a boat-shaped cart, echoing Amun's barque shrine, and go to the cemeteries to have picnics. But rather than offer food to the deceased, now considered a pagan practice, modern Egyptians share cooked meals with the area poor and homeless.

Modern and Tameran equivalents: Given its proximity of date, the Beautiful Feast of the Valley would most closely coincide with Beltane (or May Day) on May 1, though its emphasis would be different. Instead of celebrating fertility, a Tameran Beltane/Feast of the Valley would focus upon communion with loved ones.

Hab Nefer en Sekhen - *Beautiful Feast of the Reunion*
Apip 7 - May 20

Many Egyptian festivals re-enacted travels of the gods through processions of their icon statues, but the Beautiful Feast of the Reunion had to be one of the most grand. It celebrated the sacred marriage between Horus of Behdet, enshrined at Edfu, and Hathor of Denderah some 110 miles to the north. Beginning at the first half-moon during Apip, Hathor's icon was loaded onto a river barge and sailed upstream to Edfu, accompanied by a veritable flotilla of priests, dignitaries and well-wishers. At Edfu, Hathor's icon joined Horus' in a special area of the temple where their divine marriage was said to be consummated. Afterward,

Hathor returned home to Denderah to await the birth of their divine child, either Ihy the child-musician or Horus-Sema-Tawy (known in Greek as Harsomtus). The child god's birth was cause for yet more joyous celebration.

Modern and Tameran equivalents: Placing this holiday into a modern calendar presents something of a challenge. Traditionally the Feast of the Reunion began at the first half-moon of Apip; observers today could either wait for the first half-moon in late May or June, or else find a fixed date for the occasion. Because months began at the new moon, the first half-moon would fall about one week later, or around Apip 7. This would be on May 20 on the calendar used here, June 2 if you started from August 1.

For Tameran purposes, this would put the Feast of the Reunion roughly between Beltane and Litha, or Midsummer. Adapting the observance would be up to individual or group discretion. For a Kemetic observance, Memorial Day weekend in the United States or Victoria Day weekend in Canada would be convenient holiday weekends to use for a modern celebration of Horus and Hathor's Reunion.

Hab Nit - *Feast of Neith*
Apip 13 - May 27

This festival, held in the southern Egyptian town of Esna, commemorated a tale about how Neith saved Ra. According to the story, Neith took the form of Mehet-Uret, the "Great Flood" or primeval cow goddess, and lifted Ra above the waters of Nun with her horns to keep him safe from the dangerous crocodiles that were also her children. For the feast, the temple priests lined up in two rows for a purification with water as Neith's statue was taken into the sunlight in her barque shrine. Then there was a great procession, with feasting and singing that lasted long into the night.

Modern and Tameran equivalents: The Feast of Neith could serve as an alternative theme for a Tameran Midsummer, or for a Victoria/Memorial Day weekend observance.

Holidays Not Otherwise Covered

Wiccan readers might notice that no major Egyptian holiday is listed that corresponds to the Wiccan Sabbat of Imbolc, or Candlemas, which occurs on either the first or second day of February. To find a rough equivalent, we must tap into the much broader pool of minor Egyptian festivals. One source of reference for such observances is the Cairo Calendar, a Ptolemaic-era astrological calendar that includes a forecast for each day of the year based on mythological events. Using July 18 as our reference point, February 1 on the Cairo Calendar refers to a "Feast of Nut" – a possible alternative to the Celtic goddess Brighid honored in mainstream Wicca during Imbolc. Alternatively, February 16 was said to be the date on which Isis gave birth to Horus in the Delta marshes (his birth date in the Epagomenal Days notwithstanding), and February 20 on the Cairo Calendar alludes to a "Feast of the Sound Eye [*Udjat*]". Both of these could also provide possible themes for a Tameran Imbolc observance.

Another holiday popular among the Kemetic Orthodox presents its own issues. The "Aset Luminous", from *Isut Ubenut* or "Shining Isis", is generally celebrated in early July, drawing from a relatively obscure feast date reputedly found in the temple of Edfu's liturgical calendar. The event is commonly observed by floating tealight candles onto water in small paper boats (and many lovely photos of these are posted online). But this modern practice is actually reminiscent of elements from two other, better-documented feasts honoring Isis/Aset. One of these, the Hellenic feast day honoring Isis, Mistress of the Seas, took place in March at the start of the sailing season. For this festival, which was celebrated beyond Egypt itself, townspeople would brightly paint a wooden boat and load it with offerings, then push it into the harbor and watch it float to sea as a prayer for safe maritime travel. Meanwhile, Herodotus wrote about a Festival of Light that was celebrated in Sais, in which oil lamps were burned outside people's homes in order to light Isis' way as she searched for the body of Osiris - which is precisely what observers of the Aset Luminous cite as the theme of their holiday. The calendar of Philocalus recorded the date of this festival, called *Lychnapsia* in

Latin, as August 12; interestingly, the Cairo Calendar cites that day as one of 'fighting between Horus and Seth', related to the theme of avenging Osiris. So while the Aset Luminous feast has developed a 'local flavor' among Kemetic Orthodox observers, it has been omitted from the main holiday list here because of its similarities to other, more widely documented feasts honoring the goddess Isis.

One last feast not covered above is the Feast of Drunkenness, which took place on Djchutet 21 (August 7). This festival commemorated the Myth of the Destruction of Mankind, and much beer was consumed to honor and appease Sakhmet, Mut, Bast or Hathor as the Eye of Ra. Hatshepsut's Porch of Drunkenness at the temple of Mut in Karnak was built specifically for this holiday. The raucous feast of Bast described by Herodotus may have been the Bubastis version of the Feast of Drunkenness. Observing this feast today presents more problems than the ancient Egyptians would have had; "drunk chariot-driving" probably didn't happen very often, for one thing. They also did not know alcoholism as we do today. Pagans seeking to maintain sobriety would probably choose to either skip this holiday, or modify it substantially to eliminate the alcohol consumption aspects.

No truly comprehensive calendar of Egyptian holidays exists because no two regions of the country celebrated the same festivals. If you have an interest in feast days honoring a particular deity or tradition not mentioned here, one possible source you can consult is the reproduction of the Cairo Calendar in Ancient Egyptian Magic by Bob Brier. His version of the calendar begins on August 1, but with a little persistence and scratch paper it can be used to reference dates from a July 18 starting point, or anywhere in that vicinity. Other sources can be found in the bibliography of this book. Do your own digging, but be cautious of Web sources, as these are not always as well-documented as printed sources. But above all, have fun! The whole purpose of holidays is celebration, and the ancient Egyptians were known for partying every bit as hard as they worked.

A Tameran Wheel of the Year

My Kemetic readers will probably protest at this point that an Egyptian/Tameran/Kemetic Wheel of the Year - being Eight Sabbats observed at the Solstices, Equinoxes and Cross-Quarters - would be impossible. Indeed, I explained above that the ancient Egyptians had no major observances that coincided neatly with the dates of Yule or Imbolc, and didn't even seem to observe anything especially important at the solstices and equinoxes, unlike the pre-Christian Europeans. But having said that, Wiccans and Pagans in non-specific traditions still regularly ask online for ideas on how to observe Sabbats honoring Egyptian deities. Strict Kemetics always respond with some variation of "there is no Egyptian *insert Sabbat here*", but that doesn't stop the questions from being asked or offer much friendly advice for the people asking. What's more, the popular Tameran Wiccan book Circle of Isis offers a few basic rituals but no comprehensive list for the Wheel of the Year. (Overall I would rate the book as not great, but not bad; their scholarship relies on outdated sources but their personal accounts have a strong 'ring of truth' for the most part.) So Wiccan readers still get left with no template for observing a Tameran liturgical year. Since I cover a Kemetic version in Circle of the Sun, here I offer a Tameran Wiccan version, beginning with Lammas instead of Samhain.

I give a fuller explanation of my version of Quarter Calls, which do not run the typical Deosil (clockwise) direction of traditional Wiccan Quarter Calls, at the end of the next section on Iru for feast days. Feel free to adapt these rituals to your own needs - I keep them fairly general for this reason. Customize them and make them yours.

Lammas (Lughnasadh)

This ritual adapts from a New Year's observance I held with a local coven. The focal point of our altar was a pyramid, which is fairly easy to find in metaphysical or novelty stores. If you wish to enact the Subduing of Apophis, prepare beforehand by cutting out green paper snakes and establishing a safe place outdoors to burn them, such as a cauldron or barbecue pit.

Opening: "This is the time of year when the days are hottest and the sun seems at its strongest. But from the midst of the dryness and the heat comes a new beginning."

Purifying the Quarters - *Have each caller sprinkle water and a pinch of natron. If observing solo, walk to each quarter, sprinkle your offerings or place them in a dish, and recite the calls.*

East Caller: Duamutef, Adoring His Mother! You live on Ma'at and lean on your staff as watchman of the East! You are purified with natron, you are purified with water.

All: Hail and be welcome!

West Caller: Qebehsenuef, who Cools His Brothers! You live on Ma'at and lean on your staff as watchman of the West! You are purified with natron, you are purified with water.

All: Hail and be welcome!

North Caller: Hapy, He of Haste! You live on Ma'at and lean on your staff as watchman of the North! You are purified with natron, you are purified with water.

All: Hail and be welcome!

South Caller: Imsety, He of the Dill! You live on Ma'at and lean on your staff as watchman of the South! You are purified with natron, you are purified with water.

All: Hail and be welcome!

(To be read by either a Priest and Priestess, single officiant or solo observer where appropriate.)

Invocation to the God: Ra, Lord of the Nine, Lord of Life! Come in peace, turn Your face toward us.

All: Hail and be welcome!

Invocation to the Goddess: Sakhmet, Lady of Flame, the Eye of Ra! Come in peace, turn Your face toward us.

All: Hail and be welcome!

Main address: *To be read by either the officiant, or yourself if observing solo.*

"The Egyptian New Year, or Upet Ronpet, was considered the anniversary of creation. At the beginning of time, called the First Occasion, the sun god Ra emerged from the dark waters of chaos in the glory of the first sunrise. His birth established order, or Ma'at, over chaos. An important symbol of his worship was a shape representing the first mound of earth to emerge from the floodwaters, from which Ra was born. We know that shape as the pyramid."

Ritual Work: *Again, I'm leaving this part open for personalization. However, since the theme is Egyptian New Year's, now would be an ideal time to re-consecrate your altar statues using the Opening of the Mouth rite from pages 168-9, which is what we did when we performed this ritual in 2009. You can honor Sakhmet with hymns, chants or drumming. Another major theme of the day, which we observed and I include below, is the ritual destruction of Apophis.*

Rite of Subduing Apophis: *(Officiant reads this aloud if part of a group)*

"Another New Year's tradition was the ritual Subduing of Apophis. This terrible serpent of chaos tries to swallow Ra in His sun boat every night - but is defeated, thanks to the Goddesses of the Eye and to Ra's followers. At New Year's, Egyptians would burn an effigy of Apophis, to show their support of Ra and the order of the cosmos. As we pass around paper effigies of Apophis, write on them the negative things in your life you wish to be rid of this year."

(Once everyone is finished writing, light a fire in the cauldron or other fire area. Drop the paper snakes into the fire to burn completely.)

Officiant (or self): *Im ran en Ra, hu-nu Sebiu* - In the name of Ra, we smite the Evil One. So mote it be! (Other participants can respond with "So mote it be.")

Closing address: "Ra, Lord of the Horizon, we wish You happy birthday and ask You to see us through another year. Please help us to grow in wisdom as we continue Your work of Ma'at. Remember us, be where You like, and come again out of Your kindness toward us. *Seneb-ti!*"

Closing of the Quarters: *to be said by Quarter-callers; italics repeated by all*
East: Duamutef, Adoring His Mother! We thank you and wish you well. *Seneb-ti!*

West: Qebehsenuef, who Cools His Brothers! We thank you and wish you well. *Seneb-ti!*

North: Hapy, He of Haste! We thank you and wish you well. *Seneb-ti!*

South: Imsety, He of the Dill! We thank you and wish you well. *Seneb-ti!*

If observing as a group, make sure everyone can read from this final address. If reading solo, change pronouns where needed:

All: "As we leave to follow our separate paths, may we find our way back to this Circle, always sharing the Gods' blessings of life, vitality and health. *Seneb-ti!*"

End of ritual

Mabon

This ritual is based on the Opet Feast and honors Amun-Ra as the Lord and Mut as the Lady; if you prefer to work with different deities or give the Goddess a stronger role, you can re-tool it to invoke Hathor, Mistress of the North Wind and pattern it after the Navigation of Hathor, keeping Ra's role for the equinox largely the same.

Opening: "The heat of summer lingers still, but Ra is balanced in the midpoint of His course on this autumnal equinox. We honor His aspect as Amun-Ra, Lord of Opet, and His Lady as Mut, Queen of the Gods."

Purifying the Quarters - *Have each caller sprinkle water and a pinch of natron. If observing solo, walk to each quarter, sprinkle your offerings or place them in a dish, and recite the calls.*

North Caller: Hail, Good Power, Beautiful Rudder of the Northern Sky! You are purified with natron, you are purified with water.

All: Hail and be welcome!

West Caller: Hail, Circler of Heaven, Guide of the Two Lands, Beautiful Rudder of the Western Sky! You are purified with natron, you are purified with water.

All: Hail and be welcome!

East Caller: Hail, Transfigured One Before the Temples of the Gods, Beautiful Rudder of the Eastern Sky! You are purified with natron, you are purified with water.

All: Hail and be welcome!

South Caller: Hail, Foremost Before the Temple Sands,

Beautiful Rudder of the Southern Sky! You are purified with natron, you are purified with water.

All: Hail and be welcome!

(To be read by either a Priest and Priestess, single officiant or solo observer where appropriate.)

Invocation to the God: Amun-Ra, King of the Gods, Lord of Life! Come in peace, turn Your face toward us.

All: Hail and be welcome!

Invocation to the Goddess: Mut, Queen of the Gods, Great Mother! Come in peace, turn Your face toward us.

All: Hail and be welcome!

Main address: *To be read by either the officiant, or yourself if observing solo.*

"In ancient Thebes, the Opet Feast was a time when Amun-Ra visited His southern sanctuary - called *Ipet-Sut*, source of the name 'Opet' - to rejuvenate Himself. His consort Mut, Queen of the Gods, joined Him in secret rites of consecration. During the festival, the mortal pharaoh would perform mysteries to be consecrated as Son of Amun, partaking in His divine nature.

"Today, with the sun balanced in the autumnal equinox, we stand between worlds and seek to enter the mysteries of Amun and Mut, the Lord and Lady. We dedicate ourselves to follow what paths They have laid for us, and partake of Their bounty as the Gods' *shemsu*, or followers."

Ritual Work: *In the Kemetic Opet ritual, we re-consecrate ourselves as followers of the Gods, partaking of bread and water or wine from Amun's altar and anointing ourselves with sacred oil. You can use this as a time for initiations, thanksgiving (but as mentioned earlier, take cues from your local climate and growing conditions - try to stick with produce that's actually in* *season), or drumming and dancing if you prefer. If focusing on Hathor, read hymns to the Goddess or make music in Her honor.*

Closing address: "Hail, oh Amun-Ra, Lord of Heaven and Lord of the Two Lands! Hail, Mut, Queen of the Gods and Lady of the Two Lands! Now we must pass from the realm of Your mysteries back to the realm of everyday, but we ask that You continue to guide us and keep us. Remember us, be where You like, and may You come again in kindness toward us. *Seneb-ti!*"

Closing of the Quarters: *to be said by Quarter-callers; italics repeated by all*

North: Good Power, Beautiful Rudder of the Northern Sky! We thank you and wish you well. *Seneb-ti!*

West: Circler of Heaven, Guide of the Two Lands, Beautiful Rudder of the Western Sky! We thank you and wish you well. *Seneb-ti!*

East: Transfigured One Before the Temples of the Gods, Beautiful Rudder of the Eastern Sky! We thank you and wish you well. *Seneb-ti!*

South: Foremost Before the Temple Sands, Beautiful Rudder of the Southern Sky! We thank you and wish you well. *Seneb-ti!*

If observing as a group, make sure everyone can read from this final address. If reading solo, change pronouns where needed:

All: "As we leave to follow our separate paths, may we find our way back to this Circle, always sharing the Gods' blessings of life, vitality and health. *Seneb-ti!*"

End of ritual

Samhain

This is another ritual adapted from one I hosted with the local coven, photos of which also appear in <u>Circle of the Sun</u>. Pagans who feel a close relationship to Seth may disagree with the main address given here. You can simply omit that clause, or consult the Sokar ritual in <u>Circle</u>, which was written to celebrate with friends who honored Seth as their Patron.

Opening: "The heat of summer and early autumn is finally loosening its grip, and the leaves begin to turn golden hues. But the change on the wind carries bitter notes, for Osiris has gone to *Duat*, and the tears of Isis fall like autumn rain."

Purifying the Quarters - *Have each caller sprinkle water and a pinch of natron. If observing solo, walk to each quarter, sprinkle your offerings or place them in a dish, and recite the calls.*

East Caller: Duamutef, Adoring His Mother! You live on Ma'at and lean on your staff as watchman of the East! You are purified with natron, you are purified with water.

All: Hail and be welcome!

West Caller: Qebehsenuef, who Cools His Brothers! You live on Ma'at and lean on your staff as watchman of the West! You are purified with natron, you are purified with water.

All: Hail and be welcome!

North Caller: Hapy, He of Haste! You live on Ma'at and lean on your staff as watchman of the North! You are purified with natron, you are purified with water.

All: Hail and be welcome!

South Caller: Imsety, He of the Dill! You live on Ma'at and lean on your staff as watchman of the South! You are purified with natron, you are purified with water.

All: Hail and be welcome!

(To be read by either a Priest and Priestess, single officiant or solo observer where appropriate.)

Invocation to the God: Osiris, Lord of *Duat*, Lord of Eternity! Come in peace, turn Your face toward us.

All: Hail and be welcome!

Invocation to the Goddess: Isis, Lady of Life, Mother of Horus! Come in peace, turn Your face toward us.

All: Hail and be welcome!

Main address: *To be read by either the officiant, or yourself if observing solo.*

"The Haker Feast of Osiris, also called the Festival of Khoiakh, was one of the most important observances in ancient Egypt. It commemorated the death and resurrection of Osiris, the Corn King and Lord of the Dead who had been murdered by his jealous brother Seth. In ancient times, pilgrims from across Egypt would travel to the sacred city of Abydos to participate in the festival. A common prayer for the dead asked that their spirits continue to join Osiris in the Haker Feast throughout eternity.

"Osiris, Lord of the *Duat*, we gather this night to remember Your passage from this world to the next, for You alone among the Gods know the bitter taste of death. We ask You to welcome into Your Fields of Peace our loved ones who have shared with You that bitter taste."

Ritual Work: *When we observed this ritual in 2008, we performed the Opening of the Mouth rite (pgs. 168-9) on the statue of Osiris and had two ladies read from the Lamentations of Isis and Nephthys, given on pages 254-56 . If your physical space allows for it, another very powerful ritual element we used in a Kemetic version was a tent enclosure representing the tomb* *of Osiris. Inside the tent, we performed the Opening of the Mouth, then sat in silent communion with our loved ones before smashing a red clay pot to symbolize the defeat of chaos. The first time we observed it was especially moving.*

Closing address: "Osiris, You rule the next world as You ruled this one, with justice and plenty for all creatures. Please bless with Your enduring spirit those who have gone West to meet You, and help us to live justly and equitably; so that one day we will meet You with pure hearts and straight eyes. Remember us, be where You like, and come again out of Your kindness toward us. *Seneb-ti!*" *(Participants can also respond with, "So mote it be.")*

Closing of the Quarters: *to be said by Quarter-callers; italics repeated by all*

East: Duamutef, Adoring His Mother! We thank you and wish you well. *Seneb-ti!*

West: Qebehsenuef, who Cools His Brothers! We thank you and wish you well. *Seneb-ti!*

North: Hapy, He of Haste! We thank you and wish you well. *Seneb-ti!*

South: Imsety, He of the Dill! We thank you and wish you well. *Seneb-ti!*

If observing as a group, make sure everyone can read from this final address. If reading solo, change pronouns where needed:

All: "As we leave to follow our separate paths, may we find our way back to this Circle, always sharing the Gods' blessings of life, vitality and health. *Seneb-ti!*"

End of ritual

Yule

Despite whatever you may have read online, Horus was NOT born on December 25th, nor at the winter solstice (and certainly not to a virgin). But searching for a suitable Yule theme, I found the most logical choice in the Coronation of the Sacred Falcon, which honors Horus and Sakhmet. As described above, you could also invoke Isis if you made the Feast of Victory over Seth your primary theme, perhaps paralleling the battle between the Holly King and the Oak King.

Opening: "The air grows chill, and Ra's light has reached its shortest point on this winter solstice. But the light will soon return, for Horus comes as king of the living, aided by Sakhmet, the Eye of Ra!"

Purifying the Quarters - *Have each caller sprinkle water and a pinch of natron. If observing solo, walk to each quarter, sprinkle your offerings or place them in a dish, and recite the calls.*

East Caller: Duamutef, Adoring His Mother! You live on Ma'at and lean on your staff as watchman of the East! You are purified with natron, you are purified with water.

All: Hail and be welcome!

West Caller: Qebehsenuef, who Cools His Brothers! You live on Ma'at and lean on your staff as watchman of the West! You are purified with natron, you are purified with water.

All: Hail and be welcome!

North Caller: Hapy, He of Haste! You live on Ma'at and lean on your staff as watchman of the North! You are purified with natron, you are purified with water.

All: Hail and be welcome!

South Caller: Imsety, He of the Dill! You live on Ma'at and lean on your staff as watchman of the South! You are purified with natron, you are purified with water.

All: Hail and be welcome!

(To be read by either a Priest and Priestess, single officiant or solo observer where appropriate.)

Invocation to the God: Horus, Lord of the Living, Sun Child born of Isis! Come in peace, turn Your face toward us.

All: Hail and be welcome!

Invocation to the Goddess: Sakhmet, Lady of Flame, Guardian of Horus! Come in peace, turn Your face toward us.

All: Hail and be welcome!

Main address: *To be read by either the officiant, or yourself if observing solo.*

"At Samhain, we crowned Osiris as Lord of *Duat*, the Underworld. But now His son Horus, who represents the reborn sun, comes forth to rule the living. Guarding Him is Sakhmet, the Eye of Ra. At the temple of Edfu, litanies to Sakhmet were chanted at the Coronation of the Sacred Falcon, asking her to protect Horus as the 'sprout of Sakhmet'.

"As we mark this longest night of the year, let us celebrate Horus, the new king, with all that is good in our lives. Let us praise Lady Sakhmet, Mistress of Flame!"

Ritual Work: *In Hab Sed feasts, we wrote down good news or positive things in our lives, which would be an excellent activity here as well. You can perform an execration rite, especially if drawing upon the Feast of Victory theme. If holding a ritual outdoors, try incorporating a bonfire. You can also ring sistrums in the four directions and offer prayers and hymns to Sakhmet.*

Closing address: "Oh Horus, Lord of the Two Lands, Son of Osiris and Isis! We ask that You guide us with Your light upon our paths. Lady Sakhmet, we ask that You guard us and protect us as You protect Horus, so that we may be 'made whole for life'. May You both remember us, be where You like, and come again in kindness toward us. *Seneb-ti!*"

Closing of the Quarters: *to be said by Quarter-callers; italics repeated by all*

East: Duamutef, Adoring His Mother! We thank you and wish you well. *Seneb-ti!*

West: Qebehsenuef, who Cools His Brothers! We thank you and wish you well. *Seneb-ti!*

North: Hapy, He of Haste! We thank you and wish you well. *Seneb-ti!*

South: Imsety, He of the Dill! We thank you and wish you well. *Seneb-ti!*

If observing as a group, make sure everyone can read from this final address. If reading solo, change pronouns where needed:

All: "As we leave to follow our separate paths, may we find our way back to this Circle, always sharing the Gods' blessings of life, vitality and health. *Seneb-ti!*"

End of ritual

Imbolc

I finally found an appropriate reference for this Sabbat in the (somewhat obscure) "Great Burning" feast - a Festival of Lights, fitting for the fire themes of Imbolc. In our Kemetic Reform group, it becomes the Feast of Makhir. Here it takes on a Tameran Wiccan format. This version invokes Sakhmet, but any Eye of Ra Goddess can be invoked.

Opening: "The air grows warmer, and signs of spring are beginning to appear, while we have reached the mid-point of the Tameran year. It is time to celebrate what has come to pass, and look ahead to what will be."

Purifying the Quarters - *Have each caller sprinkle water and a pinch of natron. If observing solo, walk to each quarter, sprinkle your offerings or place them in a dish, and recite the calls.*

North Caller: Hail, Good Power, Beautiful Rudder of the Northern Sky! You are purified with natron, you are purified with water.

All: Hail and be welcome!

West Caller: Hail, Circler of Heaven, Guide of the Two Lands, Beautiful Rudder of the Western Sky! You are purified with natron, you are purified with water.

All: Hail and be welcome!

East Caller: Hail, Transfigured One Before the Temples of the Gods, Beautiful Rudder of the Eastern Sky! You are purified with natron, you are purified with water.

All: Hail and be welcome!

South Caller: Hail, Foremost Before the Temple Sands,

Beautiful Rudder of the Southern Sky! You are purified with natron, you are purified with water.

All: Hail and be welcome!

(To be read by either a Priest and Priestess, single officiant or solo observer where appropriate.)

Invocation to the God: Ra, Lord of the Nine who shines in the Boat of Millions! Come in peace, turn Your face toward us.

All: Hail and be welcome!

Invocation to the Goddess: Sakhmet, Lady of Flame, Great Eye of Ra! Come in peace, turn Your face toward us.

All: Hail and be welcome!

Main address: *To be read by either the officiant, or yourself if observing solo.*

"For the ancient Egyptians, mid-year was an important time to honor the Gods. The Book of the Dead speaks of 'filling the Sacred Eye in Heliopolis on the second month of winter, last day'. That Sacred Eye symbolizes the daughter of Ra, His Eye, which we know as Sakhmet, Bast, Hathor, and Tefnut. Ra rejoices when His Eye returns to Him, for She makes Him complete.

"Hail unto You, Great Goddess of the Eye, and hail unto Ra, who sails forth in joy! We rejoice with the Ennead, for You have been made whole again."

Ritual Work: *For the Kemetic Feast of Makhir, we offer "white loaves" and incense to a painted image of the* Udjat *eye, which in this case represents the Eye of Ra. Milk offerings, traditional to Imbolc, would also be appropriate here. You can also perform divination, pass out candles, sweet pastries (the 'white loaves') and wine, drum or chant to honor the Goddess, and so on.*

Closing address: "Oh Ra, Lord of the Ennead who placed Your daughter upon Your brow, and Sakhmet, Great One who shines in brilliance as the Eye of Ra, we thank You for being with us on this day. May You continue to shine upon us as You traverse the sky each day, and light our paths with Your wisdom. Remember us, be where you like, and come again out of your kindness toward us. *Seneb-ti!*"

Closing of the Quarters: *to be said by Quarter-callers; italics repeated by all*

North: Good Power, Beautiful Rudder of the Northern Sky! We thank you and wish you well. *Seneb-ti!*

West: Circler of Heaven, Guide of the Two Lands, Beautiful Rudder of the Western Sky! We thank you and wish you well. *Seneb-ti!*

East: Transfigured One Before the Temples of the Gods, Beautiful Rudder of the Eastern Sky! We thank you and wish you well. *Seneb-ti!*

South: Foremost Before the Temple Sands, Beautiful Rudder of the Southern Sky! We thank you and wish you well. *Seneb-ti!*

If observing as a group, make sure everyone can read from this final address. If reading solo, change pronouns where needed:

All: "As we leave to follow our separate paths, may we find our way back to this Circle, always sharing the Gods' blessings of life, vitality and health. *Seneb-ti!*"

End of ritual

Ostara

This version of Ostara uses the Feast of Min as its template; in its ancient version, Isis acted as both mother and consort to Min, which is perhaps the closest parallel in Egyptian religion to the Wiccan concept of Goddess as mother-consort. Again, if you work with different deities, here you could honor Ra and Bast (who has a feast day in March) or Amun and Mut in a similar manner.

Opening: "Ra is again in balance as we mark the vernal equinox. Green plants emerge with vigor, and we celebrate this vitality in Min, Bull of His Mother, and Isis, Lady of Life."

Purifying the Quarters - *Have each caller sprinkle water and a pinch of natron. If observing solo, walk to each quarter, sprinkle your offerings or place them in a dish, and recite the calls.*

East Caller: Duamutef, Adoring His Mother! You live on Ma'at and lean on your staff as watchman of the East! You are purified with natron, you are purified with water.

All: Hail and be welcome!

West Caller: Qebehsenuef, who Cools His Brothers! You live on Ma'at and lean on your staff as watchman of the West! You are purified with natron, you are purified with water.

All: Hail and be welcome!

North Caller: Hapy, He of Haste! You live on Ma'at and lean on your staff as watchman of the North! You are purified with natron, you are purified with water.

All: Hail and be welcome!

South Caller: Imsety, He of the Dill! You live on Ma'at and lean on your staff as watchman of the South! You are purified with natron, you are purified with water.

All: Hail and be welcome!

(To be read by either a Priest and Priestess, single officiant or solo observer where appropriate.)

Invocation to the God: Min, You with the upraised arm, born of Isis! Come in peace, turn Your face toward us.

All: Hail and be welcome!

Invocation to the Goddess: Isis, Lady of the Throne and Mother of the God! Come in peace, turn Your face toward us.

All: Hail and be welcome!

Main address: *To be read by either the officiant, or yourself if observing solo.*

"In Egypt's desert climate, this time of year when the sun grows warmer marks the beginning of the harvest. The ancients would offer the first sheaf of grain, which grew from the buried seed of Osiris, to Min, who represents the son born from the seed. They also honored Isis, eternal Goddess who is both mother and consort, great Lady who is the seat of all life.

"Today, this is the time of year when we harvest our winter crops and sow seeds for spring...or, instead of sowing crops, we are nearly through a school year, or perhaps busy with other tasks. But Min still rules our work, for He is the Lord of all that comes to fruition. Let us celebrate the good things that have already come to us, and seek the Lord and Lady's blessings for those things that have not yet come to pass."

Ritual Work: *In the ancient feast, a pole was raised for Min - so instead of a* May*-pole at Beltane, you could decorate a* Min*-pole for Ostara with red ribbons. You could also do a spiral dance, letting the ladies lead in honor of Isis who dances before Min. Red ribbons symbolize Min's power, so you can also tie red ribbon around participants' heads (your own if working solo). Since the original feast was a harvest festival, you can offer tokens of projects that have been completed, or ask for blessings on things nearing completion (students will probably have plenty* *of these at this time of year). Read prayers or hymns to Min and Isis. If you have it, offer myrrh incense, which is particularly favored by Min.*

Closing address: "Hail, oh Min, Great Bull of His Mother! Hail, Lady Isis, Great Throne who raises up the lands! We thank You for the blessings You have given us, and seek Your guidance for all the work that we continue to do. May You bless the fruits of our efforts with goodness and abundance. Remember us, be where You like, and may You come again in kindness toward us. *Seneb-ti!*"

Closing of the Quarters: *to be said by Quarter-callers; italics repeated by all*
East: Duamutef, Adoring His Mother! We thank you and wish you well. *Seneb-ti!*

West: Qebehsenuef, who Cools His Brothers! We thank you and wish you well. *Seneb-ti!*

North: Hapy, He of Haste! We thank you and wish you well. *Seneb-ti!*

South: Imsety, He of the Dill! We thank you and wish you well. *Seneb-ti!*

If observing as a group, make sure everyone can read from this final address. If reading solo, change pronouns where needed:
All: "As we leave to follow our separate paths, may we find our way back to this Circle, always sharing the Gods' blessings of life, vitality and health. *Seneb-ti!*"

End of ritual

Beltane

This ritual draws from an observance of the Beautiful Feast of the Valley we held in 2008. Just as the traditional Wiccan Beltane mirrors Samhain, a time when the veils between worlds are thinnest and magick is afoot, this Tameran version honors one of the more upbeat Egyptian feasts of the dead.

Opening: "The trees and fields are in full dress, and summer's heat is nearly upon us. The Lord, as Amun, comes to visit Hathor, Lady of the West. When we open our senses, we can feel Their powers of life and rebirth within us."

Purifying the Quarters - *Have each caller sprinkle water and a pinch of natron. If observing solo, walk to each quarter, sprinkle your offerings or place them in a dish, and recite the calls.*

East Caller: Duamutef, Adoring His Mother! You live on Ma'at and lean on your staff as watchman of the East! You are purified with natron, you are purified with water.

All: Hail and be welcome!

West Caller: Qebehsenuef, who Cools His Brothers! You live on Ma'at and lean on your staff as watchman of the West! You are purified with natron, you are purified with water.

All: Hail and be welcome!

North Caller: Hapy, He of Haste! You live on Ma'at and lean on your staff as watchman of the North! You are purified with natron, you are purified with water.

All: Hail and be welcome!

South Caller: Imsety, He of the Dill! You live on Ma'at and lean on your staff as watchman of the South! You are purified with natron, you are purified with water.

All: Hail and be welcome!

(To be read by either a Priest and Priestess, single officiant or solo observer where appropriate.)

Invocation to the God: Amun, Lord of the City of the Scepter, Lord of Life! Come in peace, turn Your face toward us.

All: Hail and be welcome!

Invocation to the Goddess: Hathor, Lady of the West, Great Mother who is the source of Life! Come in peace, turn Your face toward us.

All: Hail and be welcome!

Main address: *To be read by either the officiant, or yourself if observing solo.*

"The Beautiful Feast of the Valley began as a folk festival almost four thousand years ago in Thebes. It was a celebration of the dead in which Amun, Lord of the living, visited Hathor, Lady of the West, in her sacred desert valley. During the Feast of the Valley, families would leave offerings at the tombs of their loved ones. But this was not a somber holiday; Egyptians believed the music, dancing and drunkenness so sacred to Hathor would bring them closer to their loved ones who were with the gods.

"Lady Hathor, Mistress of the Sycamore! You rejuvenate life, and You guide us through Your realm of ecstasy into the realm of Sacred. As we commune with You this night, pass on our love and laughter to our blessed dead who are in Your care. And when it comes our time to fly West with the setting sun, may You guide us safely through the night and back to them."

Ritual Work: *The main portion of our original ritual was quite simple, involving an offering to the blessed dead, smashing a plate - always the most memorable part for participants! - and singing "We All Come From the Goddess". Offerings, especially* *water libations, drumming and chanting or singing to raise energy would be especially appropriate here.*

Closing address: "Amun, Lord of Thebes, and Hathor, Lady of the West, we humbly thank You for Your presence and Your blessings. Help us to remember that our family and friends may pass on, but they are never far from us. Remember us, be where you like, and come again out of your kindness toward us. *Seneb-ti!*"

Closing of the Quarters: *to be said by Quarter-callers; italics repeated by all*
East: Duamutef, Adoring His Mother! We thank you and wish you well. *Seneb-ti!*

West: Qebehsenuef, who Cools His Brothers! We thank you and wish you well. *Seneb-ti!*

North: Hapy, He of Haste! We thank you and wish you well. *Seneb-ti!*

South: Imsety, He of the Dill! We thank you and wish you well. *Seneb-ti!*

If observing as a group, make sure everyone can read from this final address. If reading solo, change pronouns where needed:

All: "As we leave to follow our separate paths, may we find our way back to this Circle, always sharing the Gods' blessings of life, vitality and health. *Seneb-ti!*"

End of ritual

Litha

This ritual uses the Feast of the Beautiful Reunion as its basis. Horus and Hathor, both being solar deities, fit the traditional Litha theme of fire quite well. While mainstream Pagan correspondences typically associate myrrh incense with the element of water, in ancient texts myrrh was specifically offered to Hathor during the Reunion Feast; if you can obtain some, include it in offerings during the Ritual Work.

Opening: "This day marks the Summer Solstice, when Ra is at His highest in the sky. On this longest day of the year, Hathor, the Eye of Ra and Queen of Love, rejoices with Horus, Lord of Life."

Purifying the Quarters - *Have each caller sprinkle water and a pinch of natron. If observing solo, walk to each quarter, sprinkle your offerings or place them in a dish, and recite the calls.*

East Caller: Duamutef, Adoring His Mother! You live on Ma'at and lean on your staff as watchman of the East! You are purified with natron, you are purified with water.

All: Hail and be welcome!

West Caller: Qebehsenuef, who Cools His Brothers! You live on Ma'at and lean on your staff as watchman of the West! You are purified with natron, you are purified with water.

All: Hail and be welcome!

North Caller: Hapy, He of Haste! You live on Ma'at and lean on your staff as watchman of the North! You are purified with natron, you are purified with water.

All: Hail and be welcome!

South Caller: Imsety, He of the Dill! You live on Ma'at and lean on your staff as watchman of the South! You are purified with natron, you are purified with water.

All: Hail and be welcome!

(To be read by either a Priest and Priestess, single officiant or solo observer where appropriate.)

Invocation to the God: Horus, Lord of the Two Lands, Lord of Life! Come in peace, turn Your face toward us.

All: Hail and be welcome!

Invocation to the Goddess: Hathor, Mistress of Love, Lady of Gold! Come in peace, turn Your face toward us.

All: Hail and be welcome!

Main address: *To be read by either the officiant, or yourself if observing solo.*

"In ancient times, Hathor would sail from Her home in Dendera to visit Her husband Horus at His temple of Edfu amidst joyous celebration. Today, we celebrate all forms of love which, so long as they remain true, are equal in the eyes of the Gods.

"Oh Horus, Falcon of Dappled Plumage! We honor You as King of the Two Lands, Sun King at the peak of His powers! Hathor, oh Golden One who loves the sweet scent of myrrh, bless us with Your love!"

Ritual Work: *We observed a Kemetic version of this holiday in 2016, which included a couple of lovely and moving prayers to Hathor contributed by members of the online Kemetic Reform group. If you have a sistrum, shake it in honor of Hathor, or in the Four Directions to announce Horus' kingship; incorporate a spiral dance, a bonfire, or whatever else inspiration and resources allow.*

Closing address: "Horus, Lord of the Two Lands, and Hathor, Lady of Love, we humbly thank You for Your presence on this Summer Solstice. Bless us with Your love and guidance on this day and throughout the year. Remember us, be where you like, and come again out of your kindness toward us. *Seneb-ti!*"

Closing of the Quarters: *to be said by Quarter-callers; italics repeated by all*
East: Duamutef, Adoring His Mother! We thank you and wish you well. *Seneb-ti!*

West: Qebehsenuef, who Cools His Brothers! We thank you and wish you well. *Seneb-ti!*

North: Hapy, He of Haste! We thank you and wish you well. *Seneb-ti!*

South: Imsety, He of the Dill! We thank you and wish you well. *Seneb-ti!*

If observing as a group, make sure everyone can read from this final address. If reading solo, change pronouns where needed:

All: "As we leave to follow our separate paths, may we find our way back to this Circle, always sharing the Gods' blessings of life, vitality and health. *Seneb-ti!*"

End of ritual

An *Iru* Template for Holidays

Now that we've covered some Tameran Wiccan ritual formats, let's explore a longer *Iru* format for more Kemetic-specific observances. As with the Wiccan rituals, this *Iru* leaves room for personalizing and improvisation; in the "Reading of Sacred Texts", for example, you can either read something from a translated ancient text, or your own prayers and hymns. If you're observing the Osiris Mysteries or the Feast of Victory and don't want to use an invocation naming Seth, use the Alternate Invocation instead. If you plan to do a group activity, or else private energy or spell work, simply incorporate that into the "Reading of Sacred Texts".

Extended *Iru*

(light candles, ring sistrum to start)

Opening Invocation:

Great Ennead of the Gods who are in Iunu!

Ra, in Your appearance at the First Time,

Ra's twins, Shu and Tefnut,

Geb and Nut, Lord of Earth and Lady of Heaven;

Osir, Isut, Set and Nebet-Hat,

Turn Your Faces toward us!

Our hearts are straight, our hearts are open,

No darkness is in our hearts!

Offering:

Water: "Take these, Your cool waters that are the Inundation."

Natron: "This is Your natron of Horus, this is Your natron of Djehuty, this is Your natron among the gods'."

Milk: "Milk, milk, may You taste it in Your shrine."

Incense: "I give You incense, I give You incense, great of purity."

Oil: "Receive this oil upon You, and Your scent will be sweet like Ra when he emerges from the Horizon."

Linen: "Receive this, Your dazzling garment from Ta'it-Town."

Food offering: "Take this, Your bread on which gods live."

Reversion of Offerings: "Turn Yourself to these, Your offerings; receive them from me."

Reading of Sacred Texts
Prayer (or **Voice Offering)**

Closing Invocation:
Great Ennead of the gods who are in Iunu!
Ra, Shu and Tefnut;
Geb and Nut, Osir and Isut, Set and Nebet-Hat;
We thank You and wish You well!
Remember us, be where You like, and come again in kindness!

In-un-Ma'a [Truly it Is]
Alternate Invocation:
Great and Little Enneads of the Gods!

Lords of Ma'at, united in Ma'at,

Great Ones who reject wrongdoing!

Assemble before the Lord of All,

And turn Your faces toward us!

Our hearts are straight, our hearts are open,

No darkness is in our hearts!

Alternate Closing:

Great and Little Enneads of the Gods!

Great Ones before the Lord of All;

We thank You and wish You well!

Remember us, be where You like, and come again in kindness!

Tameran Quarter Calls

The Egyptians did not perceive the world as being made of a system of five elements, as did the Greeks. Thus, they did not have elements assigned to each of the Four Directions, which today are invoked during Wiccan Quarter Calls. However, the Egyptians did have deities and demi-gods who were associated with the four cardinal directions, so as we saw above with the Wheel of the Year, it is certainly possible to adapt a Tameran system of Quarter Calls for casting a circle. Recall, though, that the Egyptians did not picture their directions in the same order that we do. The order they seemed to use was either counter-clockwise (widdershins), or a cross pattern, which does not correspond with the typical clockwise circle used in Wicca. If you'll be hosting a group ritual, advise Quarter-callers ahead of time to avoid confusion.

The Four Sons of Horus: (E W N S)

"Duamutef [doo-AH-mew-TEFF], Adoring His Mother! You live on Ma'at and lean on your staff as watchman of the East!"

"Qebehsenuef [KEB-uh-SEN-yoo-eff], who Cools His Brothers! You live on Ma'at and lean on your staff as watchman of the West!"

"Hapy [HAH-pee], He of Haste! You live on Ma'at and lean on your staff as watchman of the North!"

"Imsety [im-SET-ee], He of the Dill! You live on Ma'at and lean on your staff as watchman of the South!"

The Four Rudders of Heaven (N W E S)

"Hail, Good Power, Beautiful Rudder of the Northern Sky."

"Hail, Circler of Heaven, Guide of the Two Lands, Beautiful Rudder of the Western Sky."

"Hail, Transfigured One Before the Temples of the Gods, Beautiful Rudder of the Eastern Sky."

"Hail, Foremost Before the Temple Sands, Beautiful Rudder of the Southern Sky."

The Four Powers of Heaven (N W S E)

"Hail, Gods Above the Earth, Guides of Duat."

"Hail, Divine Mothers Above the Earth, Who Are in the Necropolis and the House of Osiris."

"Hail, Gods, Guides of the Sacred Land, Who Are Above the Earth, Guides of Duat."

"Hail, Followers of Ra, Ones of Strength in Osiris."

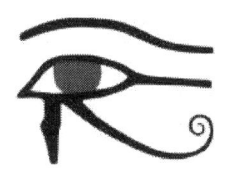

Some Sacred Texts

What follows below is but a mere sampling of the literature left to us by the ancient Egyptians. We can only imagine what vast libraries of religious books were had in ancient times, but what remains to us today speaks volumes about their sense of ethics and faith. Even their Instructional literature, which was copies by schoolboys learning to write, stresses the value of piety and honoring the gods. The selections below are adapted from Ancient Egyptian Literature, vols. I-II by Miriam Lichtheim. You can find more hymns in Circle of the Sun.

Monologue of Ra (*from Coffin Text 1130*)

Words spoken by Ra:

"Hail in peace! I repeat to you the good deeds which my own heart did for me from within the serpent's coil, in order to silence strife. I did four good deeds within the *akhet*:

I made the four winds, that every man might breathe in his time. This is one of the deeds.

I made the Inundation, that the humble might benefit by it like the great. This is one of the deeds.

I made every man like his fellow, and I did not command that they do wrong. It is their hearts that disobey what I have said. This is one of the deeds.

I made that their hearts are not disposed to forget the West, in order that sacred offerings be made to the gods. This is one of the deeds.

I have created the gods from my sweat, and the people from the tears of my eye."

From **The Lamentations of Isis and Nephthys**

Isis speaks:

Come to your house, come to your house!
You of Iunu, come to your house,
Your foes are no more!

Oh good husband, come to your house!
Behold me, I am your beloved sister,
You shall not part from me!

Oh good youth, come to your house!
Long, long have I not seen you!
My heart mourns for you, my eyes seek you,
How I search to see you!

Shall I not see you, shall I not see you,
Good king, shall I not see you?
I am your sister, your wife,
You shall not leave me!
Gods and men look for you,
Weeping for you together!

Nephthys speaks:

Oh good king, come to your house!
Please your heart, your foes are all gone!
Your Two Sisters beside you guard your tomb,
Calling for you in tears!
Turn around in your tomb!
See us women, speak to us!
Oh king, drive all pain from our hearts!

Your court of gods and men beholds you,
Show them your face, great lord!
Let your face not shun our faces,
For our hearts are glad to see you!
I am Nephthys, your beloved sister!
Your foe is fallen, he shall not be!
I am with you, your bodyguard,
For all eternity!

Isis speaks:

Your sacred image, Orion in heaven,
Rises and sets every day;
I am Sothis who follows him,
I will not depart from him!
The sky has your soul, the earth your body,
The netherworld is filled with your secrets.
Your wife is your guard,
While your son Horus rules your lands!

Nephthys speaks:
The souls of your forefathers are your companions,
Your son Horus, child of Isis, is before you;
I am the light that guards you every day,
I shall not leave you ever!

Isis speaks:
Your court of gods and men,
With Horus, perform your rites;
Come to your followers, Osiris, lord,
Do not part from them!

From a Hymn to Osiris

Hail, Osiris, son of Nut!
Two-horned, tall of crown,
Given crown and joy before the Ennead.

Whom the great powers fear,
For whom the great rise from their mats;
Fear of whom Shu has made,
Awe of whom Tefnut fashioned.

Such is Osiris, king of gods,
Great power of heaven,
Ruler of the living,
King of those beyond!
Whom thousands bless in Kher-aha,

Whom mankind extols in Iunu;
Whom the gods, when they see Him, worship,
Whom the spirits, when they see him, adore;
Who is mourned by multitudes in Thinis,
Who is hailed by those below!

From Hymn to Hapy [the Inundation]

Mighty is Hapy in His cavern,
His name unknown to those below,
For the gods do not reveal it.
You people who extol the gods,
Respect the awe His son has made,
The Lord of All who sustains the shores!

> Oh joy when You come!
> Oh joy when You come, O Hapy,
> Oh joy when You come!
> You who feed men and herds
> With You meadow gifts!
> Oh joy when You come!
> Oh joy when You come, O Hapy,
> Oh joy when You come!

From **The Instructions of MerikaRa**

"Well tended is humankind – the god's cattle,
He made sky and earth for their sake,
He subdued the water monster [Apophis],
He made breath for their noses to live.
They are His images, who came from His body,
He shines in the sky for their sake;
He made for them plants and cattle,
Fowl and fish to feed them...
He made daylight for their sake,
He sails by to see them.
He has built His shrine around them,
When they weep, He hears.
He made for them magic as weapons
To ward off the blow of events,
Guarding them day by night...
For the god knows every name."

"A man should do what benefits his soul.
In the time of service, wear white sandals,
Visit the temple, observe the mysteries,
Enter the shrine, break bread in the god's house.
Make ample the offerings of libations and loaves;
It profits him who does it.
Even one day gives to eternity,
An hour contributes to the future,
The god recognizes one who works for Him."

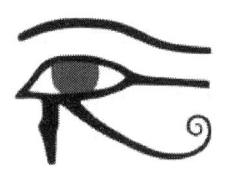

Conclusion

One evening in the course of working on the first edition of this book, I took my manuscript with me to a local Mexican restaurant to do some editing. Our waitress, ever the inquisitive and overly chatty Southern belle, grew curious about what could keep me more engrossed than my bowl of chips and salsa. When I told her I was writing a book about 'Egyptian mythology', she seemed to perk up even more.

"Oh," she said, "well then, what do you think about that whole Mayan calendar thing?"

Hopefully, by this point, you as the reader can appreciate what a hilariously non-sequiter jump in topic our poor waitress made. Despite the claims of New Age gurus and conspiracy theorists, the ancient Egyptians never made contact with the ancient Meso-Americans, and being an expert on the former culture certainly does not make one an expert on the latter simply by extension. But I reassured our curious server that the doomsday supposedly predicted by the Mayan calendar found in Mexico is simply based on a misreading of its inscriptions, just as so much Egyptian 'esoteric wisdom' is based on outdated and erroneous conclusions. She seemed almost relieved by this revelation, and went happily back to her rounds of drink refills. Indeed, the gods and goddesses of Egypt could certainly offer us reassurance about the possible end of the world, now such a popular topic in our media – They just wouldn't give us the grandly mysterious, Hollywood special-effect sort of answer we might be expecting. Instead, They would simply tell us to read carefully, think logically and not frighten ourselves by jumping to conclusions.

Egyptian Paganism in the Twenty-First Century

As a global society, we face the unknown in a world that is changing faster than we can comprehend. Ironically, the Egyptian gods might have the most to tell us about what our world might become through Their tales of how it began. As we have explored in this book, the Egyptian view of our world is one of multiplicity, of opposites in tandem, of order and dynamism occurring simultaneously. In one shining burst of energy at the first sunrise, order – *ma'at* – was established and made to prevail over chaos. Out of the dark primordial waters of Nun, teeming with confusion and what *could* be, the Creator as Atum, Ra, Ptah, Amun, Khnum, Aton and as Neith, called forth what *is*. From eternal sameness They began building differences, variety; "all people, herds and flocks, all upon earth that walk on legs, [and] all on high that fly on wings." And as Ra relates through the Coffin Texts, He created humanity from tears, which have the potential to express either the deepest of sorrow or the greatest of joy.

Such lessons are tremendously relevant for us today. For example, as our world becomes more mobile and interconnected, our own cultural identities are sometimes challenged; some respond to this change xenophobically, by rejecting anything that appears foreign or different. But if we look at such issues through the teachings of the Egyptian gods, however, we gain an added perspective. Through Them, we see yet another reason for the importance of embracing diversity, not shunning it – for the world which They have left us is *meant* to be diverse. As we travel and communicate, we are *supposed* to be forever adding new words and customs, new ethnic groups, new cultures and countercultures. Each bit of newness, difference and creativity we contribute to the world continues the process the gods began on *Zep Tepi*, the First Occasion.

The gods are also depending on us, just as They did upon the pharaohs and their subjects, to perpetuate the rule of order and *ma'at*. An abstract concept, *ma'at* nevertheless stood behind the Egyptians' legal and ethical codes. Its tenets of justice, rule of law and equality of all citizens still hold true for us today. When we work to better our society, either through our civic duty or by "clothing the naked and feeding the hungry", we advance *ma'at* and let the gods work through our hands. Just as important to *ma'at* as civil order is natural order, including the rhythm of the seasons and the life cycles of animals and plants. Increasingly, these cycles are being disrupted – perhaps irrevocably – by the forces of climate change. We owe it to the gods as well as to ourselves to act as good stewards of our environment, for if we do not use its resources responsibly, the only ones to blame for the end of the world will be ourselves.

If the Egyptian gods and goddesses have anything to say about it, our world should continue for quite a long time. For although the Coffin Texts make a brief reference to an end time when "cities will crash upon cities", far more texts speak of time in "millions of years". Even now, we know that our planet is four *billion* years old, and our sun has many billennia of lifetime left; so perhaps the old Egyptian wish for kings to celebrate "millions of jubilees" still holds meaning. Furthermore, the same Coffin Text states that two gods will survive the end of the world: Ra and Osiris, the supreme agents of creation and rebirth from death. Even this tale of an ultimate ending contains the hope of a new beginning.

From the Past Into the Future

Our inquisitive waitress' question serves as but one illustration of how indelibly ancient Egypt has become linked to notions of mystical revelation and transcendent knowledge in our popular imagination. Even now, New Age and Neo-Pagan writers and gurus are interweaving Egyptian themes with Native American, Greek, Hindu and modern mythology to create even more complex and exotic revelations. But do higher 'truth' and 'wisdom' have to be complicated in order to be valid?

As we have explored in the preceding chapters, the answer is most assuredly 'no', for simplicity holds its own power. The lowliest Egyptian peasant would never have been able to read sacred temple texts, but he would have known the story of Osiris and Isis just the same because its premise was easy to understand and its appeal was universal. While we may consider ourselves a more literate and savvy society today, we still need those same universal messages that cut across cultural and educational boundaries. Even a young child, for example, could grasp the meaning behind the stories of Isis using her magic to protect her son Horus while they hid in the Delta marshes.

It is through this immediacy, this psychological common ground between our distant forbears and ourselves, that the Egyptian gods and goddesses still have power to speak to us. The roles of comforters, guardians and teachers that They played two thousand and more years ago are roles that we still need fulfilled today. The methods in which we learn, communicate and earn a living may differ from those of pharaonic times, but as human beings our emotional, psychological and spiritual needs will always remain the same. For more and more people, when aspects of our existing culture fail to meet those needs, Egyptian Paganism will provide them with their own means to fulfill them. The gods and goddesses of Egypt are no longer simply the benefactors of Pharaoh's people; indeed, They have become benefactors for *all* people.

Online Resources

Following the Sun Discussion Forum -
http://followingthesun.freeforums.org/

Virtual Temple of Tutankhamun
(also homepage for Kemetic Reform) -
http://www.kemeticreform.org/

The **Kemetic Independent Channel** on YouTube -
https://www.youtube.com/user/KemeticIndependent

Altar Supplies: Originally I listed several localized stores for statuary, incense and altar supplies. But since the first publication of this book, a number of stores have opened on Etsy.com in particular that cater specifically to Kemetics and Egyptian Pagans. If you're having trouble locating statues or other specific items, try Etsy or log onto the Following the Sun forum and ask for pointers. You could even find artists willing to do special commissions.

Bibliography

Allen, James P. The Ancient Egyptian Pyramid Texts. Atlanta: Society of Biblical Literature, 2005.

Brier, Bob. Ancient Egyptian Magic. New York: Quill Press, 1980.

Budge, E. A. Wallis. The Egyptian Book of the Dead. New York: Dover Publications, 1967.

Collier, Mark, and Manley, Bill. How to Read Egyptian Hieroglyphs: A Step-By-Step Guide to Teach Yourself. Berkeley: University of California Press, 1998.

David, Rosalie. Religion and Magic in Ancient Egypt. New York: Penguin Books, 2002.

Desroches-Noblecourt, Christiane. Tutankhamen: Life and Death of a Pharaoh. New York: Penguin Books, 1984.

Dever, William G. Who Were the Early Israelites and Where Did They Come From?. Grand Rapids: Wm. B. Eerdmans, 2003.

------------------------. Did God Have a Wife? Archaeology and Folk Religion in Ancient Israel. Grand Rapids: Wm. B. Eerdmans, 2005.

Fairman, H. W. The Triumph of Horus: An Ancient Egyptian Sacred Drama. London: B. T. Batsford Ltd., 1974.

Fisher, Marjorie M., Lacovera, Peter, Ikram, Salima, and D'Auria, Sue, eds. Ancient Nubia: African Kingdoms on the Nile. New York: American University in Cairo Press, 2012.

Gilbert, Katharine Stoddert, Holt, Joan K., and Hudson, Sara, eds. Treasures of Tutankhamun. New York: Metropolitan Museum of Art, 1976.

Gore, Rick. "Ramses the Great." *National Geographic* 4 (April 1991): 2-31.

Hart, George. Egyptian Myths. Austin: University of Texas Press, 1990.

Hawass, Zahi. Silent Images: Women in Pharaonic Egypt. Cairo: The American University in Cairo Press, 2008.

Hornung, Erik and Bryan, Betsy M., eds. The Quest for Immortality: Treasures of Ancient Egypt. Washington: National Gallery of Art, 2002.

Hornung, Erik, trans. John Baines. Conceptions of God in Ancient Egypt: The One and the Many. Ithaca: Cornell University Press, 1996.

Lesko, Barbara S. Great Goddesses of Egypt. Norman: University of Oklahoma Press, 1999.

Lesko, Leonard H. et al. Pharaoh's Workers: The Villagers of Deir El Medina. Ithaca: Cornell University Press, 1994.

Lichtheim, Miriam. Ancient Egyptian Literature, vols. I-III. Berkeley: University of California Press, 1973, 1980, 2006.

Manniche, Lise. An Ancient Egyptian Herbal. London: British Museum Press, 2006.

------------------. Music and Musicians in Ancient Egypt. London: British Museum Press, 1991.

Muller, Hans Wolfgang, and Thiem, Eberhard, trans. Pierre Imhoff and Dafydd Roberts. Gold of the Pharaohs. New York: Barnes and Noble Books, 2005.

O'Connor, David. Ancient Nubia: Egypt's Rival in Africa. Philadelphia: The University Museum of Archaeology and Anthropology, 1994.

Pinch, Geraldine. Egyptian Mythology: A Guide to the Gods, Goddesses, and Traditions of Ancient Egypt. New York: Oxford University Press, 2004.

Pinkowski, Jennifer. "Egypt's Ageless Goddess". *Archaeology* 5 (Sept.-Oct. 2006): 44-49.

Quirke, Stephen, et al. "Festivals in Ancient Egypt." Digital Egypt for Universities. 2003. University College London. 30 December 2009 <http://www.digitalegypt.ucl.ac.uk/ideology/festivals.html>

------------------. "A late Middle Kingdom Account, listing festivals." Digital Egypt for Universities. 2003. University College London. 30 December 2009 <http://www.digitalegypt.ucl.ac.uk/lahun/festivallistmk.html>

Roberts, David. "Egypt's Old Kingdom." *National Geographic* 1(January 1995): 2-43.

Robins, Gay. The Art of Ancient Egypt. Cambridge: Harvard University Press, 1997.

Roerig, Catharine H. et al. Hatshepsut: From Queen to Pharaoh. New York: Metropolitan Museum of Art, 2005.

Roth, Ann Macy. "Ancient Egypt in America: Claiming the Riches." Archaeology Under Fire: Nationalism, politics and heritage in the Eastern Mediterranean and Middle East, ed. by Lynn Meskell. New York: Routledge, 1998: 217-229.

Sauneron, Serge, trans. David Lorton. The Priests of Ancient Egypt. Ithaca: Cornell University Press, 2000.

Scott, Joseph and Lenore. Egyptian Hieroglyphs for Everyone. New York: Barnes and Noble Books, 1993.

Silverman, David P., and Wegner, Josef W. and Jennifer Houser. Akhenaten and Tutankhamun: Revolution and Restoration. Philadelphia: University of Pennsylvania Museum of Archaeology and Anthropology, 2006.

Smith, Ray Winfield. "Computer Helps Scholars Re-Create an Egyptian Temple." *National Geographic* 5 (1970): 634-655.

Sullivan, Elaine. "Processional Routes and Festivals." Digital Karnak. 2008. University of California - Los Angeles. 2 September 2009 <http://dlib.etc.ucla.edu/projects/Karnak/assets/media/resources/ProcessionalRoutesAndFestivals/guide.pdf>

Watterson, Barbara. The Gods of Ancient Egypt. Bicester, England: Facts on File Publications, 1984.

Other Works Cited:

Ali, Abdullah Yusuf, trans. The Qur'an. Elmhurst: Tahrike Tarsile Qur'an, Inc., 2000.

Dasa, Shukavak N. "Ways of Worship: *Puja* and *Archana*". A Hindu Primer. 2007. Sanskrit Religions Institute. 25 June 2008<http://www.sanskrit.org/www/Hindu%20Primer/whatispuja.html>

------------------------. "The Offerings of Food and Lamps (*aarati*)". A Hindu Primer. 2007. Sanskrit Religions Institute. 25 June 2008 <http://www.sanskrit.org/www/Hindu%20Primer/offerings.html>

------------------------. "Installing a Sacred Image (*Murti Sthapana/Prana Pratishta*)". <u>A Hindu Primer</u>. 2007. Sanskrit Religions Institute. 25 June 2008 <http://www.sanskrit.org/www/Hindu%20Primer/murtisthapana.html>

Gideons International. <u>The Holy Bible</u>. Chicago: The Gideons International, 1958.

Index

A'apep. *see* Apophis, 67, 89, 90, 126, 148, 152, 155, 156, 227, 241, 243, 283

Afrocentric, 8, 14, 15, 21, 36, 44, 46-47, 51-52

Akhenaton, 29, 32, 35, 38, 39, 40, 41, 43, 44, 71, 80, 94, 96, 152, 153, 232

Amun, 23, 31, 32, 36, 40, 41, 42, 43, 45, 51, 67, 68, 69, 70, 71, 72, 74, 76, 77, 80, 95, 100, 102, 107, 127, 128, 130, 134, 135, 136, 137, 138, 141, 143, 152, 154, 171, 229, 230, 235, 245, 246, 247, 261, 265, 266, 267, 286

Amun-Ra, 31, 43, 68, 72, 77, 107, 135, 229, 245, 246, 247

Anubis, 17, 19, 51, 66, 114, 115, 119, 124, 125, 150, 166, 191

Apophis, 67, 89, 90, 126, 148, 152, 155, 156, 227, 241, 243, 283

Aset Luminous, 237

Aton, Atonism, 32, 38, 39, 40, 42, 43, 44, 45, 72, 80, 94, 109, 152, 153, 154, 286

Atum, 86, 106, 107, 108, 109, 128, 142, 144, 151, 179, 184, 286

Bast, 17, 19, 75, 136, 140, 145, 147, 150, 151, 168, 199, 238, 258, 261

Bes, 33, 44, 140, 148, 152, 153, 154, 199

Book of Imy-Duat (Am-Duat), 73, 148

Book of the Celestial Cow, 132, 140

Book of the Dead, 19, 38, 47, 73, 119, 155, 164, 185, 258, 291

Destruction of Mankind, Myth of, 110, 132, 136, 145, 238

Distant Goddess, Myth of, 110, 151

divination, 190

Djehutet (month), 225, 226, 227, 228, 238

Drunkenness, 136, 238

Ennead, 105, 109, 114, 184, 259, 273, 274, 281

Exodus, the, 5, 27, 28, 29, 30, 31, 33, 34, 36, 39, 72

Eye of Ra, 109, 123, 137, 144, 150, 238, 242, 253, 254, 257, 258, 259, 269

Fellowship of Isis, the, 11, 12

Forty-Two Declarations of Innocence, 73, 97

Geb, 105, 109, 110, 111, 112, 115, 184, 273, 274

269

Haker, 230, 231, 232, 233, 235, 250
Hathor, 14, 59, 77, 79, 85, 117, 127, 129, 136, 138, 139, 140, 144, 147, 151, 154, 167, 188, 218, 225, 230, 235, 236, 238, 245, 247, 258, 265, 266, 267, 269, 270, 271
heka, 18
henotheism, 45
Heriu Ronpet, 225, 226
Horus, 12, 20, 21, 28, 40, 59, 75, 77, 78, 86, 90, 93, 95, 104, 106, 114, 115, 117, 118, 121, 122, 123, 124, 127, 130, 132, 139, 145, 148, 149, 162, 166, 181, 182, 183, 184, 185, 226, 227, 232, 233, 234, 236, 237, 238, 250, 253, 254, 255, 269, 270, 271, 274, 276, 280, 281, 288, 291
icon, 167, 170, 190, 227, 231, 232, 235
incense, 168, 182, 274
Iru, 174, 175, 180, 182, 184, 240, 273
isfet, 88, 90
Isian, 12, 14
Isis, 11, 12, 14, 20, 45, 76, 78, 79, 95, 105, 114, 115, 116, 117, 118, 119, 121, 122, 125, 126, 130, 136, 138, 139, 140, 155, 180, 184, 185, 186, 190, 221, 227, 237, 240, 249, 250, 251, 253, 254, 255, 261, 262, 263, 279, 280, 281, 288
ka, 91, 92, 93, 96, 141, 154, 179, 186, 187
Kemetic Reconstructionism, 7, 14, 163
Khnum, 85, 91, 107, 127, 140, 141, 149, 286
Khonsu, 76, 127, 135, 137, 138, 225, 229, 234
meditation, 187
Mehet-Uret, 85, 236
Min, 41, 84, 127, 129, 130, 135, 207, 234, 261, 262, 263
monolatry, 44
monotheism, 34, 38, 39, 42, 44
Montu, 127, 128, 129
Mut, 36, 44, 51, 76, 111, 117, 127, 134, 135, 136, 137, 138, 144, 145, 151, 229, 230, 238, 245, 246, 247, 261
natron, recipes for, 87, 170, 180, 181, 182, 193, 194, 195, 196, 241, 242, 245, 246, 249, 250, 253, 254, 257, 258, 261, 262, 265, 266, 269, 270, 274
Nefertem, 20, 86, 141, 143, 144, 145, 151
Neith, 76, 85, 126, 146, 147, 148, 149, 155, 236, 237, 286
Nephthys, 105, 114, 118, 119, 125, 126, 185, 227, 251, 279, 280

netjer, meaning of, 45, 104, 131, 187
New Year's, 199, 221, 227, 228, 234, 243
nisut, 21
Nun, 86, 89, 102, 105, 106, 109, 113, 148, 149, 155, 237, 286
Nut, 85, 105, 109, 110, 111, 112, 115, 117, 120, 139, 140, 184, 227, 237, 273, 274, 281
Opet, 225, 228, 229, 230, 245, 246, 247
Osiris, 3, 14, 20, 41, 65, 66, 67, 71, 72, 73, 78, 84, 85, 86, 87, 88, 90, 91, 97, 105, 107, 114, 115, 117, 119, 120, 121, 123, 125, 126, 132, 143, 146, 148, 149, 154, 156, 179, 180, 184, 185, 186, 187, 189, 221, 227, 228, 230, 231, 232, 238, 249, 250, 251, 254,렘 255, 262, 273, 277, 281, 287, 288
Peret (season), 84, 187, 222, 225, 233
Peret Sopdut, 222
personal shrines, 171, 289
possession, 22, 191
prayers, 5, 142, 143, 177
Ptah, 20, 23, 76, 135, 137, 141, 142, 143, 144, 145, 146, 151, 230, 286
Pyramid Texts, 40, 65, 91, 92, 109, 111, 112, 115, 121, 126, 150, 152, 163, 164, 174, 181, 185, 291

Ra, 3, 19, 23, 24, 31, 40, 42, 43, 64, 67, 68, 70, 72, 73, 77, 86, 87, 88, 89, 90, 92, 93, 95, 96, 105, 106, 107, 108, 109, 110, 111, 112, 116, 118, 122, 123, 125, 128, 129, 132, 135, 137, 139, 140, 141, 143, 144, 146, 148, 149, 150, 151, 152, 155, 179, 183,렘 184, 186, 225, 227, 229, 236, 238, 242, 243, 245, 253, 258, 259, 261, 269, 273, 274, 277, 278, 286, 287
Ra-Horakhety, 40, 42, 70, 106, 123, 179
Reunion, 269
Sakhmet, 14, 17, 20, 35, 36, 136, 137, 140, 141, 143, 144, 145, 150, 151, 227, 238, 242, 243, 253, 254, 255, 257, 258, 259
Sed, 224, 232, 233, 255
Serket, 114, 126, 127, 148, 155, 166
Seth, 31, 65, 67, 72, 89, 90, 104, 105, 114, 115, 118, 119, 120, 121, 123, 125, 148, 149, 155, 156, 180, 183, 184, 185, 191, 226, 227, 233, 238, 249, 250, 253, 273
Shomu (season), 84, 225
Shu, 42, 105, 108, 109, 110, 184, 273, 274, 281
Sirius (Sopdut), 221, 222, 223, 224, 226
Sobek, 86, 106, 147, 148, 149

Sokar, 141, 143, 146, 231, 249
Tameran Wicca, 12, 13, 163, 223, 233, 240, 257, 273
Tawret, 44, 152, 153, 154
Tefnut, 105, 108, 109, 110, 112, 132, 144, 145, 150, 151, 181, 184, 258, 273, 274, 281
Thoth, 15, 62, 75, 108, 110, 127, 131, 190, 225, 226

udjat (wedjat), 12, 123
Uret Hekau, 117
Valley, 85, 234, 235, 265, 266
Victory, 93, 233, 234, 253, 255, 273
Wagy, 224, 228
Wepwawet (Up-Waut), 147, 231
Zep Tepi, 86, 102, 227, 286